INDIAN ANTHROPOLOGY

INDIAN ANTHROPOLOGY

Nadeem Hasnain

Former Professor of Social Anthropology
Department of Anthropology
University of Lucknow,
Lucknow

PALAKA PRAKASHAN
palakaprakashan@gmail.com

ISBN 9788185799773

₹ 290/-

FOR SALE IN INDIA ONLY

1st Edition	:	1991
6th Edition	:	2001
16th Reprint (6th edition)	:	2017
7th Revised, Expanded & Updated Edition	:	2019
8th Revised, Expanded & Updated Edition	:	2022
Reprint (8th edition) Jan	:	2023

Editor (Social & Biological Series)
N.K. Vaid
Director, **VAID'S ICS,**
Delhi

PALAKA PRAKASHAN

AC-177B, Shalimar Bagh, Delhi - 110088
1244A/84, Shanti Nagar, Tri Nagar, Delhi - 110035
Ph. : +91 - 8744884844 /9873921850
palakaprakashan@gmail.com **www.palakaprakashan.com**

Printed at Sanjay Printer, Delhi.

PREFACE TO THE PRESENT EDITION

I write these lines for the Eighth revised and expanded edition with pleasure as well as sadness. As the author I feel so happy to share with you that Tribal India and Indian Anthropology have been enjoying popularity and trust of the readers for more than 30 years with eight editions and dozens of reprints and during this period no other book on the same topic could replace these books. Obviously, it is a matter of great pride and happiness for any author. The sadness has also crept into my mind as the dishonest and unscrupulous elements, taking advantage of the new technology, are not only spreading the illegal pdf version of the text but also producing and selling it in the print format causing financial losses to the publisher of the book. Obviously, if this is not checked no publisher will be publishing such useful books bearing losses and the authors shall not be writing and revising the text. It is the responsibility of the readers/buyers not to buy such pirated versions.

Besides incorporating latest data wherever required additions have also been made in the existing chapters. More contributors to Indian anthropology, especially from the west, have been added whose concepts and contributions will now be better understood. In the chapter on Fieldwork a detailed note on Ethnography and Ethnographic Method have been added to give the readers a comprehensive view of place and importance of fieldwork in anthropology. Some new and latest information to the chapter on Population gives edge to the existing text, chapter on Scheduled Castes and OBCs has been further enriched by new additions, and in the chapter dealing with Village India rich content has been added in the form of Peasant Movement, Changing Mode of Production in Indian Agriculture,and Green Revolution and Social Change.

I hope that you would find this revised and expanded edition more useful. I would continue to welcome your feedback and suggestions for making the book more helpful and useful for you. I shall also expect you to spread the word against buying illegal and pirated editions and tell your friends and others in your circle not to do this for the sake of saving some money at the cost of the author and the publisher.

Happy reading

January, 2022 Nadeem Hasnain
Lucknow (nadeemhasnain@gmail.com)

PREFACE

It gives me great pleasure in writing these lines. First published in 1988, **Indian Anthropology** rose to become one of the most popular and sought after books of anthropology of recent times. I am overwhelmed by this response of my readers. I take it as a compliment to the growing popularity of anthropology in the country.

Indian Anthropology because of its sweep and style of narration shall continue to help its readers—aspirants for Civil Services and students at University level — is a firm belief of mine.

ACKNOWLEDGEMENT

My valued friend Mr. N.K. Vaid (Director, Vaid's ICS) has helped me in a variety of ways. I am grateful to him. My wife Nishat, son Aseem and daughter Samta have also contributed in their own ways. Mr. Kamal Kishore Gupta of Palaka Prakashan has really worked hard to bring out a nice edition. He deserves kudos.

Lastly, I shall be waiting for the suggestions and comments of my readers for further improvements in the next edition.

15 August, 1991
Lucknow

Nadeem Hasnain
(nadeemhasnain@gmail.com)

Other Published Books of The Author

- Sociology of Marginalised Communities and Weaker Sections of India, 2021
- Shia Muslims of India, 2021
- Handbook of Sociology, 2020
- Indian Society: Themes and Social Issues, 2019
- The Other Lucknow: Ethnographic Portrait of a City of Undying Memories and Nostalgia, 2016
  (Also available in Hindi)
- India's Current Social Problems (co-authored), 2014
  (Also available in Hindi)
- Contested Identities in the Globalised world (co-edited), 2013
- Anthropology in India (co-edited), 2010
- A Study of Women's Problematic (co-edited), 2009
- Towards Empowering Indian Women (co-edited), 2007
- The Indian State and Womens' Problematics (co-edited)
- Beyond Textual Islam, 2007
- Aspects of Islam and Muslim Societies, 2006
- Islam and Muslim Communities of South Asia, 2005
- OBC's in the Process of Change (co-edited), 2005
- Indian Society and Culture: Continuity and Change, 2004
  (Also available in Hindi)
- Introducing Social and Cultural Anthropology (co-authored), 2004
  (Also available in Hindi)
- General Anthropology, 1997
  (Also available in Hindi)
- Tribal India, 1982
  (Also available in Hindi and Telegu)
- Bonded for Ever, 1982
  (Also available in Hindi)

CONTENT

Preface to the Present Edition v
Preface vii

SECTION ONE — Aspects of Indian Anthropology

1. Origin and Growth of Indian Anthropology : A Brief Review 17 - 54
   (i) Social/Cultural Anthropology
   (ii) Physical/Biological Anthropology
   (iii) Prehistoric Archaeology/ Archaeological Anthropology
   (iv) Some Important Contributors to Indian Anthropology
2. Fieldwork and Fieldwork Tradition : Defining Features of Anthropological Reseach 55 - 70
   - Ethnography
3. Anthropology in the Service of Man : Applied Anthropology in India 71 - 78
4. Moving Towards Complex Societies : Urban Anthropology in India 79 - 84
5. Secularism: Some Sociological/Anthropological Implications 85 - 88

SECTION TWO — Cultural Reconstruction of the Past

6. Prehistoric and Protohistoric Dimensions of Indian Culture 91 - 150
   (i) Palaeolithic
   (ii) Mesolithic
   (iii) Neolithic
   (iv) Prehistoric Art
   (v) Indus Civilization

(vi) Chalcolithic Culture
(vii) Megaliths and Megalithic Age
Ethnoarchaeology
How Archaeologists Work
Stone Tools: The Indelible Markers
7. Contributions of Tribal Cultures to Indian Civilization 151 - 154
8. Anthropological Museums and Museology in India 155 - 164

SECTION THREE — Colourful Mosaic of India's population

9. Racial / Ethnic Elements in Indian Population 167 - 172
10. Linguistic Elements in India 173 - 176
11. Population of India and Indian Population Policy 177 - 190

SECTION FOUR — Understanding Indian Society and Culture

12. Approaches to the Study of Indian Society 193 - 198

SECTION FIVE — Indian Civilization and It's Cultural Process

Introductory Note — Folk society, Peasant Society, Folk-Urban Continuum 201 - 208
13. Little and Great Traditions (with the concept of Tradition, Little Community and Great Community) 209 - 218
14. Universalization and Parochialization 219 - 224
15. Sacred Complex 225 - 230
16. Tribe-Caste Continuum 231 - 236
17. Nature-Man-Spirit Complex 237 - 240

SECTION SIX — Indian Social System

18. Traditional Bases of Indian Social System 243 - 262
Ashram, Purushartha, Rina, Karma, Rebirth
Joint Family,
Caste (Varna and Jati)

19. Scheduled Castes & OBC 263 - 284

20. Impact of Buddhism, Jainism, Islam and Christianity on Indian Society 285 - 294

SECTION SEVEN — Dimensions of Social Change in India

Introductory Note 297 - 300

21. Sanskritization and Westernization 301 - 316
Secularization
Modernization

22. Dominant Caste 317 - 322

23. Social Change in India: Some Dimensions 323 - 332

SECTION EIGHT — Aspects of India's Villages and Social Organization of Agriculture

24. Rural Society in India 335 - 376
(i) Traditional Characterstic Features of Villages and Change
(ii) Indian Village as a Social System
(iii) Village Study in India and its Significance
(iv) Rural Cosmopolitanism
(v) Traditional Culture
(vi) Agrarian Social Structure
(vii) Peasant Society
(viii) Power Structure and Class, Stratification
(ix) Jajmani System and its decline
(x) Kisan Sabha
(xi) Telangana Movement
(xii) Naxalbari Movement
(xiii) Changing Mode of Production in Indian Agriculture

(xiv) Green Revolution and Social Change
(xv) Impact of Market Economy on Villages
(xvi) Impact of Globalization on Village India

SECTION NINE — Religions and Religious Communities in India

25. Religions and Religious Minorities 379 - 404
26. Linguistic Minorities 405 - 410

Select Bibliography 411 - 426

SECTION ONE

ASPECTS OF INDIAN ANTHROPOLOGY

1

Origin and Growth of Indian Anthropology : A Brief Review

Any discussion on the rise and growth of Anthropology in India is not without considerable difference of opinion. Thankfully the areas of dispute are mostly confined to the origin and not to the development and growth of the discipline as such.

Vidyarthi (1972, 1980) has been advocating that the beginning of anthropological investigation in India should be traced back to the year 1774 - the year of establishment of the 'Asiatic Society of Bengal' by William Jones. The scope of the Society as defined by the founder, was to study nature and man. "Since then, the British administrators, missionaries, travellers, and a few other anthropologically oriented individuals collected data on tribal and rural groups and wrote about their life and culture in the *Journal of Asiatic Society of Bengal* (1784), *Indian Antiquary* (1872), and later in the *Journal of Bihar and Orissa Research Society* (1915) and *Man in India* (1921). Alongwith other historical and geographical information they also collected ethnographic data and published a series of district gazetteers, hand books on tribes and castes and then a number of monographs especially on the tribes off Assam" (ibid).

Gopal Saran (1973, Saran & Sinha, 1976) does not agree that the beginning of Indian Anthropology can be traced back to 1774 when the Asiatic Society of Bengal came into being. "It is true that the Asiatic Society was responsible for the publication of materials concerned with antiquarian and anthropological interests. In our view the origin of anthropology in India goes back to the days of British colonial administration in the latter half of the nineteenth century. The British administrators gradually realized that a good acquaintance with the natives and their culture was a basic pre-requisite for governing them properly without falling foul of their customs and thus causing avoidable irritations. Therefore, the administrative needs of the British rulers forced them to use official machinery to gather information about the social institutions, economic conditions and religious beliefs and practices of the native Indians who could be grouped easily into tribes and castes" (ibid, 1976). Saran (1983) further supplements his contention by pointing out that Abbe Duboi's *Hindu Manners, Customs and Ceremonies* was first published in 1816 in London while J. Compbell published an account of the Ethnography of India in 1856 and R.G. Latham's book of the same name appeared in 1859. But these ware only stray attempts. The generally recognised anthropological works in India were written by the anthropologically oriented British administrators like Blunt, Crook, Dalton, Grierson, Ibbeston, Mills, Nesfield, O'Malley, Risely, Russel, Senart, Thurston and the administrator turned academician Hutton, in the latter half off the nineteenth century. Risley, who published his account of tribes and castes of Bengal in 1891, became famous as head of census operations and later on created a place for himself in Indian anthropology with his most celebrated book *'The People of India'*.

As already stated, anthropological studies in India were the off-shoot of colonial rule. These were undertaken by British administrators to enable "the rulers to take the stock of their position and to see how it has fared with the people committed to their charge" (Risley & Gait, 1903). Drawing our attention to an important landmark in the history of the rise of anthropology in India, Saran & Sinha (ibid) opine that in some cases anthropological studies were motivated by genuine curiosity about the variety of different peoples of India and their 'exotic' customs. A few notable consequences of these studies are worth mentioning. The early anthropological studies were not academic but utilitarian in their nature. The contributors were all foreigners who were studying the cultures of the 'natives'. They were all based in India and did not have direct contact with the academic anthropologists like Tylor, Frazer, and others who were conducting researches at Cambridge, Oxford and London universities. Thus, their work did not become a part of British anthropology, which would have been the case had they been inspired by the British academic anthropologists or the colonial office in London. This early affiliation of anthropology with government agencies continued even after independence mostly under the banner of applied anthropology.

Among the earliest Indian anthropologists the name of S.C. Roy stands as a colossus. Roy published his first exhaustive monograph on the Munda Tribe (1912), Oraon (1915), Birhor (1925), Kharia (1937) and many other pioneering works and was subsequently called "*Father of Indian Ethnology*". R.P. Chandra's work on the Indo-Aryan race (1916) also generated a lot of interest specially among the students of the cultural history of India. It has been a worldwide phenomenon including India, that the earliest anthropologists were specialists in diverse fields like natural history, medicine, law etc. and in the systematic study of man they were merely "Gifted Amateurs".

Before moving to the discussion on the establishment of academic anthropology in India it will be very significant to describe the 'image' of the earlier anthropologists (as cultivated in the mind of intelligent of those times) because for those readers not coming from anthropology background, it may help clear some cobwebs of misgivings. In a highly absorbing description Saran (1983) says that both the common man and the intellectual of the 19th century considered the contemporary anthropologists as eccentrics. This was primarily due to the anthropologists' interest in "bizarre" and "inconsequential" things. The so called liabilities, namely, the study of oddments, the so called eccentricity of the pioneering anthropologists and romanticism which led most of them to take interest in distant places and exotic peoples, have proved to be most advantageous to anthropology. The 19th century anthropologist studied the oddities out of pure interest in them and not to reform the world or to earn a living. Consequently a sense of detachment and a tradition of relative objectivity have become the distinctive attributes of anthropology since its very inception. Anthropology was dubbed a science of left-overs. Left-overs were many and varied. Therefore, unlike economics or political science, anthropology escaped being stamped with preoccupation with only one aspect of life of man. Although it is true that anthropology began with the study of life and customs of primitive people, it diversified and included such branches as physical (biological) anthropology and prehistoric archaeology (archaeological anthropology) and a vast number of sub-branches and fields of specializations.

A discipline cannot be said to have made its mark until it is accorded recognition as a subject of teaching and research at the university level. On the academic side the master's degree had been started at Calcutta University in 1921 and the department of sociology at Bombay University (started in 1920) had included in its syllabi a fair bit of social anthropology. K.S. Mathur (1971) says that this was under the inspiration of A.C. Haddon and W.H.R. Rivers. Calcutta had produced some find anthropologists, prominent amongst them were K.P. Chattopadhyay, T.C. Das, D.N. Majumdar, N.K. Bose and P.C. Biswas. These scholars had done extensive work on the tribes and castes of eastern and middle India and produced theory oriented monographs and papers based upon first hand field data. Of these, Chattopadhyay Das and Bose continued teaching at Calcutta; Majumdar came to Lucknow in 1928 and succeeded in slowly building up a nucleus of anthropology in the department of economics (a full fledged department of anthropology was established only in 1951 with Majumdar as first head of the department). Biswas taught at Calcutta for a while and then came to Delhi where he built up at the university a department of anthropology with emphasis on physical anthropology. B.S. Guha with his academic training in anthropology at Harvard joined Government service and became the first director of the Anthropological Survey of India when it away from the Zoological Survey of India in 1946. All of them were after the Calcutta pattern, general anthropologists, though Chattopadhyay, Das, Majumdar and Bose did more social anthropology while Guha and Biswas did more physical anthropology.

During these decades two persons stood like colossus. They were S.C. Roy and Verrier Elwin. Both of them were not academically trained anthropologists but their contributions to Indian anthropology can never be forgotten. Roy was a lawyer by training, who during his stay at Ranchi, developed fascination for the tribal people. Elwin came from England and started as a missionary but his love for Indian tribal people eclipsed all other considerations. He choose to stay in India even after independence and, enjoying full rapport with Jawaharlal Nehru, became the main planner and policy maker vis-a-vis tribal people of India.

The forty four years after independence have witnessed rapid growth in the teaching and research in anthropology. It is no more an unknown discipline dealing with the quaint, the 'exotic' and the curious. It is now the recognised science of man whose growing utility as an applied science has been acknowledged. More than three dozen universities in the country are imparting teaching in anthropology at various levels. The syllabi are less descriptive and more analytical-theoretical. Research in anthropology is now problem-oriented and covers human society in various phases of its growth and development. Besides the university departments of anthropology, some part or the other of the discipline is included in the syllabi of such other subjects as sociology, political science and social & preventive medicine. In specialised courses in physical (biological) anthropology, papers common to most universities are human evolution and human genetics; some departments are paying greater emphasis on primatology and comparative anatomy, others on cytogenetics, biochemical anthropology, and population variation.

Among the research institutions - governmental, semi-autonomous and autonomous - Anthropological Survey of India is, probably, the largest of its kind in the world. It has several regional stations and employs hundreds of professional anthropologists who are engaged in research in social as well as physical anthropology. The application role of anthropology has come to be recognized in the fields of such state programmes as family welfare, public health, adult education, community development, environmental sanitation, regional development, etc. Anthropologists are working in tribal research institutes, office of the Commissioner for Scheduled Castes and Scheduled Tribes (Now National Commission of Scheduled Caste and Scheduled Tribe), officer of the Registrar General of India, Indian Agricultural Research Institute. Space Applications Centre, museums, various constituents of C.S.I.R., Planning Commission and many other diverse and important institutions. Anthropology also has a separate section in Indian Science Congress. India is second only to the U.S.A. in the number of professionally trained anthropologists working in divergent institutions.

(i) Social-Cultural Anthropology

Among the three major branches of anthropology, social anthropology in India has come of age. This is clearly reflected in reviews of its history and development undertaken by Majumdar (1956,58), Ghurye (1956), Dube (1962), Bose (1967), Saran (1973),

Saran & Sinha (1976) and Vidyarthi (1966). Majumdar categorised the development of social anthropology in India into three phases - Formulatory (1774-1911), Constructive (1912-1937), and Critical (1938 onwards). Vidyarthi made some minor adjustments - Formative period, constructive period and analytical periods. However, in the present discussion the journey of Indian social anthropology has been described without any labels encompassing salient points and issues raised by the above mentioned scholars.

As already state, during the earliest phase (last quarter of the nineteenth century and first quarter of the twentieth century) the anthropologically oriented British administrators posted in different parts of India wrote descriptive accounts of the life and culture of people of different regions. Among such scholar—administrators Risely, Dalton and O'Malley were posted in Eastern India; Russel in Middle India; Thurston in South India and crooks in north India. The main objective behind this exercise was to acquaint the government officials with classified description about the people of different regions to ensure effective colonial administration. Some of the notable works of this kind are *Tribes and Castes of Bengal* by Risley, *Tribes and Castes of Oudh and United Provinces* by Crooks and such other works. These generalised works in descriptive ethnography gave rise to a more rigorous exercise of preparing more detailed accounts of specific tribes followed by accounts of some specific castes. Some of the remarkable works of this phase are *the Khasi* by Gurdon, *The Lhota Naga* by Mills, *The Lushai Kuki Clans* by Shakespeare and *The Chamars* by Briggs. The First Indian ethnographer to write such monographs was S.C. Roy who published very good monographs on some of the important tribes of Chotanagpur such as Munda and Oraon. Roy's work had a different flavor. L.K. Anantha Krishna Iyer, like the British administrators, worked on a serial publication on the tribes and castes. His major works are *Cochin Tribes and Castes* (1908, 1912) and *The Mysore Tribes and Castes* (1918, 1930 & 1935).

Pointing towards a major weakness of the works of Roy's genre Saran & Sinha (1976) very correctly says that even these very able pioneering anthropologists of Indian origin did not think that their work should be different from that of the British administrator-anthropologists who were studying an alien culture. Roy was not a foreigner, but he quickly adopted the prevailing fashion of the day of studying tribals who were called animists by Tylor. Both Iyer and Roy thought that a study of tribal people through first hand field work was central to anthropology. Other anthropologists of Indian origin followed the lead of these pioneers by choosing to work among the tribal people. Thus, for a fairly long time (until the end of the 1940s) Indian anthropology was primarily a study of tribal people of India who were considered separate from the rest of the Indian population and thus could be studied with the same kind of detachment that the western anthropologists had adopted in studying simple societies usually outside their own national boundaries. In those days anthropology's exclusive concern was with exotic and non-literate peoples.

It would be fairly appropriate to comment that the first full-fledged exposure to the academic world of universities changed the face of social anthropology. As stated earlier when it was introduced in the universities of Calcutta (in the department of anthropology) and Bombay (in the department of sociology) it was exposed, for the first time, to the glare of academics. It not only attracted trained scholars but also opened avenues for training young anthropologists (including social anthropologists). The horizon of social anthropology widened radically. For the first time such areas of study as social institutions (family, kinship, political organisation, etc.) were taken up seriously, Chattopadhyay, Das, Majumdar, Irawati Karve, Aiyappan and others provided the long needed impetus to the growth of academic social anthropology by conducting extensive field work, lecturing and publishing on the new emerging themes. Vidyarthi *et al*, (1980) opined that a big jump came in 1938 when a joint session of the Indian

Science Congress Association and the British Association reviewed the progress of anthropology in India, and eminent anthropologists and discussed plans for future anthropological researches in India. For the first time some theoretical leads were provided in social anthropological researches. Majumdar's *The Changing Ho*, Srinivas' *Marriage and Family in Mysore* and Bose's *Hindu methods of Tribal Absorption* may be described as a turning point in the growth of social anthropology in India. At this juncture entered Elwin, the poet-visionary-romanticist-expert on tribal affairs, with his problem-oriented works on the tribes of Madhya Pradesh and Orissa. Elwin's *The Baiga* (1939). *The Agaria* (1943) and *The Muria* and *Their Ghotul* (1947), are classics in the problem oriented ethnography. Haimendrof's *The Chenchus: Jungle folk of Deccan* (1943), *The Reddis of the Bison Hills: A study in Acculturation* (1945) and other publications on southern tribes provided models for future scholars for problem oriented studies.

After World War II and Indian gaining independence the scenario underwent a qualitative change. Previously ethnography was the domain of administrators but now foreign as well as Indian anthropologists were academicians. Moreover, after a long time the attention of social anthropologists was attracted toward the institution of caste. In due course interest shifted from the study of tribes to that of castes. The transition was natural and smooth for both the foreign as well as Indian academic anthropologists who succeeded such pioneers as Iyer and Roy.

In the post-independence phase (described by Vidyarthi as analytical period) contacts with American social (cultural) anthropologists increased rapidly and many American anthropologists such as Morris Opler, Oscar Lewis and David Mandelbaum along with their students came to India, did field work, tested many of their hypotheses in the village social structure and thus created an atmosphere in which village and caste studies along with studies on the dimensions of Indian civilization were taken up. The whole social science scenario (including that of social anthropology) was in ferment.

Now independent India posed a challenge to the genius of Indian social scientists. They were supposed to join in the planning of economic development and social reconstruction of the country. Indian anthropologists had another gigantic task to perform they were to shed their colonial legacy. They tried hard to clear the cobwebs of misgivings vis-a-vis the role of anthropology in colonialism. But they were destined to pass through an agonizing period of humiliation and ruthless criticism. Headed by Thakkar Bapa, a close associate of Gandhiji and a fighter for the case of the suppressed tribals, an influential group of leaders maligned Indian anthropology and anthropologists and tired to ensure their total isolation from the affairs of the tribal India by accusing the anthropologists of nurturing a vested interest in the perpetuation of backwardness and isolation of the tribal people. It took about a decade in combating this propaganda and only then social anthropologists were involved, to a respectable extent, in the planning process of the backward segments of Indian population.

Before moving further it would be in the fitness of things to make a few comments on the contributions of one of the all time greats of Indian anthropology. He is the legendary D.N. Majumdar. Precisely, it is during this period that Majumdar's contribution seems most important. He was a student of Malinowski at Cambridge and he was the first Indian anthropologist to use the holistic-functional approach in his trend setting study of the Ho tribe. The establishment of a separate department of anthropology at Lucknow University in 1950, a result of Majumdar's untiring efforts, provided a great and timely impetus to the development of anthropology. For more than a decade (till his sudden death in 1960) Lucknow occupied a very important place in Indian anthropology. In fact many persons started using the term *Lucknow school of anthropology* as a mark of acknowledgment of his great contribution. Dozens of anthropologists trained by him are occupying prestigious positions in India and abroad. Lucknow was a highly respected centre of anthropology during this period. The establishment of Ethnographic & Folk Culture Society and the initiation of a research journal, The Eastern Anthropologist, as the organ put Indian anthropology on the international scene. His contribution in developing a new identity for Indian Social anthropology is without any doubt.

As already stated, after studying tribes almost exclusively, social anthropologists moved to the study of communities, castes and other more complex segments of Indian population without losing their identity as anthropologists. The role of caste in politics has also attracted the attention of social anthropologists and much of the empirical research on caste deals with the relationship between castes, status, power, stratification and economic dimensions of these factors.

Thus, some headway has also been made in political anthropology. After taking up folk and peasant communities (obviously inspired by the researches of Redfield, Milton Singer and Mckim Marriott of Chicago School of Anthropology) social anthropologists started the study of traditional and modern cities to understand the interaction between the great and *little* traditions and as dimensions of Indian civilization. Several useful studies of the processes of urbanization and industrialization have been undertaken. During this phase we started confronting such terms as *Industrial Anthropology* and *Urban Anthropology*. The impact of industrialization on tribal populations of India has also been studied in some detail. But the pioneers in Urban anthropology were Bose who studied Calcutta (1958); Majumdar studied Kanpur (1961), and Gaya and Ranchi were studied by Vidyarthi (1961, 1969).

Social anthropology has also entered in the field of management in its zeal to study organizations. Sheth's *Social Framework of an Indian Factory* (1968) and Chattopadhyay & Sinha's work (1970) on the socio-cultural relevance of new educational technology and the study of authority and dependency in Indian culture (1975) are some of the examples of this trend. Even the field of space research is also not without contribution of social anthropology. B.C. Agrawal and his associates have been associated with Space Application Centre, Ahmedabad since the days of Satellite Instructional Television Programme (SITE) launched in 1975 -- hence, another field of study - Space Anthropology.

The moment of glory should not hide the weaknesses. Self assessment and self criticism must form part of any frank and honest appraisal. The practitioners of Indian social anthropology have demonstrated the utility of detailed, indepth and long term face to face field work. Participant observation has been a hallmark of anthropology and this is responsible for the distinctiveness of anthropological contributions. We have done it in our own culture. "One of our greatest drawbacks is the lack of 'other culture' studies by Indian anthropologists. It is high time that we did develop expertise in this field because research among other cultures has been the forte of anthropology. Such research will broaden the vision of Indian anthropologists and will help them understand their own culture better" (Saran & Sinha. ibid). However, what has until now been our weakness will prove to be source of strength in the future. There is hardly any country in the world where anthropological self-study has been conducted by native-born anthropologists for almost seven decades. Before long, anthropologists of all countries, particularly the developing countries, will have to start studying their own culture. We cannot anticipate the kind of problems these native anthropologists will face. This new aspect of anthropology in almost every country will encounter growing pains. The only exception then will be anthropology in India, which has long passed that stage.

For the last two decades or so an agonising process of re-appraisal has been growing on in Indian anthropology specially in social anthropology. Because of the British influence during the pre-independence period and the American influence in the post-independence era, there is a general feeling of a persisting crisis of identity in Indian social anthropology. It is said that it lacks a personality of its own. It must get away from western models which are unsuited for our purposes. K.S. Mathur (1972) rightly draws our attention to the need of Indian social anthropology being bunt upon home made designs and models. We should develop our own different approaches, traditions, symbols, and culture patterns. For bringing about greater 'Indianness' in Indian social anthropology we should make greater use of ancient Indian literature along with interactional patterns between Islamic and local Hindu traditions for understanding Indian society. But this urge for identity should not let us ignore developments in the west and we should adapt the research strategies and models developed there to our own social problems.

The whole of Indian society is in ferment and our country is passing through a difficult phase of its independent existence. British colonialists used social anthropological knowledge to promote their colonial interests. But it is time we should sharpen its tools to improve our own administration. It is heartening to see that anthropology has been introduced as an optional subject in the central civil services examination and the aspirants are opting anthropology in large numbers. It should be adopted as an essential part of the training of administrative personnel at all levels.

(ii) Physical/Biological Anthropology

Physical anthropology is the second major branch of anthropology. Its beginning may be traced back to the later half of the 19th century when, under the British administration, attempts were being made to study physical traits of the native people side by side with the cultural characteristics. Physical anthropological investigations thus began with simple anthropometry. The main objective behind anthropometric exercises during that period was to give metric expressions to observable human physical features for ethnic differentiation, their possible origins, an affiliation and the resulting admixtures between populations. Its techniques have been simple but very effectively employed by the competent persons working in this field.

Prior to its use in India, in the seventeenth and eighteenth centuries when missionaries from western countries and travellers were giving descriptive accounts of morphological features along with cultural traits of various people they met with in different lands, scientists were grappling with the problem of giving metric expression to those visually observable morphological traits. "Historically, the available records on anthropometric studies in India indicate that J. Shrott was the first to embark on such a study. He measures three tribes from the Nilgiris in Tamilnadu, mostly for their stature, and included only the necessary dimensions of the head and the nose for the calculation of *cephalic* and *nasal* indices. The results were published jointly with Col. Ourchterlony in 1868. He was followed by Risley in 1891 who organized and supervised the most comprehensive survey for most of the provinces of the then British India, including Baluchistan, Ceylon and Burma" (R.D. Singh, 1987). Surgeon Captain Brake-Brockman measured most of the castes and tribes of Uttar Pradesh an published his accounts in 1896. Thurston worked on a large number of groups from all over the south and published the results in 1909 onward in several volumes.

Around 1930s some advances were made in the field of human genetics in general and human serology in particular. Thus physical anthropology was enriched considerably. This period and the period that immediately followed witnessed physical anthropology engaged in racial surveys which included beside anthropometric measurements, anthroposcopic observations, ABO blood groups surveys and finger and palm print studies (dermatoglyphics). Notable among these are Risley's anthropometric surveys of India on the basis of which he gave a racial classification of India, Guha's racial survey of India as a part of the Census of India 1931. Majumdar's racial surveys of Bengal, U.P., and Gujarat, Blood group surveys of Macfarlane, Chatterjee and Mitra, and genetic and racial studies of Sarkar. At this juncture, "mathematicians and statisticians joined physical anthropologists in the efforts to standardize the tools and techniques for meaningful comparative evaluations, and also to provide new tools in the form of mathematical formulae to meet these requirements" (Mathur, 1977). Majumdar's racial surveys were helped by such statisticians as Mahalanobis and C.R. Rao. Human palaeontological (search and study of fossils) researches remained within the jurisdiction of the Geological Survey of India. With the establishment of Anthropological Survey of India and University departments engaged in physical anthropological research the skeletal remains of prehistoric and historic period got competent patrons. Large series of skeletal remains are available from Mohenjodaro and Taxila. Rupkund Series (Himalayas) collected and reported by Majumdar and his associates, Anthropological Survey of India and a few others from another collection of the mid 1950s. So far, more than twenty sites have yielded human remains for the interpretation of ethnic elements from mesolithic to megalithic periods in India. S.R.K. Chopra took up the pursuit for early man in the *Siwaliks* and has been rewarded with some important finds including that of *Gigantopithecus bilaspurensis.*

Physical anthropology in India has made rapid advances after 1960. It has moved into more specialized and problem oriented areas. With the knowledge of the genetics of blood groups, genetical studies of various populations with the focus on blood groups received tremendous impetus. Serological studies though primarily designed to understand population variation, distinction between individual groups, their origin and admixtures, have now focussed attention on the processes of genetic adaptations in response to varying environmental stresses. Human haptoglobins and haemoglobins, particularly the sickle-cell have been tested on about two hundred groups. The association of blood groups with different diseases like eosinophilia, asthma, renallithiasis, filarisis and syphilis have also been reported by physical anthropologists. Studies of genetic variation in different Mendelian groups have also been conducted. Some genetical traits like PTC testing, colour blindness, mid phalengeal hair and hypertrichosis have been studied. Disease in relation to morphological traits, hair histology, human adaptability, immunization and Rh incompatibility and growth studies are no more alien to Indian Physical Anthropology.

Although demographic studies in physical anthropology did begin in fifties, they received impetus only during sixties. "These studies aimed at obtaining information with regard to size of a mating group, preferential mating patterns, marriage distances, inbreeding and outbreeding and other minor associated aspects" (Mathus *et al.*, 1987). Research programmes in physical anthropology have got a big boost with the help of sponsorship and financial support by such national research organizations as Council of Scientific and Industrial Research, Indian Council for Medical Research and National Institute of Sciences. Among the University departments, physical anthropology has figured prominently at Delhi, Chandigarh, Patiala and Calcutta. This branch of anthropology is making rapid strides but in the process its line of demarcation, in several areas, with related branches of sciences is getting blurred.

(iii) Prehistoric Archaeology / Archaeological Anthropology

Indian prehistory or prehistoric archaeology may be said to have begun in 1863 when Robert Bruce Foote, a geologist, discovered some stone tools of Palaeolithic age. This discovery was made at Pallavaram near Madras. In the course of next two decades he reported many prehistoric sites in the Southern Peninsula and Gujarat. Still earlier, Colonel Meadow Tylor carried out meticulous excavations of some south Indian megaliths and in their scientific approach and precision his excavation accounts were far ahead of his times. Around this time there emerged several scholars who began to probe into the remains of man's prehistoric part; these amateur scholars were either geologists or civil servants; T.J. Newbold examined the now well-known Neolithic ashmounds of south India; H.K. Le Mesuriar discovered neolithic ground celts south of Jabalpur and so on. However, among all these persons Foote's interest was entirely different. He was not a mere collector of antiquities. He reported his findings before Indian and European fora of scholars, published them in academic journals, and tried to reconstruct the life of the makers and users of these tools and other antiquities.

Although, the Archaeological Survey of India had been established in 1861 but, its efforts were restricted to the historical period. It was much later-precisely in the third decade of the present century-that the Survey entered the field of prehistory (more correctly protohistory). Thus, it was left to the anthropologically oriented prehistorians to explore new fields and areas of study to understand man's prehistoric past.

The Yale-Cambridge Expedition may be described as the turning point in prehistoric studies. They carried out very significant work in Kashmir Valley, the Potwar plateau, Narmada valley and the Madras coast. "This expedition proposed the scheme of a fourfold glaciation in the Himalayas and brought out the evidence of a new Palaeolithic culture-the Soan-in the Potwar plateau. In the meantime a department of anthropology was established at Calcutta University in 1922 and prehistory was made a component of anthropology in the teaching syllabus. D.Sen of this department had taken part in the Yale-Cambridge Expedition" (V.N. Mishra, 1985). De Terra and Patternson (1939) made the Yale-Cambridge Expedition immortal in the annals of Indian prehistory. K.R.U. Todd (1939) published a short account of the Palaeolithic industries along the Bombay coast and Krishnaswamy (1938) did a similar study around Madras. Giving an immaculate chronological narration of the sequence of studies Misra & Nagar (1972) tell us that perhaps the first excavation of Palaeolithic deposits was carried out by Bose and Sen (1948) of Calcutta University at Kuliana in Mayurbhanj, Orissa. In the early forties an expedition was organized by the Archaeological Survey of India under the leadership of H.D. Sankalia of Deccan College Research Institute at Pune for follow up of the work of Bruce Foote in Gujarat. This expedition led to the discovery of extensive remains of Acheulian culture in the Sabarmati valley and to the first regular excavation of a Mesolithic site at Langhnaj.

As Malti Nagar (1985) very correctly opines, the basic framework of prehistoric culture sequence of India had already been established by 1940 as a result of the pioneering work of many individuals in the preceding hundred years. However, there was little organised institutional research in prehistory at this stage. The Archaeological Survey of India, after its brilliant discoveries of the *Indus Civilization* in Sind and Punjab in the twenties and thirties, had relapsed into inactivity and there was hardly any other activity in the field of prehistoric archaeology in the beginning of 1940s.

In the pre-independence period, the principal agency of pre-historic-indeed all archaeological work in the country-was the Archaeological Survey of India. Outside it only Calcutta University and Deccan College Research Institute had done some work. Two important developments took place at this stage and these were to shape the course of prehistory in India in the coming years and decades. The first of these was the appointment of H.D. Sankalia as professor in the department of archaeology of the newly created Deccan College. The other significant event of this period was appointment of R.E.M. Wheeler as Director General of the Archaeological Survey of India in 1944.

Sankalia undertook a spate of excavations and transformed the Indian prehistoric scene with his discoveries. Further, Ph.D. students working under him extended exploration for the Palaeolithic and Mesolithic remains into all parts of the country. Another of Sankalia's major contributions was to open the field of protohistory in peninsular India.

Wheeler, as Director General of Archaeological Survey of India put new life into the declining fortune of the Survey. He trained many young Indian archaeologists who later made significant contributions to Indian archaeology. Among the important contribution by the Survey during this period are (i) Rao's excavation of the Harappan sites of Lothal and Rangpur of Gujarat, (ii) Lal's excavation at Hastinapur in U.P. and discovery of Painted Grey Ware cultures, (iii) B.K. Thapar's excavations at the Chalcolithic site of Prakash in Dhule district, (iv) Deshpande's excavation at the chalcolithic sites of Bahal in jalgaon district, (v) Sharma's excavation at the Harappan site of Ropar and (vi) Lal's excavation of the Mesolithic of Birbhanpur in Burdwan district.

Reviewing the growth of Prehistoric archaeology after 1947 Misra & Nagar (1972) say that in contrast with the limited work of the first three quarters of this century there has been a phenomenal expansion of prehistoric activities in the country. The virtual monopoly, on archaeological research, of Archaeological Survey of India is now over, though it still continues to be an important agency of research. Universities, on the other hand, are now playing an increasingly bigger role in teaching and research. In more than a dozen universities of the country prehistoric archaeology (Archaeological anthropology) forms an integral part of teaching at the post-graduate and under-graduate levels in anthropology departments though only two of them-those at Calcutta and Gauhati- are actively engaged in research. Prehistory also finds a place in teaching in an equal number of archaeology departments in the universities. But while the emphasis in anthropology courses is on Palaeolithic and Mesolithic, in archaeological courses it is on Neolithic and Chalcolithic. The Archaeological Survey of India has now, for may years, an independent prehistory unit which concerns itself exclusively with stone age while other branches of the Survey restrict themselves largely to Neolithic-Chalcolithic and historical periods.

Other than the Survey the biggest contribution to archaeological researches, specially of prehistory, has been that of Deccan College and its towering patriarch Sankalia. His illustrious student V.N. Misra (coming from Lucknow with pure anthropological background) has made significant contributions in not only excavations but also training a devoted band of students thus continuing the work of the late patriarch. Among such students the names of Malti Nagar for her work in ethno-archaeology and Yashodhar Mathpal for the reconstruction and study of rock art (cave art) may be cited in support of the gigantic contribution made by the famous Deccan College, Pune.

Last two decades or so have witnessed a phenomenal increase in our knowledge of Indian prehistory. While the term Anthropological Archaeology has been formalized in the United States, we have moved from Prehistory to Archaeological Anthropology. Two professional organizations namely, *The Indian Archaeological Society* and *The Indian Society for Prehistoric and Quarternary Studies* have firmly emerged on the horizon of Indian prehistory with their research journals. The contents of these journals reflect the growing trend towards interdisciplinary research and a shift from the traditional history-oriented one. This seems to be a very healthy shift because of the fact that Indian archaeology does not have its roots in anthropology; it is a child of history. Though least developed and popular among all the branches of anthropology in India, the future of archaeological anthropology is definitely not black. Last three decades bear testimony to this statement.

Life Sketches and Contributions of Some Indian Anthropologists

L.K. Ananta Krishna Iyer

L.K. Ananta Krishna Iyer is one of the pioneers in the realm of Indian Anthropology. He was born in 1861 in the Palghat district of Kerala. After completing his BA he joined the local land settlement office as a clerk but soon took up the assignment of a college teacher.

Ananta Krishna Iyer, right from the beginning, was fascinated by the study of evolution of human society and thus he developed a keen insight into human society. Impressed by his interest, the State assigned him the responsibility of carrying out a systematic ethnographic survey. This was a turning point in his life. This survey resulted in the publication of several monographs of castes and tribes. When the first volume of the hand book on the "*Tribes and Castes of Cochin*" was published in 1908 it earned laurels for him. Similar volumes followed later. In the year 1914, he was elected President of the Ethnology section (now Anthropology and Archaeology Section) of the 'first Indian Science Congress' held at Kolkata. In the same year he was appointed as curator of the State Museum and Superintendent of the Zoological Gardens at Trichur. In the year 1920, he joined the first department of Anthropology opened at Calcutta University, where he continued upto his retirement in 1933. He toured Europe extensively and delivered lectures in Indian Ethnography in Paris, Vienna, Berlin, Cambridge, etc. Among his best known works come Anthropology of *the Syrian Christians and Lectures on Ethnography*. Author of five books and dozens of papers, he dies in 1937 in Madras (Chennai).

S.C. Roy

Rai Bahadur Sharat Chandra Roy is also known as 'Father of Indian Ethnology'. He was a master ethnographer, S.C. Roy was born in 1871. He got his schooling and college education at Calcutta. He did his honours degree in English and graduated in Law from the Rippon College, Calcutta. He began his career as a lawyer in Calcutta but later shifted to Ranchi where he proved himself as a highly respected legal practitioner.

S.C. Roy, by virtue of his residence at Ranchi, was attracted towards the local tribal population. He was greatly moved by the plight of the tribals all around him and started writing on them. The result of this labour appeared as *The Mundas and their Country* in 1912. He devoted himself to the study of the tribes of Chotanagpur and rose to become an undisputed authority on the subject. His systematic but descriptive ethnography gave a new lead to the future ethnographics. He was elected honorary member of Folklore Society of London. Another laurel came in 1932 with his election as President of the Anthropology and Archaeology Section of the Indian

Science Congress; he was also elected a member of the Council of honour of the International Congress of the Anthropological and Ethnological Sciences. Back to home, he was elected a member of the Legislative Council of Bihar and Orissa. He was also a member of the Provincial Committee that sat with the Simon Commission.

The journey into ethnography continued and came out *The Oraons of Chotanagpur* in 1915, followed by *The Birhor, Oraon Religion and Custom, The Hill Bhuiyas of Orissa and the Kharia.* He founded, in 1921, a research journal '*Man in India*' which has been a highly respected journal of anthropology. His interests were multifarious. Besides tribal ethnography in which he excelled, he also lectured on 'Principles and Methods of Physical Anthropology' and excavated several Asur' sites of Chotanagpur. A prolific writer, he published several books, tribal monographs and dozens of articles and research papers. He died in 1942 at Ranchi.

B.S. Guha

Like his predecessor, Biraja Shankar Guha also came from a non-anthropology background; he was a student of philosophy and obtained his master's degree from Calcutta University. His other interests were natural history, antiquarianism and primitive tribes. Having been inspired by one Prof. Dixon, he switched over to anthropology, went to Harvard University on a fellowship and did his Master's and Ph.D. in anthropology from the same university. At Harvard he studied all the major branches of anthropology and also worked under E.A. Hooton. He did his Ph.D. thesis on '*The Racial Basis of the Caste System in India*'.

When he came back to India after four years, anthropology had made it's debut as an independent discipline in Calcutta University where he joined the department. The big break came in 1927 when the government created a post of 'anthropologist' in the Zoological Survey of India and he joined it. Ultimately his post became a nucleus of the growth of anthropology in India. In 1936, he founded the Indian Anthropological

Institute at Calcutta with the help of amateur ethnographers. He was also a fellow of the Royal Asiatic Society of Bengal and it's honorary secretary. He also presided over the section of Anthropology and Archaeology in the Indian Science Congress in 1938.

Due to the persistent efforts of Guha and several civil servents sympathetic to the cause of anthropology, in 1946 a new organization called *"Anthropological Survey of India"* was carved out from the parent organization of Zoological Survey of India. Guha became it's first Director. and organized several training and extension programmes for the social workers and social scientists. He persistently worked to make Indian Anthropology a holistic discipline and propagated it as an integrated or united science consisting of ethnology, physical anthropology, prehistory, linguistics, maintaining close affinities with the allied sciences like psychology, zoology, paleobotany etc. Three of the most prestigious organizations of anthropology in India namely *Anthropological Survey of India* with it several stations, *Indian Museum*, Calcutta and the *Tribal Research Institute*, Ranchi, which were founded with the help of significant contributions of Guha, bear testimony to his genius and untiring spirit a San organizer. His contribution in the reconstruction of the racial map of India can never be forgotten. Though, he was not a prolific writer (he published about fifteen papers and books) whatever he has written still retains lot of importance. B.S. Guha was born in 1894 and died in 1961.

N.K. Bose

Nirmal Kumar Bose is a highly familiar and respected name in Indian Anthropology. He was born in 1901. He got his schooling at Patna and Ranchi and higher education at Calcutta. He did his Master's in Anthropology in 1925. He was involved in freedom struggle and his academic career was interrupted several times by certain nationalist events. He taught anthropology at Calcutta University.

N.K. Bose also served as a visiting scholar in the University of California, Berkley and Chicago. He also acted as the Director, Anthropological Survey of India during 1959-64 and served as advisor on tribal affairs, Government of India. He retired in 1964 and from then onwards served in various capacities. He distinguished himself as a devoted social worker and was involved with several philanthropic organizations. Bose had multifarious interests outside anthropology. Beside being author of books like *Cultural Anthropology* (1929) and *Problems of Indian Nationalism* (1969). He also published works such as *Canons of Orissan Architecture* (1932), *Excavations in Mayurbhanj* (1949) and *Calcutta : A Social Survey* (1964). He also served as editor of Man in India. He also wrote profusely in Bengali and helped popularizing anthropology and making it more relevant to the contemporary society. He died in 1972.

D.N. Majumdar

Dhirendra Nath Majumdar occupies a unique place in Indian Anthropology. To many he was a father figure, a patriarch and an institution into himself. If one is asked to name the persons dedicated to the cause of Anthropology in India. Majumdar shall definitely be included in such a category or persons known for his fierce devotion to the subject and his passion for the expansion of anthropology so dear to his heart.

D.N. Majumdar was born in 1903 at Patna and pursued his education at Dacca, Calcutta and Cambridge. He obtained a Master's in anthropology from Calcutta University in 1924 and was recipient of several prestigious awards. In 1928, he joined the Department of Economics and Sociology, Lucknow University, as a lecturer in '*Primitive Economics*'. In the mid-twenties, Majumdar had turned down his nomination for a sub-deputy collectorship and preferred to do anthropological fieldwork in Chotanagpur. He was initiated into fieldwork by the great ethnographer S.C. Roy and he always acknowledged this profusely. In 1933, he went to Cambridge to write his doctoral thesis on culture contact and acculturation among the Ho of Kolhan under Hodson. He was awarded Ph.D. in 1935. He was invited to deliver a course of lectures at Cambridge during this period. This was a rare honour for any Indian. He was also elected as a fellow of the Royal Anthropological Institute of Great Britain and Ireland.

Though he specialized in social anthropology. He also maintained active interest in physical anthropology and prehistory. He got advanced training in physical anthropology from Morant and Gates. He was greatly influenced by Malinowski and regarded his as his teacher. On his return in India, he joined his old post in Lucknow University. In 1939, he presided over the Anthropology and Archaeology section of Indian Science Congress. The number of medals and honour conferred on him were countless.

D.N. Majumdar was also involved in the decennial census of 1941 and he carried out an anthropometric and serological survey, for then the United Provinces (now Uttar Pradesh). The legendary statistician P.C. Mahalanobis collaborated with him in this endeavour. His involvement and devotion to the subject may be gauged from the fact that he was the most knowledgeable anthropologist about the tribes and castes. His knowledge of the Ho of Chotanagpur and the Khasa (Jounsari) of Jounsar Bhawar was amazing. The people of Bengal, Gujarat and Uttar Pradesh and the tribals of Bastar were intimately known to him. Alongwith Verrier Elwin, he initiated 'problem oriented ethnography'. He founded the Ethnographic and Folk Culture Society, U.P. in 1945 and later on brought a journal '*The Eastern Anthropologist*'. The society as well as the journal still remain to remind the world of his immense contribution to anthropology. He lectured at several prestigious universities of the world.

D.N. Majumdar may be regarded as a pioneer among Indian anthropologists to do '*village studies*'. The study of non-tribal peasant society was a new trend. "He not only came forward with a 'model' of what anthropological village studies ought to be but even undertook the unconventional task of demarcating the social contours of an industrial city. Alongwith these he also undertook and completed the evaluation of administratively engineered social change" (Gopal Saran, 1961). He always remained in the forefront in Indian anthropology. He was the innovator of acculturation studies as well as 'theoretically oriented ethnography'. We do not known of any Indian anthropologist, other than D.N. Majumdar, who besides writing tribal monographs, studied various tribes in transition presented a model of anthropological village study, delineated the social contours of an industrial study, delineated the social contours of an industrial city, carried out anthropometric and serological survey, carried out excavation, influenced and moulded a whole generation of anthropologists, a popularised anthropology in every department and acted as patriarch. D.N. Majumdar is the greatest academic anthropologist, India has produced so far. At the time of his death in 1961, he was head of the department he founded and Dean, Faculty of Arts. True to his life style and philosophy he expired after an extremely busy day's work. His bibliography runs into several pages and his works are too well known to be enumerated here again.

M.N. Srinivas

Mysore Narasimbachar Srinivas (popularly known as M.N. Srinivas) is a highly respected name in the contemporary sociology/social anthropology. He was born in 1917 and received his early education in Karnataka. He did his Masters in sociology from Mysore University, Ph.D. in Sociology from Bombay University and D. Phil. in Social anthropology from the Oxford University. Srinivas has taught at Delhi University, M.S. University, Baroda and Oxford University. He has been a recipient of many prestigious awards and fellowships.

The first systematic attempt to define the processes of social change in Indian Society was attempted by Srinivas through his pathbreaking concept of Sanskritization and Westernization. These concepts were evolved by him in the course of his study of Coorgs of South India, later published as '*Religion and Society among the Coorgs of South India*' (1952). By providing lead in this direction, Srinivas inspired several Indian Sociologists and social anthropologists to do empirical research on Indian Society to understand the direction and the process of change hastened by the independence of the country. Later on, when he published his paper *Dominant Caste in Rainpura* (1959) in American Anthropologists, he gave further lead to the social scientist to understand the contemporary ground realities in village India. The phenomena of power and dominance in village India, to be understood through the concept of dominant caste provides the basis to understand the nature of socio-economic political change in village India. When linked with twin concepts of Sanskritization and Westernization, these concepts provide the crucial basis to understand the dynamics of social change in Indian society. His *'Remembered Village'* is a unique work in ethnography in which the whole data were derived from memory after the whole text was lost in a dormitory fire where Srinivas was staying in the Stanford University U.S.A. Some of his other very well-known works are *Caste in Modern India* (1962), *Social Change in Modern India* (1966) and *India's Village* (ed.) (1955). Besides these and some other books he has also published more than hundred research papers.

M.N. Srinivas was very active and academically productive. He died in 1999, Benguluru. He has trained a whole generation of sociologists and social anthropologists some of whom are occupying prestigious positions in India and abroad.

S.C. Dube

Shyama Charan Dube belongs to that category of social anthropologists who did not do their master's or Ph.D. specifically in anthropology and yet, like M.N. Srinivas is considered top ranking social anthropologist. S.C. Dube obtained his master's degree in political science (with a special paper on social anthropology). He wrote his doctoral dissertation in sociology on the 'Kamar', a tribe of Madhya Pradesh. He taught political science at Lucknow University and sociology/social anthropology at Nagpur and Osmania. He also served for some time in Anthropological Survey of India and National Institute of Community Development. He also taught at Sagar, London and Cornell Universities.

A fine field researcher, he did his fieldwork in Chattisgarh (Madhya Pradesh), Telangana region (Andhra Pradesh) and West Orissa. He is best known for his theoretical interest and contributions in the field of social structure and '*Sociology of Economic Development*'. Social change and economic development has been the major theme of his several works like *India's Changing Villages: Human Factors in Community Development* (1958). *Power and Conflict in Village India* and several research papers. His *Indian Village* (1955) is considered a major work in village studies.

S.C. Dube has always advocated for a dynamic social science responsive to the contemporary challenges. His *Social Science in Changing Society* is an important contribution in this field. The theme of development and modernization has been uppermost in the work of Dube for the last two decades. It began prominently with the publication of his collection of articles titled "*Contemporary India and its Modernization* (1973) and *Explanation and Management of Change* (1971) and *Culminated in Modernization and Development: The Search for Alternative Paradigms* (1988)". He was born in 1922 and continued to be highly productive in the academic world. He passed away in 1996.

L.P. Vidyarthi

Lalitha Prasad Vidyarthi, popularly known as LPV is a familiar name in contemporary Indian anthropology. Vidyarthi did his masters in anthropology from Lucknow University and Ph.D. from Chicago. He was a student of D.N. Majumdar at Lucknow and Robert Redfield at Chicago. Perhaps, his last Ph.D. thesis supervised by the great patriarch of Chicago.

L.P. Vidyarthi joined Ranchi University and almost single handed he raised the status of the anthropology department and added multifarious dimensions to it. A major department of anthropology in the country, centre of advanced studies in anthropology and a very productive area of anthropological research. Expansion of anthropology in the country was a passion with him.

The concept of '*Sacred Complex*' is an original contribution of Vidyarthi through which the cultural processes in the Indian Civilization is sought to be understood. His Rise of Anthropology in India, a two volume narration of the growth of Indian anthropology is perhaps the only detailed treatise on this subject. He did fieldwork mostly among the tribes of Bihar and developed new insights into applied anthropology. When he headed the 'Task force for the Development of the Backward Area's', appointed by the Planning Commission on the eve of the Fifth Five-Year Plan, it brought great honour to applied anthropology in India. The concept of 'Tribal Sub Plan' (TSP) now in vogue is a product of his effort. He has published several books and research papers on applied anthropology. By writing extensively on the impact of industrialization and urbanization on the tribes of Chotanagpur region, he contributed immensely to an 'Industrial Anthropology' in India. When the 'Tenth International Congress of Anthropological and Ethnological Sciences' was held in 1978 in India, it not only brought a singular honour to India (because it was the first time when this congress was held in any Asian Country) but also to L.P. Vidyarthi, who chaired the Congress.

Andre Beitelle (1934)

Andre Beitelle is one of the leading sociologists/ anthropologists of India. Besides having been visiting professor is several prestigious universities of Europe, he has spent most of his time in University of Delhi as professor in the department of sociology. He obtained his Masters degree in anthropology from Calcutta University and then joined the department of of sociology, university of Delhi as lecturer. His name has always been a matter of curiosity to those who did not know of his parentage-coming from a French and Bengali parentage. He was conferred Padma Bhushan in 2005, as a mark of recognition for his scholarship.

Beitelle's Caste, Class and Power: Changing Patterns of Stratification in a Tanjore Village (1965) is regarded as a classic. His area of specialization is social stratification, inequality, social change and political sociology. Agrarian class relations thus has been his major area of interest. Because of his orientation in anthropology he had a natural inclination to compare different cultures. Among the British anthropologists he was most influenced by

Evans-Pritchard followed by Max Gluckman and Edmund Leach. MN Srinivas, his teacher, had also a great impact of these anthropologists. Beitelle's critical contribution has been his understanding of caste, class, hierarchy, inequality and justice. Some of his important published works are Six Essays in Comparative Sociology (1974), The Backward Classes in Contemporary India (1992), The Idea of Natural Inequality and other Essays (1983) and some others. He is also a public intellectual and writes in popular newspapers and magazines, beyond purely academic circles.

Verrier Elwin (1902 - 1964)

Elwins life, personality, and anthropology is unique in several ways. He came to India as a Christian missionary in 1930s and was attached to the church in district Mandla, Madhya Pradesh. In his first counter with the tribal people living around the place he was so moved by their plight that he left the church and the clergy and decided to devote himself for their upliftment. Elwin was not an academically trained anthropologist but he soon realized that he was destined to develop an anthropological perspective to highlight the problems of the tribal communities. His first major work The Baiga (1939) may be understood as his statement on what was wrong with the whole situation and what should be done for the tribal communities. This led to his considered view that the tribal people are to be saved from exploitation by the non-tribals through 'reserved national parks'. This isolationist approach did not win the support of even fellow anthropologists. In his later years he virtually gave up this approach and wanted the integration of the tribal people with the larger society with all the necessary safeguards. He then moved to study the Muria tribe of Bastar and published his well known work Muria and their Ghotul which was the first full fledged study of a tribal youth dormitory. This study was followed by a number of other studies on the religion, myths and folklore of the tribal communities. In the course of his studies he developed friendship with Jawahar Lal Nehru, who among the national leaders, was perhaps most sympathetic to the tribal cause. In the second stage of his work among the tribals he moved to the north eastern region especially North East Frontier Agency (NEFA) and settled in Shillong. Meanwhile he took Indian citizenship and married a tribal woman. Because of affinity of ideas he appreciated Nehru's Panchsheel (five point charter for the tribal people) and supported Nehru's idea of allowing and encouraging the tribal communities to develop along their own genius. His A philosophy for NEFA and Loss of Nerve are recognized as outstanding works for understanding the tribal problems. After independence he was appointed as an adviser on tribal affairs. He also served as the Deputy Director of the Anthropological Survey of India. His autobiography The Tribal World of Verrier Elwin gives a calourful account of his experiences with the tribal communities. In recognition of his services to India he was conferred Padm Bhushan in 1961.

One of his very important contributions, less talked about, is popularization of anthropology in India. He carried the message of anthropology through his motto, 'The Art and essence of anthropology is love, without which nothing is fertile and nothing is true'.

Irawati Karve (1905-1970)

Irawati Karve is regarded as the first female anthropologist of India. Born in 1905, her first name 'Irawati' comes from the river Irawaddy of Burma where she was born. She obtained her masters in sociology in 1928 from Bombay University and did her Ph.D. from Berlin University in Germany. Her joining Deccan College, Pune facilitated her entry into anthropology. In her own unique way she pioneered the use of Indology for the study of Indian society despite fairly oriented torwards anthropology. Her works on kinship is considered both in sociology and anthropology, as a pioneering contribution in creating a multidisciplinary corpus of knowledge. Though the father figure of sociology GS Ghurye was her mentor but she was not a blind follower of his teacher-mentor. Her study Kinship Organization of India (1953) is respected as a classic. It was followed by Hindu Society:

An Interpretation (1961). In her work on kinship organization, she divided India's kinship pattern into four zones, Northern Zone, Southern Zone, Eastern Zone and Central Zone. With this study she opened the door for future studies on kinship system in Indian society.

Surajit Sinha (1926-2002)

SurajitSinha obtained his Masters in anthropology in 1949 from Calcutta University and Ph.D. in North Western University, U.S.A. He was also visiting professor at various universities in Europe and U.S.A. In his academic life he belonged to a period of Indian anthropology when Indian anthropologists were under the profound influence of both British as well as American anthropology and anthropologists. Yet, gradually the influence of British anthropology was dwindling and American anthropological academia was becoming favourite with Indian anthropologists. Surajit Sinha, trained by both NK Bose and T.C. Das and later by Robert Redfield at Chicago, had a fairly good exposure to the global anthropology too. He was very critical of Indian anthropologists and sociologists borrowing and leaning heavily on the non-Indian and western models.

His important contribution may be seen in the field of tribal transformation in India with reference to the tribe-caste continuum and how several tribal communities, especially of central India, were being drawn towards the Hindu caste system. His research findings on the integration of Bhumij tribe within the Hindu caste system is regarded as a landmark research. He continued with his Ph.D. dissertation on the acculturation of the Bhumij: A Study in Inter-ethnic Integration and Stratification and on the basis of his further research among the central Indian tribal communities especially the Gonds, he came out with the process of Kshatriyization and Rajputization of these tribes. He widened his research further by conducting researches on an anthropological study of Indian civilization and of cultural evolution. Summarizing, his original contribution to Indian anthropology may be seen in his studies, 'Tribe-caste and Tribe Peasant continua" in Central India (1965), 'State formation and Rajput Myth in Tribal Central India' (1962) and 'Bhumij-Kshatriya Social movement in South Manbhum (1959). Thus, he may be seen as a pioneering historical anthropologist of India.

Christoph von Furer-Haimendorf (1909-1995)

An Austrian, deeply interested in India and Indian Culture, Haimendorf contributed immensely to the tribal issues in India. It is said that he developed interest in Indian culture after reading Rabindranath Tagore during his student days. He was trained in anthropology and archeology in Vienna and obtained his Ph.D. on the tribal social organization of Assam and North-West Burma. After completing his Ph.D. he moved to London to have interaction with Malinowski and other anthropologists.

Haimendorf travelled to India in 1936 and worked among the Nagas. He wrote a travelogue in 1938 titled The Naked Nagas on the basis of his observations and experiences in that area. This publication described the life of the Konyak Nagas, a relatively lesser known tribe at that time. Unlike others he learnt the local language and worked without an interpreter. On the outbreak of the IInd world war, he was arrested by the British authorities on the suspicion of a Nazi sympathizer. Because of his friendship and contact with several British officers, he was released but ordered to confine himself to Hyderabad state in the South. After winning the trust of the ruler Nizam of Hyderabad he was assigned the task of studying the local tribal communities to understand their problems and suggest remedial measures. That is how he studied the Chenchu, Bhil, Reddi and RajGond tribes of the present Telangana state. After sometime he was allowed to return to the north-east where he was given the post of special officer to NEFA where he studied Apatanis.

After the war was over, Haimenderf was formally appointed by the Nizam's government as advisor for tribes and backward classes. Later he went to Nepal and became the first foreigner to do research on the peoples of Nepal. Haimendorf was an ethnographer par excellence. Some of his most important works are The

Naked Nagas (1939), The Chenchus (1943), The RajGonds of Adilabad (1948), The Sherpas of Nepal (1969) and Tribes of India: The Struggle for Survival (1982)

David Mandelbaum (1911-1987)

Mandelbaum was an American anthropologist and an associate of Melville Herskovits, another well known anthropologist. He belongs to a group of anthropologist whose name and fame in Indian anthropology rests on just one book – Society in India published in 1970 in two volumes. The sub-titles of these two volumes are very meaningful – continuity and change and change and continuity. This two volume work is one of the most comprehensive and important studies on Indian society. Mandelbaum was professor of anthropology at the University of California and a prominent scholar on Indian society.

His study of Indian society began with a field survey of Kota society in 1937. Since then he continued to visit India many times till old age got him. In his magnum opus, Society in India he understood and interpreted the principal institutions of Indian society- family, jati and village both as "systems and sub-systems of the larger society." His analysis of the Indian social system and caste order, the general nature of Indian society and the customary relations among members of different groups was laudable. According to his view, the family in Indian society is both a model and as mould for the jati and its relations. Very few scholars of Indian society could be credited to have done such an incisive analysis in such a lucid manner.

Louis Dumont (1911-1998)

A formidable scholar in modern sociology/ anthropology, Louis Dumont was French and taught at Oxford University during the 1950s. Later he became the director at the prestigious Institute Ecole des Hautes Etudes in Sciences Sociales (EHESS), Paris.

Dumont studied under the great sociologist Marcel Mauss in 1930s and because of his Sanskritist and indological expertise developed deep interest in this field of knowledge. He studied several societies including India and did an inter-civilizational comparison. He spent several years in India wandering from north to south and focused on Hindusism, kinship and caste in ancient India along with socio-political movements in modern India.

Homo Hierarchicus: The Caste System and its Implications published in 1966 is taken as his magnum opus. When the English translation of this French work came, it became one of the most debated works in Indian sociology/anthropology. In this classic Dumont moves from the ethnographic data to hierarchical ideology in ancient religious texts. On another plane of analysis he contrasts this work with his modern western antithesis, Homo Aequalis. After lot of debate and criticism the new edition of Homo Hierarchicus came with a lengthy new preface as answer to his critics. Louis Dumont remains one of the few scholars of Indian society whose only one book is considered so important and indispensable.

Milton Singer (1912-1994)

Milton Singer was a leading American anthropologist whose scholarship is based mainly on Indian society He was a professor at the University of Chicago. He started coming to India since 1954 and did intensive study for the next ten to fifteen years. Because of his interest in India he created a leading centre of South Asian Studies at the University of Chicago.

Singer's field work in India prompted him to challenge the popular American contention that India would not be able to advance economically because its people were too tied to their traditions of caste and Hindu spirituality. He studied industrialists and industrial culture in Madras and published an outstanding work When a Great Tradition Modernizes: An Anthropological Approach to Indian Civilization (1972). He also worked with his senior Robert Redfield in Chicago on an inter-disciplinary project. His another important work is Traditional India: Structure and Change and another one Structure and Change in Indian Society co-authored with Bernard

Cohn. The phrase "Semiotic anthropology" was first used by Milton Singer. As a research programme, its goal is the establishment of a "Cultural theory of signs" and the development of an analytical tool for cultural messages such as painting and architecture.

Mckim Marriott (1924)

Marriott was professor of anthropology at Chicago University and was trained by Robert Redfield, the patriarch at Chicago. Following the structural-functional approach and influenced by the model of Redfield and Milton Singer, he conducted pioneering studies of village India. He focused on social change in India's villages. In his landmark work, Village India: Studies in the Little Communities (1955) he refined the concept of interaction between Little and Great Traditions. The whole approach of Marriot is historical and cultural. Through his evolutionary understanding of civilization and structure of tradition he came out with the twin concepts of universalization and Parochialization. Marriott's edited Village India is one of the pioneering and best known collection of village studies down in 1950s carrying, besides his own, contributions from both foreign and Indian anthropologists. He did not stop at this study but continued with intensive field work in India resulting in two more important works, Caste Ranking and Community Structure in the Five Regions of India and Pakistan (1960) and India through Hindu Categories (1990). In the former dealing with caste ranking he takes the position in this path breaking study that the Muslims operate within the framework of the Hindu caste system. It was a new idea of that time.

HD Sankalia (1908-1989)

Sankalia's contribution to archaeological anthropology and prehistory in India is unparalleled. After doing his masters in History he want to England in 1934 to do his Ph.D in Ancient Indian History at London University. He wrote his thesis on the archaeology of Gujarat and returned to India in 1937. He admits the role of Robert

Bruce Foote, regarded as father of Indian Prehistory, in his training in archaeology through Foote's two volume magnum opus Prehistoric Antiquities in India.

Joining Deccan College, Pune, the most prestigious institution for archaeology in India, now a university, he not only himself carried a number of excavations but also trained a whole generation of prehistorians. He excavated Langhnaj, the famous Mesolithic site with Irawati Karve discovering microliths and other tools. Among his other famous excavations, Maheshwar, Navdatoli, and Inamgaon should be placed at the top. He developed Deccan College from scratch, transforming it into an area of excellence with a number of laboratories. In 1963, he published his monumental work Prehistory and Proto history of India and Pakistan. Besides having been conferred several medals and awards, he was conferred Padm Bhusahn in 1974. It must be highlighted that almost all the Indian anthropologists specializing in prehistory/archaeological anthropology were motivated, inspired and several of them trained by HD Sankalia. Without his contribution this relatively lesser known branch of Indian anthropology would have been further poorer.

❑

2 Fieldwork and Fieldwork Tradition: Defining Features of Anthropological Research

Fieldwork, more than anything else, characterises the discipline of anthropology. It advocates face to face experience with its subjects. Gopal Saran (1983) puts it brilliantly by stating that, "this is due to the anthropologists' desire to receive phenomenon through his own senses because of his great love of facts". The anthropologist is different from the other social scientists. Anthropology would not be what it is today but for the insights fed into it by intensive field work. "It was not, however, always so; fieldwork was not what interested our founding fathers" (beteille & Madan, 1975).

Anthropology, in its earliest stages, was mainly concerned with the study of primitive society. In the absence of any scientifically collected data by professionals the image of primitive man was determined by the descriptions of such narrators as travellers and hunters. "Hence there seems to have been pendulum swing from extreme to extreme in speculations about primitive man.

First he was a little more than an animal who lived in poverty, violence, and fear; then he was a gentle person who lived in plenty, peace and security. First he was lawless; then he was a slave to law and custom. First he was devoid of any religious feelings or beliefs, then he was entirely dominated by the sacred and immersed in ritual. First he was an individualist who preyed on the weaker and held what he could; then he was a communist who held lands and goods in common. First he was sexually promiscuous; then he was a model of domestic virtue. First he was lethargic and incorrigibly lazy; then he was alert and industrious" (Evans-Pritchard, 1956). There were all sorts of distortions and contradictions. Subjectivity was sometimes stretched to absurdity and fantasy.

Sixteenth century onwards saw a beginning of sober, factual and balanced accounts of native life. During the middle of the eighteenth century and the middle of the nineteenth century, knowledge of primitive peoples and societies was greatly increased. The European colonization of America, establishment of British rule in India and settlement of Australia, New Zealand and South Africa by European emigrant were largely responsible for this trend. The logical consequence of these developments was that the character of ethnographic descriptions of the people of these regions began to change. It was no more hunters'/ travellers' tales now and these were detailed studies by missionaries and administrators who not only had better opportunities to observe but were intellectually more equipped to understand and rationalize many an 'exotic and strange' ways and customs. Even at this point of time, with the sole exception of Morgan, all the notable anthropologists (and of course, researchers of allied disciplines too) were 'armchair scholars'. They relied on the secondary data and secondary sources. Their main tool of data collection was mailed questionaire. For non-professionals a standardized format provided in Notes and Querries on Anthropology, first published by Royal Anthropological Institute in 1874, was the most reliable guide for observing and recording the data through extensive use of interpreters. The towering professional anthropologists of this period (the earliest ones) such as McLennan, Tylor, Maine and Frazer were content with producing important treatises based on secondary sources. The classic on religion *The Golden Bough* by Frazer was also based on the data collected through secondary sources.

By that time it became pretty clear to the ethnographers and anthropologists that if the study of social anthropology was to more forward the researchers would have to go to their subjects and make their own observations. Evans-Pritchard (ibid) very rightly comments that it is indeed surprising that with the exception of Morgan's study of the Iroquois, not a single anthropologist conducted field studies till the end of the nineteenth century. It is even more remarkable that it does not seem to have occurred to them that a writer on anthropological topics should atleast have a look, if only a glimpse, at one or two specimens of what he spent his life writing about. This was also the time when scholars from natural sciences background started joining the discipline of anthropology. Bose was physicist and geographer Haddon a marine zoologist, Rivers a physiologist, Seligman and a pathologist, Elliot Smith and amatomist and Malionowski a physicist. These men had been taught that in science one tests hypothesis by one's own observation. One does not rely on laymen to do it for one.

The *Jessup North Pacific Expedition* led by Franz Boas in 1897 and the *Cambridge Expedition* to the Torres Straits in 1898-99 comprising Haddon, Rivers, Seligman and others mark the beginning of formal anthropological fieldwork. Seligman's remark that fieldwork was to anthropology what the blood of the martyrs was to church indeed proved prophetic. From this time onward anthropology became a whole time professional study and field experience an essential part of anthropological study. Fieldwork almost completely eliminated speculation.

Among the pioneer field researchers, the man who did more than most others in defining the nature of field work was Rivers. He distinguished between intensive and survey work. Intensive empirical studies from the core of anthropological studies today. Rivers had himself engaged in both types of research, survey work in Melanesia and intensive fieldwork among the Toda tribe in India. However, the early empirical research suffered from some weaknesses. The short time researchers spend among the people they studied, their ignorance of the subject's language and their casual approach did not permit deep investigation. Radcliffe-Brown, a student of Rivers and Haddon provided an important thrust to the anthropological field work. His field work among the Andaman Islanders in India between 1906 to 1908 is considered to be the first genuinely intensive fieldwork in a primitive society to describe the social life of a people in "*such a way as to bring out clearly what was significant in it for sociological theories*" (Evans-Pritchard, ibid). He lived among the Andaman Islanders intimately, learnt their language and collected the data through *participant observation.*

Bronislaw Malinowski, the great British social anthropologist of Polish origin transformed the Fieldwork in anthropology to such an extent that things could never be the same again. As Saran (ibid) correctly remarks, "with the publication of Malinowski's Argonauts of the Western Pacific amateur ethnography ws totally eclipsed. The ethnographic fieldwork became a highly professionalised activity. It was no more mere data collection. It turned into deeper analysis of particular social structure and cultural patterns". He was a thorough fieldworker. He not only spent a longer period than any anthropologist before or after him in a single study of aprimitive people but he was also the first anthropologist to conduct his whole research through the native language. It is he who proclaimed what may be called the philosophy of fieldwork' and there is little that has been added to the principles of fieldwork given by Malinowski half a century ago. "We certainly use more technical aids today, increasingly rely upon statistical tools but the essential definition of the nature of fieldwork remains substantially the same as Malinowski's description of it" (Beteille & Madan, ibid). Among his other works *The Sexual Life of Savages* (1929) and *Coral Gardens and Their Magic* (1935) are regarded as classics in fieldwork.

As already stated, Malinowski transformed the fieldwork into an art. Thus certain basic conditions have been laid down for a good field investigation.

Enumerating the attributes of a good field investigation Evans Pritchard (ibid) says that anthropologist must spend sufficient time on the study, he must throughout be in close contact with the people among whom he is working, he must communicate with them solely through their own language and he must study their entire culture and social life. The earlier professional fieldworkers were always in a great hurry. Their quick visits to native peoples sometimes lasted only a few days, and seldom more than a few weeks. Survey research of this kind can be useful preliminary to intensive studies but it is of little value for an understanding of social life. The position is very different today when one to three years are devoted to the study of a single people. This permits observations to be made in every season of the year, the social life of the people to be recorded to the last detail and conclusions to be tested systematically. However, even given unlimited time for his research, the anthropologist will not produce a good account of the people he is studying unless he can put himself in a position which enables him to establish ties of intimacy with them, and to observe their daily activities from within and not from without, their community life. He must live, as far as possible, physically and morally as part of the community. He then not only sees and hears what goes on in the normal everyday life of the people as well as less common events, such as ceremonies and legal cases, but by taking part in those activities in which he can appropriately engage, he learns through action as well as by ear and eye what goes around him. This is very unlike the situation in which records of native life were compiled by earlier anthropological fieldworkers and also by missionaries and administrators, who living out of the native community in mission stations or government posts, had mostly to rely on what a few informants told them. A good field researcher is not there to change their way of life but as a humble learner of it. What is perhaps even more important for his work is the fact that he is all alone, cut off from the companionship of men of his own race and culture and is dependent on the natives around him for company, friendship and human understanding. An anthropologist has failed unless, when he says good bye to natives, there is on both sides the sorrow of parting. It is evident that he can only establish this intimacy if he makes himself in some degree a member of their society and lives, thinks, and feels in their culture since only he, and not they, can make the necessary transference.

The essential requirements and conditions of a good fieldwork described in the preceding paragraph by another great field researcher Evans-Pritchard may be covered within the parameters of two terms—intensive field work and participant observation—so distinctive of anthropological studies. Unfortunately very few people have published their field experiences. "The implication of this general neglect would seem to be that what matter are the results of fieldwork rather than the techniques that one might employ for data collection, so long as certain basic requirements of objective investigation have been met. This is a pity, because the importance of self-analysis by the investigator becomes very valuable for himself and for others in the absence of standardizaton of fieldwork techniques" (Beteille & Madan, ibid). One way to meet this situation is obviously to try to standardize research techniques and to prepare formal guides fieldwork. The argument is simple: anthropology as a social science can hardly afford to be personal adventure; it has to be a collective endeavour united shared understandings in respect of both purpose and methodology. Methods of social research should be communicable to students in the classroom and replicable in the field. The problem of subjectivity and objectivity should also be faced likewise. An emphasis on the freedom of the individual observer must not be allowed to become an excuse for lack of methodological regiour and a pre-occupation with technical virtuosity should not be permitted to drive underground, as it were, the role that the observor's personality plays in what he observes, the links that he forges between data, and the kinds of structure that he prefers to fabricate to make sense out of the multitude of observed roles and relationships, however, the study of human society would indeed become a dull affair if some magic formulae could be devised which would enable the fieldworker not only to foresee all possible problems but to solve them in the ordinary course of his work. If our experiences in our own or in other societies were never a source of puzzlement or doubt, there would hardly be any stimulus for sociological research (ibid). It would be contrary to the spirit of scientific enquiry if we were to write up our research experiences as a series of success stories. The actual experiences of research are made up of failures as well as successes, of trials as well as joys. There are times when the surest procedure fails to produce results, and times when the most obscure facts reveal their true significance, unasked as it were.

At this point it would be important not to miss the mention of field investigation in one's own culture and in 'other cultures'. As the precedings pages reveal when the anthropologists, British as well as American, initiated anthropology into the realm of social research based on fieldwork they were concerned with studying primitive peoples whose life radically differed from their own. It was much later that they started studying their own societies and cultures. In India, on the other hand, fieldwork for Indian anthropologist has largely meant the study of one's own society. This was a unique situation not faced by anthropologists of Britain and United States. Further, the categorisation of 'insider' and 'outsider' is also full of dilemmas. When a researcher brought up in North India goes to do fieldwork in a South Indian village, is he an outsider or an insider? Dozens of such situation may be perceived.

Whatever has been described in the preceding pages mainly concerns with fieldwork in social-cultural anthropology and of course most of the anthropological field research is concerned with this branch of anthropology. However, research in physical biological anthropology also requires fulfillment of some of the conditions laid down for social-cultural anthropology. Earlier physical anthropological research was mainly confined to the study of morphological criteria for racial classification. The present day physical anthropology (sometimes referred to as biological anthropology due to its widened horizon) involves extensive research in dental anthropology, population genetics, cytogenetics, molecular and biochemical generics and host of other spceializations. Some of these fields required detailed knowledge of the environment and kinship system of the human groups under study. All these rquire atleast some of the methodological fineness and vigour demonstrated by social-cultural anthropology. The physical anthropologists too are required to established rapport with their subjects and respondents and sometimes have to resort to participant observation technique to elicit required data. However, a prehistoric archaeologist or archaeological anthropologist does not have to worry about such problems because he is not dealing with living human beings. Their work mostly requires digging or collection from the surface for the material (and physical) remains of prehistoric man.

Fieldwork has been accepted as an indispensable *rite de passage* in the making of a modern anthropologist sometimes referred to as an act or feat of *living with strangers*. The anthropological approach, to use Xluckhon's term, is that of "attached detachment". Fieldwork is considered, in Koreber's words, "an opportunity, a privilege and the professional catchet". Levi-Strauss has the last work when he says that "indeed, the field research with which every anthropological career begins is the mother and wet-nurse of doubt, the philosophical attitude par excellence. This 'anthropological doubt' does not only consist of knowing that one knows nothing, but of resolutely exposing what one thought one knew, and indeed one's very own ignorance, to the buffetings and denials which are directed at one's most cherished ideas and habits by other ideas and habits which must need contradict them to the highest degree".

Ethnography and Ethnographic Method

The most characteristic feature of anthropological field work is Ethnographic Method, the most important tool of 'qualitative research. In simplest terms, ethnography is the systematic description of a contemporary culture through fieldwork. In loose and broad sense, the goal of ethnography is to provide a detailed, in-depth description of everyday life and practice of a people. Many scholars referred to it as "thick description", a term attributed to Clifford Geertz (1973) who was developing the idea of an interpretive theory of culture in the 1970s. From another angle, the term ethnography has come to be equated with virtually any qualitative research project. Thus, traditionally speaking, ethnography may be described as the best tool of qualitative research in anthropology and now being used in sociology too, whose aim is cultural interpretation, Thus an ethnographer is supposed to go beyond reporting events and details of experience but to attempt to explain how these represent "webs of meaning" (Geertz, ibid).

As rightly suggested by Alan Barnard & Jonathan Spencer (1996) the word 'ethnography' has a double meaning in anthropology: ethnography as product (ethnographic writings) and ethnography as process (participant observation or fieldwork). The product depends upon the process but not in any simple relationship. In constructing ethnographies, anthropologists do more than merely 'writing up' the field notes they record as part of the process of doing fieldwork. If ethnographies can be seen as the building blocks and testing grounds of anthropological and sociological theory, ethnographies and the ethnographic process from which they derive are also shaped and moulded by theory. As a category of anthropological research, ethnography is characterized by the first hand study of a small community or ethnic group. "Such studies combine, to a varying degree, descriptive and analytical elements, but the central characteristic of conventional ethnographies is that they focus on one specific culture or society and consider theoretical or comparative generalization from the stand point of the ethnographic example" (Macmillan's Dictionary of Anthropology, 1986). Interestingly, anthropologists have generally paid little explicit attention to ethnographies as texts, often treating ethnography as synonymous with fieldwork or as a method rather than a product of research.

History and Development of Ethnography

When we look at the history of anthropology we find that it has complex intellectual roots in the enlightenment and the European discoveries of non-western peoples. Empiricism or empirical tradition was the byproduct of this historical development. The pioneering anthropologists were not field researchers and were basing their conclusions on secondary sources. They may be described as 'arm chair anthropologists' but the later developments helped develop the tradition of fieldwork and that is how ethnography becomes a part and parcel of anthropological field research.

Before moving further let us refer to the work of a young French philosopher, Citizen Joseph -Marie Degerando who, according to P.J. Pelto and G. H Pelto (1997), wrote the first field guide for ethnographers. His Considerations on the various methods to follow in the observation of savage people was intended as a guide for members of the Societe de observateurs de I' Homme as they embarked on expeditions to Africa and Australia. Degerands (1969) discussed the principal weaknesses in the ethnographic observations of earlier explorers, and argued that "the first means to proper knowledge of the 'savages" is to become like one of them, and it is by learning their language that we shall become their fellow citizens". He was especially clear about the importance of studying primitive people within the context of their social systems. He gave detailed suggestions concerning ethnographic observations. But his excellent fieldwork instructions had little effect on the French explorers." The long forgotten suggestions of Degerando and the earlier ethnographic work provide us with a perspective from which to view contemporary ethnographic activities" (Pelto & Pelto, ibid).

Bernard & Spencer (ibid) points out that ethnographies as they have evolved over the past century and a half constitute a genre, a form of writing conditioned by the process of knowledge construction epitomized in this anthropological triangle - process/product, comparison and contextualization. Ethnographies consequently differ from travel writing, gazetteers, interview based surveys, or even the personal fieldwork accounts of anthropologist(which form a separate genre). Ethnography, both as product and process, has a history and pattern of development of its own.

Essentials of Ethnography

Modern ethnographic fieldwork involves living in close contact with a population in order to observe their daily routine, ritual and social acts, economic activities, and other aspects of cultural behaviour. This could be possible through "participant observation". Malinowski is often credited with being the originator or at least the major developer, of this style of fieldwork that involves intensive and long term immersion in the daily lives of native people.

Though some anthropologists even before Malinowski conducted fieldwork through native language, spent substantial time in the field and in the process got involved emotionally with the people they studied, yet it was Malinowski who raised the ethnographic fieldwork to the status of an art or craft. The ethnographer Frank Cushing lived for about five years (1880-85) at Zuni Pueblo participating in the life of the people but the strong emphasis on participant observation, owes much to Malinowski.

As the main technique of an ethnographer, participant observation involves living with the people one studies. He/she learns their language and through it learns about their belief and behaviour. Much of his/her research is therefore based on subtle inference that he/she derives from informal situations. The ethnographer may interview formally for particular kind of information or may use questionnaires, psychological tests, or other standardized and relatively rigorous techniques. But regardless of what other methods one may be following he/she is always alert to record the events going on around him/her and understand their significance for particular problems for his/her general understanding of the life of the people. Thus, the ethnographer himself/herself is the most important instrument and the value of the work depends on his/her participating broadly in the life of his/her hosts and sensitively observing what is happening around him/her.

New Trends in Ethnography

When we look at the autobiographical accounts of ethnographers we notice that changes have come in fieldwork objectives, techniques, and styles. Pelto & Pelto (ibid) make the following generalizations about recent trends in contemporary ethnographic work:

1. Quantification of field observations and increasingly sophisticated "operationalizing" of field data have become more usual in ethnographic investigations than they were earlier.
2. Much ethnographic research is now focused on urban social systems, complex segments of peasant societies, and other types of 'non primitive' literate populations.
3. The study of social change, modernization, and social processes looms large in contemporary research partly overshadowing earlier concerns with static, 'equilibrated' social and cultural systems.
4. The tendency of ethnographer to identify with 'their people' and to find positive values in their cultural practices has continued but more and more anthropologists now go beyond this passive partisanship, seeking to foster social changes that would improve the socio-economic situations of their research communities. This trend is related to a series of ethical questions
5. In connection with the tendency to press for social action, some contemporary ethnographers are beginning to see themselves as carrying out research for the local communities themselves, rather than simply for their academic peers and perhaps for governmental agencies. Thus, anthropologists and sociologists have assumed the responsibility of making their research results relevant for and available to the people whose ways of life they have studied.
6. Although there continues to be a large number of general descriptive ethnographic studies, many fieldworkers focus their data gathering on one specialized aspect of the socio-cultural system, or on some theoretical problem.
7. A general ecological orientation is becoming more common in ethnographic work, bringing with it a

much needed reemphasis on physical and biological environment.

8. Self-conscious concern and writing about the techniques of field research must also be considered a significant characteristic of the contemporary ethnographic scene. Autobiographical accounts of field experiences are a recent phenomenon.
9. Complex ethical and practical questions are posed by anthropologists' involvements in research related to American foreign policy (involvement of some anthropologists in the ongoing war in Afghanistan is a case in point. It generated heated debate in American Anthropological Association and the majority censured such anthropologists).

Global and Multi-sited Ethnography:

Globalization is now impacting the entire world.lt poses a challenge to the existing social scientific methods of enquiry and units of analysis by 'destabilizing' the embeddedness of social relations in human groups and places.lt thus poses problems for ethnography upsetting ethnographers' claim to understand social relations by being there and thus demands that the practitioners of ethnography rethink the character of a global ethnography. Ethnographic sites are now globalized by means of various external connections across multiple spatial scales and porous and contested boundaries. The extension of the site in time and space poses conceptual and practical problems for ethnographers. However, by locating themselves firmly with the time and space of social actors 'living the global' ethnographer can reveal how global processes are collectively and politically constructed, demonstrating the variety of ways in which globalization is grounded in the local and how the social becomes transnational. Thus a global ethnography may be taken as a response of the ethnographers to the impact of globalization process that has engulfed all the regions of the world.

Traditional ethnography typically situates a researcher-ethnographer in one field/site for a long period of time. The researcher does not move across many spaces and thus gets to know one setting extremely well. Differing from the traditional ethnography, multi-sited ethnography follows a research topic across numerous spaces for shorter periods of time. Thus, multi-sited ethnography may be described as a method of data collection that follows a topic or social problem through different field sites geographically and/or socially. George Marcus(1995)proposed multi-sited ethnography as a way to examine global processes and the increasing interconnectedness of all people through the process of globalization. Marcus maintains that multi-sited ethnography solves the need for a method to analytically explore transnational processes, groups of people in motion, and ideas that extend over multiple locations. Since multi-sited ethnography is concerned with movement of ideas, people and commodities, it is closely related to a world systems theory, influenced by Immanuel Wallerstein, which views capitalism as a process without geographic boundaries. He argues that multi-sited ethnography allows for a macro-level understanding of a topic.lt allows researchers to understand a variety of perspectives.lt also enhances our understanding of how power structures from seemingly disconnected spaces ultimately impact a specific population. On a macro level, policies of one nation impacts people in another. The obvious limitation of multi-sited ethnography is that it has multiple sites and thus prevents researchers from getting to know of one site in depth and if a researcher does not get to know a site in depth, the quality of the data may not be as good as the researcher expects. Managing access to multiple sites can also be challenging. Moreover, when using multi-sited ethnography to compare different groups' answers to the same research questions, there may be problems in obtaining comparable data and difficulties related to translation and cultural appropriateness of questions asked.

New Ethnography

Recently, a new approach in the field of Anthropology has come to be recognized as Cognitive Anthropology or 'Ethno -Science' or even 'Ethno- Semantics'. This entails a relatively new and some controversial perspective in cultural and social anthropology It's major emphasis is on the development of structuralism, but it accords crucial importance to the empirical data 'as well as theoretical abstraction. It's conceptual mould is adopted from 'Phonemics', the branch of linguistics that seeks an objective, value free means of recording the sound systems of language. Ethno- science has important epistemological links with ethno-semantics as they both entail extensive methodological attention to ascertaining the meaning ascribed to the various aspects of culture or elements of language by the natives themselves i.e. by the participants of culture and users of the language being studied. A major objective in this ethnographic approach is the development of an ethnography that states the rules of appropriate or acceptable cultural behaviour in much the same way as a grammar can be used to state and predict linguistic behaviour. The adequacy of the anthropologists' ethnographic description is measured by the extent to which it provides an accurate and economical basis for prediction of natives responses under all culturally possible circumstances. As Charles Fralke (1964) wrote:

"An ethnography should be a theory of cultural behaviour in a particular society. It's adequacy should be evaluated by the ability of a stranger to the culture (who may be the ethnographer) to use ethnographic statements as instructions for appropriately anticipating the scenes of the society". "A similar view is also adopted by Conklin (1964) who also specifies 'appropriate anticipation' rather than prediction".

This new approach to ethnography, Strutvant is tempted to call the 'New Ethnography'. In one sense this is not the New Ethnography but the 'New old Ethnography'. It is a better operationalized but narrower version of a research strategy, which has already proved itself incapable of solving the major substantive issues of social sciences.

In the 20th century, many prominent spokesmen, representing a nominally vide variety of theoretical positions, have exhorted anthropologists to give priority to 'emic' analysis. While Lowie stressed upon understanding the 'inwardness' of the beliefs and practices of the people being studied by a field worker, Kluckhohn talked about 'setting down of events as seen by the people under study as the primary task of anthropologists. In the same vain, Malinowski wrote about grasping 'natives point of view' as the final goal of the ethnographer'. In British social anthropology, the overwhelming commitment to the analysis of descent, affirmity, filiation, prescriptive and preferential alliances sufficiently establish the 'emic thrusts' of their research interests.

The emic bias of New Ethnography got infused with a mentalism of recent origin. Linguistics was the source of this mentalism. Del Hymes has traced this influence in terms of Sapir's 'complimentary distribution', Jackhobson's 'distinctive features' and Chomskyian 'generative grammar'. The linguistic model has also influenced French and British anthropologists who are converging towards an emic strategy where logic and reason have upper hand replacing empathic humanist emic approach. The mentalism of Levi-Strauss and his American counterparts, stressing upon logical functions of mind as opposed to emotional and irrational components, have shown a departure from the previous emic approaches. This new approach has also the notion as it's basis that anthropology must be emic if it is to be anything at all.

In New Ethnography, culture is a timeless system of logical categories. The Ethno-semantists insist that the cultural field of inquiry is only definable in emic terms, emic in new linguistic sense. Thus, the goal of New Ethnography is to arrive at a description and analysis of a culture as a member of that culture would see it free from the biases of the outsider. It promises to achieve precise and highly operationalised renderings of cultural phenomenon which have come to be associated with the linguistic descriptions of phonology and grammer. With an imprint of new scientific credibility, it carries forward the tradition of cultural idealism in anthropology.

❑

3

Anthropology in the Service of Man: Applied Anthropology in India

In plainest terms 'Applied Anthropology' refers to the actual application of anthropological knowledge. The genesis of applied anthropology may be traced to the days of the earliest British colonialist. Anthropology was one of the subjects taught at the Haileybury College where the British civil servants going out to serve in India under the East India Company were trained. As early as 1807 the East India Company realized that anthropological knowledge would be of much use to the administration. "Dr. Francis Buchannan was appointed by the then Governor General to enquire into the life and culture of the people of Bengal. After the middle of 19th century a number of administrators like Dalton, Thurston and Risely were commissioned to prepare handbooks and gazetteers on the castes and tribes of India. These, however, did not make any recommendations to the government about the solution of any specific problems of the people they described. "It was only in 1931 that J.H. Hutton, Census Commissioner, writing in the context of the culture contact suggested the creation of self governing tribal areas with the power of self determination in regard to joining the adjacent provinces or states" (Sachchidanand, 1980). Obviously, in the initial stages, the administrators and scholars were more concerned with "fact collection" and not with problem oriented analysis.

In the course of their journey to academic excellence Indian anthropologists were confronted with the challenge to apply anthropology's knowledge for the benefit of the society. They were supposed to act as 'social doctors' to help the administration at various levels in "diagnosing social ills, in prescribing appropriate remedies, and smoothening the course of transformation from traditional to transitional and then perhaps to 'reorganisational' phase of our society" (Vidyarthi, 1978). In the post-independence period the first systematic attempt towards problem oriented - problem solving type of research was made in the context of the tribal problems in the special issue of *The Eastern Anthropologist* (1949) founded and edited by the great D.N. Majumdar from Lucknow. Among the contributors to this special tribal number were such anthropologists as Haimendorf, Chattopadhyay, Naik, Dube, Srivastava, Majumdar, Ehrenfels and social workerslike Thakkar Bapa and Wandreker. From this point onwards papers dealing with tribal problems continued to appear in growing numbers in other anthropological journals too like *Man in India* and *Journal of Social Research.* In fifties appeared a few publications by Dube, Oscar Lewis, Srinivas, Surajit Sinha and others "with a certain amount of sophistication that provided a strong base for the theory and methods of applied anthropology in India" (Vidyarthi, ibid).

During this period anthropologists broad approach to the tribal problems as guidelines were put forward as state policy by Jawahar Lal Nehru. The five principles of tribal development said to be the article of faith with Nehru were the result of Elwin's influence upon him vis-a-vis tribal policy. These run as follows:

(i) People should be allowed to develop on the lines of their own genius and nothing should be imposed upon them;

(ii) tribal rights in land and forests should be respected;

(iii) induction of too many outsiders into tribal areas should be avoided;

(iv) there should be no over-administration of tribal areas as far as possible; work should be done through their own social and cultural institutions; and

(v) the results should be judged not by the amount of money spent but by the quality of human character that is involved.

In the early fifties the Commissioner for Scheduled Castes and Scheduled Tribes advocated the setting up of tribal research institutes to tackle the problems of the tribals and suggest remedies. Thus, till now such tribal research centres have been established in Bihar, Orissa, West Bengal, Madhya Pradesh, Rajasthan, Assam and Uttar Pradesh. The various other national organizations like National Family Planning Institute, the Programme Evaluation Organisation of Planning Commission, National Institute of Community Development and a few voluntary organizations including Institute of Gandhian Studies, Adimjati Sevak Sangh and the progessional organizations like Indian Anthropological Association, Indian Sociological Society, Institute of Applied Anthropology, the Indian Society of Extension Education etc. have also been promoting the cause of applied research in anthropology and related fields.

The applied anthropologists with their general background in anthropology have to specialise in diverse fields such as tribal development, urban planning, demography, family planing, education etc. They are collaborating, along with other applied social scientists, with the policy planners and administrators. Vidyarthi (ibid) views such collaboration in terms of five categories. The first category of applied anthropologists acts as consultants on the staff of the administration and usually functions under the control of the administration. The second type is that of the anthropologist who is consultant primarily to the administrators but is an outsider and is not on the regular payroll of the organisation. The third type is represented by a category in which the researcher and the administrators work together as co-administrators. The fourth and fifth categories an anthropologists is at least temporarily in actual charge of the development programme. The fifth category is represented by *Action Anthropology* as propounded by Sol Tax (1959) which can function only in the independent manner and in institutions where an action anthropologists can combine both *action* and *research*. An action anthropologist as a social doctor, combines in himself the responsibility for diagnosing the disease, prescribing the medicines, following up the treatment, changing the prescription if need arises and finally bringing about health and happiness in the society. Obviously in such type of research monitoring, evalution and the consequent shift in the strategy goes on simultaneously. However, in view of limitations in personnel and resources on the one hand, and the magnitude of the task of national development on the other, there are numerous difficulties in the implementation of action research programmes in India. This is a role to which an action social scientists should aspire.

II

Since applied anthropology was first put to use in India vis-a-vis tribal problems it would be in the fitness of things to make some comments on this sector first before moving on to newer fields and horizons explored by applied anthropologists in India.

Much has been written on applied anthropologists' efforts for economic upliftment of the tribal population of the country. Problems of land alienation and indebtedness have been dealt with in great detail. Among the lesser known problems special attention has been given to the educational uplifement of the tribal people. Studies have also been made on the reasons of heavy dropouts in the schools of the tribal areas. Some work has also been done on tribal languages. However, a lot remains to be done by the applied anthropologists in the sphere of educational anthropology.

In the field of health and sanitation, there has been increasing realisation to pinpoint the local cultural factors. The applied anthropologists, through their studies, have demonstrated that the attitude, beliefs and value system etc., affect the willingness of people to take voluntary action with respect to their own health and that of the members of their family. Now we are richer in understanding about the place of culture in health and medicine. Dialogue has been established between behavioural scientists and the public health administrators. Now one can find several anthropologists in the National Family Planning Institute, ministry of health and its associate bodies where they are making important contributions. Apart from health, sanitation and family planning programmes the applied physical anthropologists have also been involved in the problems of genetically controlled diseases, forensic science, dermatoglyphics etc.

The Indian Council of Agricultural Research, agricultural research universities and other organisations have also been benefiting from applied anthropology in their efforts to introduce innovations and modernisation in agriculture: social anthropologists along with sociologists and other social scientists have been working in the field of extension to study the behavioural pattern of peasants to solve a number of problems in the sectors of agriculture, dairy practices, horticulture and related activities.

Although, traditionally, anthropologists have been concerned with small scale primitive communities, of late they have also turned their attention to the process of urbanisation and industrialization. Applied anthropology is also being utilized in the field of town and country planning, relationship between man and his environment, neighbourhood, conflict and tensions, political process in the cities and a host of other fields. Though, urban anthropologists have been relatively new entrants they have started making their presence felt.

In the labour sector, specially among the unorganised labour, social anthropologists and sociologists have been doing important work. The National Commission on Labour under the chairmanship of L.P. Vidyarthi has made important studies - about the cultural factors involved with the tribal labour force in middle India. There is also ample scope for studies of the effect of the caste system on occupational mobility and efficient mobilization of manpower, role of socio-cultural factors in the emergence of entrepreneurs, productivity of industrial workers and so on. Issues in tribal and student unrest have also been dealt with by applied anthropologist. Studies in tribal movements and leaderships have given us new insights. Increasing campus unrest has also been studied in terms of social control and student-society relationship. In one such study it was concluded that the "student of present day India is torn between tradition and modernity, the sacred and secular, individuality and collectivity, inner-directed man and outer-directed man; all in all a marginal, man".

Defence organisation is another field where applied anthropology entered recently. Although contributions in this sphere have not been very substantial mainly because of secutiry reasons, whatever has been done is full of promise. The study of the economic, social and political implications of the military organisation is really a fascinating field.

To many people the contribution of applied anthropology in our space programmes may sound strange. The Space Applications Centre, Ahmedabad has developed a sizeable social research plan of programme production for telecasting. B.C. Agarwal and his band of young and devoted anthropologists have done a pioneering work. Satellite Instructional Television Experiment (SITE) was one of the most advanced and probably the largest experiment conducted in human communication. SITE was one such experiment in which anthropologists were induced to conduct in depth, qualitative and descriptive studies for undertaking the process of communication. This group is still involved with various programmes of Satellite Communication.

The preceding pages have presented only a brief and somewhat sketchy description of various fields where applied anthropology is playing its role. A number of relatively less important fields have been skipped. Yet the reader must have got the idea that the scope of applied anthrpology is very wide.

III

The government or administration and anthropologists have been carrying a strange love-hate relationship since the very inception of applied anthrpology. Anthropologists and administrators do not, generally, get along very well, "some administrators argue that they can very well act as their own anthropologist. Administrators certainly know the area they serve better than the anthropologist. They also know the local people and their language well. But howsoever valid this argument may have been in the early days of anthropology it surely does not hold good in the present age of specialization. In recent years, there have been very rapid advances both in the theory and fieldwork techniques of modern anthropology. The fieldwork today is full time Job" (H.M. Mathur, 1980).

There is a great deal of mis-understanding between anthropologists and administrators. The administrators demand quick and certain prediction from the anthropologists who are generally reluctant to be hastened. The dilemma of anthropologists working on the pay roll of the government is pitiable. They are afraid to make recommendations which are unpalatable to the government in power.

In a brilliant and ruthlessly frank analysis Sachchidanand (ibid) comments that in India the applied anthrpologists would have to be content with a rather modest role. he can claim to be present at high level discussions, but his voice cannot be decisive. On the basis of the special knowledge he can provide to the administrator data which would be helpful in the formulation of policy. Whether his advice would be accepted or rejected depends upon administrative exigencies and political considerations. The anthropologist no longer offers a blue print but offers a map on which pitfalls are marked but he cannot claim to decide the direction of change. In spite of the hurdles enumerated above, applied anthropology has left an impact on government policy.

Taking a somewhat wishful stand Vidyarthi (1978) laments that the role of social anthropologist has not been well definited in the bureaucratic machinery of the state and central governments. it seems that applied anthropologists in India should gracefully, accept the various roles if certain conditions are satisfied. Firstly, he should have appropriate status in organisational set up, and secondly, once a subject for investigation is agreed upon through consultations, he must be free to draw up design and the tools of investigations, and thridly he must be able to present his findings at the highest policy making level. Sadly, what Vidyarthi forgets to add here is that the anthropologist's finding and recommendations, product of his hard labour and endeavour, should not be allowed to gather dust or be consigned to the dustbin by an arrogant bureaucrat without providing a better alternative. Applied anthropology, or for that matter any other academic pursuit, cannot flourish to its desired heights unless an unfettered and arrogant bureaucracy is made to realise that it is not the only fountain-head of knowledge.

❑

4 Moving Towards Complex Society: Urban Anthropology in India

Social anthropology has traditionally been concerned with the intensive study of small scale primitive and peasant societies. However, its preoccupation with simple societies hardly means that it, at any point of time, gave up its claim of being the total study of man. That is why urban centres have been interesting the anthropologists, from time to time, as the locales of social problems, hub of a civilization or the region or segments of human societies embodying particular sorts of social structure and social relationships. A number of anthropologists have begun to turn their attention to the study of complex societies and have begun to write on what is called urban anthropology. Obviously, this is in conformity with the traditional claim of anthropology of dealing with man everywhere and as a whole.

Under the influence of the 'Chicago School of Anthropology'. Indian anthropologists turned their attention towards cities - traditional as well as modern. This venture had twofold purpose i.e., study of cities as part of Indian civilization and then to analyse them in terms of the folk-urban continum.

The process of urbanization, industrialization in city planning interested our planning bodies to an extent that they allocated separate funds for their studies. The National Planning Commission sponsored and financed several such studies. Milton Singer's study of Madras, Marriot's study of Wai Town near Pune and Martin Oran's study of Jamshedpur provided the necessary fillip to the growing recognition of the cultural roles of cities. However, before a systematic and serious trend to study urban centres emerged, some anthrpologists have been making occasional 'forays' into urban centres. Harold Gould's work on Lucknow's Rickshawpullers and some such other works in the late fifties and early sixties "appeared to arise from particular opportunities open to a fieldworker rather than an articulated theoretical view point and, therefore, did not lead to substantial developments in urban studies" (Saberwal, 1973). Early in the 1960s American anthropologists turned their attention to commercial centres and groups; Richard Fox in a market town in eastern Uttar Pradesh, Mattison Mines among the Muslims merchants in a Tamil town near Chingelpet, Leighton Hazlehurst among traders and refugee entrepreneurs in a town in Haryana and so on.

Milton Singer's *When a Great Tradition Modernizes: An Anthropological Approach to Indian Civilization* (1972) may be regarded as a landmark study. Derived from Chicago's folk-urban, Great Tradition - Little Tradition model he sought, in Madras, the adaptations being made by the Hindu Great Traditions in a new metropolis.

Enumerating important urban studies Indrani Ganguly (1986) opines that these studies emphasise the sociological aspects of city life. In a pioneering venture D.N. Majumdar took up the study of Kanpur (1960), an important industrial centre of Uttar Pradesh, to assess the "complex conditions of urban life in an industrial metropolis". In the light of his training as a social anthropologist, Majumdar (ibid) promises "to make a departure from the routine type of socio-economic surveys that have been carried out in different parts of India" and to "initiate a major probe into factory/life with all its sociological con-comittance, for the social background and antecedent social conditions shape labour and the success or failure of industrialization would depend upon the recognition of such sociological contents". This work covers a detailed discussions of the city's civic amenties, migration, and division of the population of Kanpur into different occupational categories and a section on fertility. The glaring weakness of this study is that the cultural content of urbanization was not discussed in any considerable details. Also, little attempt was made to identify the various strata of the city and the corresponding differences in life style that might be presumed to exist between them.

Vidyarthi's *The Cultural Configuration of Ranchi* (1969) may also be cited as an example of Indian anthropologist's attempts to come to terms with urban realities. This is an empirical study of the origin, morphology, function and influence of Ranchi as a city. He has also examined the interaction of two somewhat distinct cultures, the fold and the urban, or the tribal and the non-tribal. Since Ranchi has a large contagious tribal area, significantly a section on the social pattern of urban tribal life has also been added.

Owen Lynch's 'The Politics of Untouchability' (1969) however, may be taken as a landmark study. In this work the Jatav-an untouchable caste engaged in leather work -- have been studied in the traditional city of Agra. Lynch shows that the Jatav had a well knit mohalla (ward) organisation which was similar to village community of this region in many ways. *The mohalla Panchayat* functioned as a unit of social control, co-operation and commensality. Their residential segregation was due to the Jatav monopoly over the shoe industry. Significantly, the Jatav were not bound to upper caste by *Jajmani* (patron-client) relationship and, therefore, could afford to stay allof from them. The influence of the ward *Panchayat* is however declining due to the introduction of parliamentary democracy and a number of other factors.

Bose's Study of Calcutta (1968), Vidyarthi's Gaya (1961), Guha & Roy Chowdhry's Calcutta (1964) and Roy Chowdhry's Bhowanipur (1964) are some other studies in the Indian anthropologist's quest for the fuller understanding of complex urban societies. However, to begin to cope with the urban complexity the field researches appear to have taken a strategic decision : simplify the complexity by locating 'isolable' problems which would enable one to continue with the tried and tested micro-techniques even in 'unfamiliar' field setting. This is also not a bad idea because in the later stages such an experience may prove very valuable in grappling with the urban complexity at macro level.

The study of occupational groups and settings are case in point. Morrison's work on lawyers and their *munshis* in Ambala's courts, Madan's on doctors in a medium sized town, Sinha's on research scientists, Singh's on University academics, Rosenthal's on corporators and their setting in two cities and a host of other studies may be cited as important examples of this thinking.

The fairly rapid growth of industrialization and the resultant 'industrial culture' have added yet another dimension to the growth of urban anthropology in India. During the last two decades some anthropologists have turned their attention to the study of various aspects of industrialization. Sheth's Social Framework of Indian Industry (1968) is particularly important. He analysed the structure of relationships among people working in a factory in relation to the social and cultural milieu in which they live and work. Some other scholars have covered such topics as social effects of industrialization, worker-management relations, trade unionism etc. Such studies obviously are going to break new ground.

Urban anthropology does show potentialities of its own. Despite some ambiguity and ambivalene with regard to such questions as (i) Is the overall goal of anthropology still the same as in traditional tribal and peasant society studies? (ii) Are we still interested in a holistic point of view? (iii) How do we achieve this in large scale societies?

(iv) How does the anthropologist's concept of community fit into the study of complex societies? (v) How can the concept be applied in the urban setting? (vi) How can the time honoured methodological tools be applied in the urban setting? and so on, it may be said with a good degree of fairness that anthropologists everywhere are trying to break new ground in the study of urban life and evolving their distinct approach to the study of urban centres. If they don't succeed in their endeavour, the "urban anthropologist", as Ferriera (1978) rightly opines "can point to his special knowledge of tribal and peasant cultures which would undoubtedly prove exceedingly useful when these tribals and peasants are over taken by the urbanization process". Even in such an eventuality the contribution of anthropologists shall be unique and distinct as in other fields.

❑

5 Secularism: Some Sociological/ Anthropological Implications

Popularly speaking religion and secularism or religious and secular are complimentary terms. Hence, before making any comment on secularism it seems appropriate to think of religion at least a little bit. In the whole of the animal kingdom man alone prays. Man's cultural world embodies also a conception of the mysterious unknown. He has nourished an astonishing variety of beliefs and practices. Beliefs constitute the cognitive part of religion, practices (rituals) represents its' expressive and instrumental aspects. Though them man acquires a system of meanings and motivations.

On a theoretical plane, as Emile Durkheim puts it, all that is there in the world-beliefs, myths, dogmas, actions, persons and beings-are either sacred or secular. All that is related with religion is covered under 'sacred' and according to this scheme of things all traditional societies are basically 'sacred societies' because they are governed, in crucial segments and in varying degrees, by laws of religion. It is the religion that controls the activities of the members of such societies.

Among the characteristics of secularism the following are the most important ones:

(i) separation of authority between 'church' and the 'state';

(ii) emphasis on 'this world' as opposed to the 'other world'; and

(iii) ratonalism and scientific outlook.

Secularism implies that the state will not be governed by the church, i.e., by religious authorities such as bishop, *pundit*, *Mulah* or *Khalifa*. The doctrines promoting social inertia such as fatalism and divine retribution have no place in secularism. A secular mind is characterized rationality. A secular and modern society is not against religion as such, but it has to fight superstition and intolerance as well as bigotry and obscurantism. "Areas of personal beliefs that are not inconsistent with the larger needs of the society can be upheld and protected by society. But beliefs and practices that bring about discord and disharmony between different religious groups will required resolute action" (S.C. Dube, 1974).

Societies are not born secular. Instead, the societies that are practising varying degrees of secularism had to undergo transformation from traditional to secular. The process of secularization has played its part in this transformation.

Broadly speaking, the process of secularization operates through three factors :

(i) Education;

(ii) Legistlation; and

(iii) Social reform.

Education when imparted on scientific and rational lines gives rise to rationality in the thinking process. If we take the case of India, education was imparted through religious institutions- pathshala, Madarsa and seminaries- attached to temples, maths, mosques and churches. When the scope of acquisition of formal education was widened and secular educational institutions were opened, it brought about a sea change. The change in the content of education and medium of instruction was largely responsible for it. That is why the role of formal education in social transformation cannot be minimized. The legislative action is also a crucial factor in the process of secularization. But mere legislative action not supported by proper motivation and social environment may not achieve the desired results. Many developing countries may be cited as examples of this situation. Take the case of India, our country has gone secular by legislative flats without the backing of sufficient infrastructure for the emergence of true secularism. Behind our country's facade of secularism and national unity lurk a bewildering variety of parochial, narrow minded, obscurantist and unscientific feeling that threaten to tear the fabric of our 'secular' country apart. Casteism, tribalism, linguism and religious communalism are painful facts of our day to day existence. The so called 'do gooders', 'godmen' and religious bigots are flourishing at will. In the face of these factors secularism is reduced to just a paper tiger. In reality, secularism should be a way of life. It is not a slogan but an article of faith. Social movement for social reform is a potent weapon for the promotion of the process of secularization. It does mental conditioning. It prepares us to accept social change. Whatever degree of secularism our society has achieved and absorbed owes a lot to various social reform movements launched from time to time.

Two subsidiary factors in the secularization process are urbanization and industrialization. Both these factors owe a lot to technological innovations. It has been observed that as the area of scientific knowledge and technology widens, the area of religion shrinks. This hardly means that religion and science are incompatible. As Dube (ibid.) rightly points out on a higher spiritual and moral plane, religion is not necessarily inconsistent with the idiom of science and the ethos of progress. Moreover, urbanization and industrialization helps loosen the grip of 'in group' feeling and presents newer alternatives to man. Further, it promotes rational cause-effect explanations and the hold of religious beliefs over different aspects of life declines, although interest in religion as a phenomenon persists. It sheds much of its' collective and communal overtones and becomes largely a personal concern.

The state of India seeks to promote the secularization process by :

(i) abloshing such symbols of ritual inequality as untouchability, the practice of which has been declared a penal offence;

(ii) throwing open all religious places and institutions to all classes and sections of the people;

(iii) reform of the Hindu Personal Law eventually aiming at evolving a common personal law for all communities in the country;

(iv) forbidding all such agencies as shops, public restaurants, hotels and places of public entertainment from discriminating against any citizen of the state;

(v) throwing open all educational institution to members of all communities;

(vi) secularizing the content of text books by including such material as could be helpful in the promotion of a scientific-rational outlook by deleting such material as was likely to poison young minds, which smacked of traditionalism, obscurantism and religious orthodoxy; and

(vii) developing a sound economic base so as to eradicate poverty and ensure an equitable distribution of wealth among the people.

Secularism is one of the basic elements in the process of modernization. Thus, if our society is to become modernised to cope with the worldwide changes we are left with no other option but to adopt 'secularism in practice' by speeding up the process of secularization.

❑

SECTION TWO

CULTURAL RECONSTRUCTION OF THE PAST

6 Prehistoric and Protohistoric Dimensions of Indian Culture

Latest researches and studies tell us that man is approximately 3 million years old. Finds of fossil human and sub-human remains along with material remains consisting mainly of stone tools have been made that go to prove not only the antiquity of man but also the story of his cultural evolution. Whereas most of the early discoveries were, to a great extent, accidental during the last 4-5 decades the search for the ancestors and cousins of *Homo Sapiens* and their material and cultural achievements is being conducted increasingly by trained scientists mainly anthropologists and archaeologists.

This collaborative endeavour has been joined by geologists, paleontologists, chemists and a host of other specialists required in various spheres and areas of this mission. Yet even today when the search of stone age cultures and fossil humans is more scientifically orgnized than even before, luck or chance still plays a major part in most discoveries of importance. "After all, the surface of the earth is immense and a very large part of the earth's crust is covered by vegetation and by surface deposits of humans and hill-wash and other superficial deposits, so that, to a considerable extent, the search for evidence of man's past in geological deposits is governed by change. River and other forces of nature cut through geological deposits containing the evidence which we seek, and it is a matter of luck whether this erosion takes places at a time when some trained scientist is on the spot to recognise the hidden treasure so exposed. Similarly, commercial undertaking carried out for the exploitation of river gravels and brick earths, or alluvial deposits containing gold or diamonds or tin are often the means by which deposits containing missing parts of the grans jigsaw puzzle are revealed. Here again it is a matter of pure luck whether a person, qualified to recognise the stone tools and fossils, is present before they are destroyed" (Leakey, 1960). [Table given on page no. 93].

Climate and geographical position have always played the most important part in determining where man made his home, where he hunted and where he lived, just as they do today, and since neither climate nor the geogrphy of the world has remained the same over the long period of time since man first became man, and the still longer period when man's apelike ancestors were slowly evolving to a human status, we must study the world changes of climate and geogrphy, before we can appreciate details of the story of man's past. Leakey (ibid) has very rightly commented that ordinary common sense is a very important factor in the interpretation of the past. To this must be added a great deal of scientific knowledge if we are to obtain a proper picture of the climate, geography, and general environment which existed in the days when stone age man lived.

Palaeolithic Culture

Man faced great climatic changes during the period of his development but his highly developed, complex and intelligent brain helped him to invent tools, to face climate fluctuations and to continue to live. He had to

Climatological Periods of the Pleistocene

YEARS AGO	TIME PERIODS	EUROPE	NORTH AMERICA	SOUTH AND EAST AFRICA
	HOLOCENE	Postglacial		Postpluvial
9,000	UPPER PLEISTOCENE	Late Würm Glacial	Late Wisconsin Glacial	
		Middle Würm Glacial		
40,000		Early Würm Glacial	Early Wisconsin Glacial	
75,000		Third Interglacial		Gambian Pluvial
105,000	MIDDLE PLEISTOCENE	Riss Glacial	Illinolan-Lowan Glacial	Interpluvial
200,000		Second Interglacial		Kanjeron Pluvial
				Interpluvial
200,000				Kamasian Pluvial
		Mindel Glacial	Kansan Glacial	
225,000				Interpluvial
	LOWER PLEISTOCENE	First Interglacial		
				Kangeran Pluvial
		Günz Glacial	Jerseyan Glacial	
		Villafranchian		
2,000,000+	PLIOCENE			

work hard to get food. In the initial stages he was merely food gatherer. He learned, to join his fellow men and go in search of the fruits and games that nature provided. he learned to make tools of stone, use animal skins for clothes and built shelter. He learned to makefire and developed the power for speech. But he still lived hunting, fishing and gathering edible roots, fruits and any other things that nature provided. This period in early man's development is commonly known as old stone age or the Palaeolithic age. By definition the cultural debris recovered from the entire period of pleistocene (approximately 3 million years to 10,000 B.C.) is termed as Palaeolithic culture.

Man has been living in India roughly for 500,000 years. The Palaeolithic culture of India developed in the Pleistocene period that comes immediately before the geological period Holocene or current period in which we live and which began about 10,000 years ago. Scientists are not sure as to when Pleistocene period exactly began. The period was characterised by major climatic fluctuations. For thousands of years climate used to become so cold and chilly that everything used to be frozen and big boulders of ice (glaciers) were formed. This phase has been termed as **Glaciation**. Thus, Europe and America passed through four Glaciations and three **Inter Glaciations** (the periods of moderate climate in between two glaciations). However, the tropical regions, excepting the mountains, were free from ice. On the other hand they underwent period of great rainfall; interspersed by dry climate termed **Pluvial** and **Inter-Pluvial** respectively.

The process of cultural development may be said to have started when our sub-human ancestors had acquired the skill to produce crude tools that often looked like stones chipped or shaped under natural conditions. Man was still in the process of evolution and was more or less of the status of Australopithecus africanus - a semi-erect ape like creature. Nearly a million years ago *Homo erectus* evolved and after words Homo *sapiens* or modern man came on the scene to conquer this earth. They were much better equipped to interact and hence adapt to ground living. Fire was also tamed by them at a later date. "Gathering around fire for equal traditional benefits may have been usually practised and this may have also helped in consolidating the social bonds in these early human bands" (Bhattacharya, 1984). The natural flaking might have suggested to man that he could also make stones into tools for different purposes. The earliest tool maker gradually learned just how to hold a piece of stone or rock and just how forceful a blow to deliver precisely at what angle in order to remove flakes of the right size from the desired spot.

Robert Bruce Foot was the first to discover a Palaeolithic stone tool in Indian in 1863. Palaeolithic research in India is, therefore, more than a hundred years old. But it got a boost only with the coming of Yale-Cambridge Expedition in 1935 led by De Terra and Patterson.

Till some time back Palaeolithic in India had only two divisions:

(i) Early Stone Age or Lower Palaeolithic

(ii) Middle Stone Age or Middle Palaeolithic

Since India did not have an independent character of Upper Palaeolithic like Europes', the available scanty and fragile evidences of the Upper Palaeolithic were lumped with the Middle Palaeolithic. On the basis of several recently excavated sites an outline of Indian Upper Palaeolithic has definitely emerged thought it is still not comparable with that we know as European Upper Palaeolithic. Thus in the present description of Palaeolithic in India has been described through the three familiar phases —Lower Palaeolithic, Middle Palaeolithic and Upper Palaeolithic.

Lower Palaeolithic

Except for the northern alluvial corridor and Kerala, the archaeological evidences of Lower Palaeolithic have been found throughout India. However, no human fossils of so early a period have so far been discovered. In other regions, Palaeolithic tools been found from plateaus, river terraces, and even hilly slopes.

The Indian Lower Palaeolithic can neither be arranged in any definite sequence or chronological order nor it should be considered as a uniform cultural stage. This is because of the fact that it's character, in terms of time and cultural features, varies from region to region. The bulk of information we have of Indian Lower Palaeolithic is based on the study of the following sites: Soan valley located in Potwar plateau of north-west; Sabarmati Valley, Nagri, Chittorgarh and Didwana in Western India; Narsinghpur and Hoshangabad in narmade Valley of Madhya Pradesh; Singrauli basin of Uttar Pradesh; Kuliana and Kamarpada in Odisha; Sisunia Hills of Bankura district in West Bengal; and Kurnool, Giddalur Karempudi Nagarjunakinda and Chingelpet in Peninsular India.

The Soan valley is one of the most important sources of Lower Palaeolithic in India. Potwar is an elevated undulating land of about 100 sq. kms. lying between the rivers Indus and Jhelum. Rawalpindi (now in Pakistan) is located almost centrally in this region. Soan is a tributory of the river Indus whose valley (along with Kashmir region) was excavated by De terra and Patterson. Later on, some Indian prehisotians also excavated this region. The whole region demonstrates a predominance of chopper—chopping tools made on pebbles but at the same time some hand axes, and in relatively larger numbers, flakes have also been found. The Palaeolithic tools of the Soan valley may be divided into four main phases:

1. Pre-Soan
2. Early Soan
3. Late Soan
4. Evolved Soan

The layer or stratum of the Pre-Soan has yielded a number of heavily rolled and blunted pebbles of quartzite rock. Most of these are split or broken and are of different shapes. The human workmanship of these 'tools' is doubtful because the presence of man in this region at such an early date is still not confirmed. It is still a matter of debate whether these heavily rolled and blunted pebbles are the handiwork of certain natural factors or the earliest manifestation of human workmanship. Many scholars put these 'tools' under the category of '*Eoliths*'. The layers of the early-Soan have yielded very important tools. These are mainly two types of tolls described as choppers and chopping tools. The only point of difference between these two is flaking on one/both sides. When it is unifacial it is chopper and when flaked from both the sides (bifacial), it is chopping tool. These are very crude looking tools and indicate the use of a crude and unsophiscated technology in their fabrication. These must have been 'generalized tools' and beside cutting or chopping some other usages of these tools may also be thought of Pre-Soan and Early Soan may be put under Lower Palaeolithic. The tools of Late Soan are not basically different from those of the Early Soan except that now tools were lighters and neater and flakes/flake tools increased in number. The layers of the Evolved Soan have also yielded blades and blade tools but their number is not large enough to indicate any radical change in the life style of the people. Hence, parallels from the European Upper Palaeolithic should also not be drawn because its' European counterpart is characterized by the presence of blade tools and a large number of other tools made on bone and other non-lithic materials.

A very striking feature of Soan culture is the discovery of some hand axes and cleavers along with the chopper/chopping tools made on pebbles. Most of these handaxes and cleavers look heavily rolled and blunted. A site called *Chauntra* is considered unique in this respect. Such sites have added an element of uniqueness to Indian Palaeolithic because nowhere in the world chopper/chopping tools of pebbles and handaxes-cleavers have been found together. Even in the Indian subcontinent chopper/chopping tools and handaxes-cleavers belonging to such an early date have not been found together except in the Soan valley. It may be indicative of a co-existence of two different human populations in close proximity living with different tool technology and typology. But it cannot be substantiated in the absence of skeletal remains.

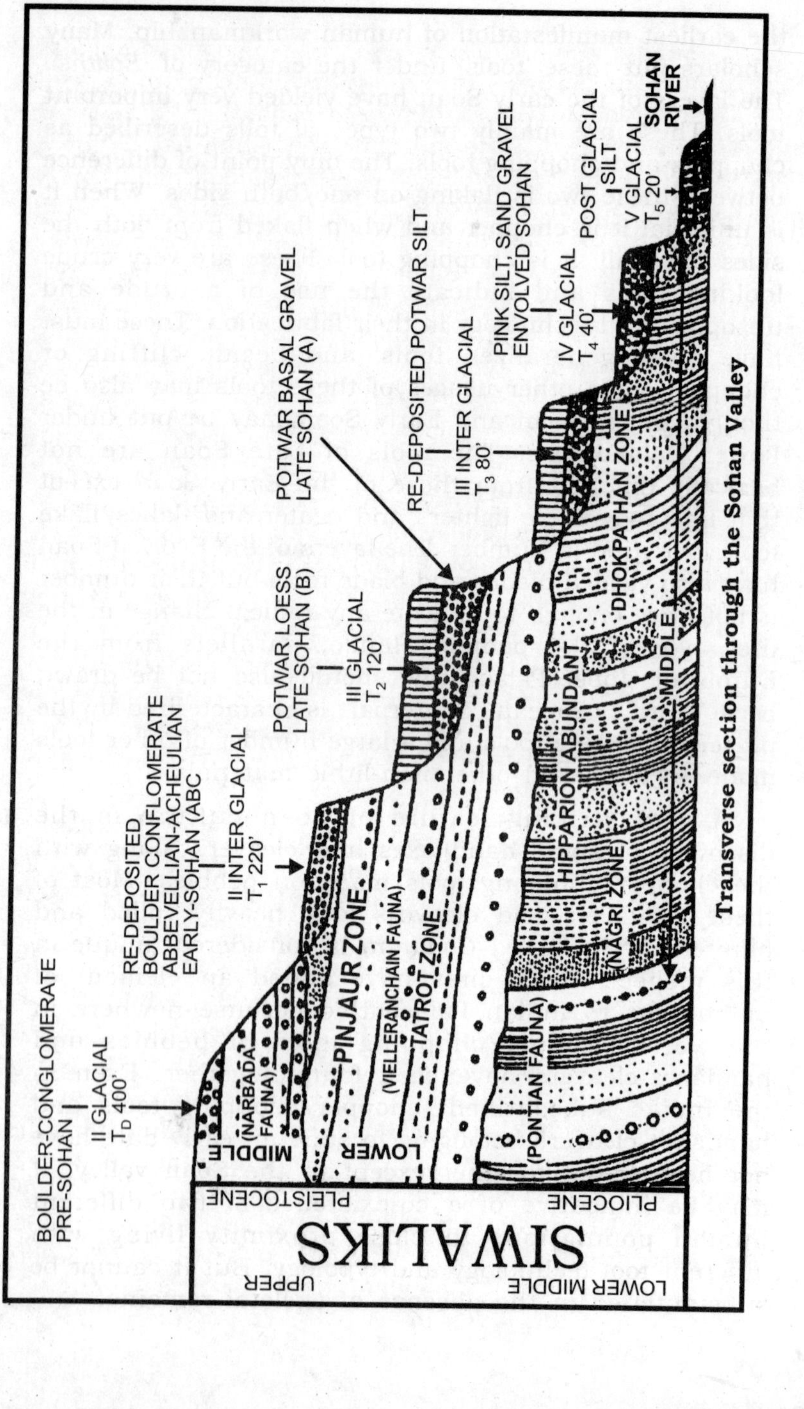

Transverse section through the Sohan Valley

Lately, the western region has also emerged as an important source of Palaeolithic culture in India. Excavations in Saurashtra and Rajasthan have opened new avenues of information. The Chambal valley has yielded a number of large Lower Palaeolithic tools. The excavation of Didwana near Jodhpur has yielded evidences of substantial human settlements. Here, one comes across large deposits of chopper and chopping tools with some relatively large hand axes; significantly no cleavers have been found. In Gujarat, Lower Palaeolithic sites have been found along almost all the rivers which indicates that the climatic conditions were definitely conducive for human existence. Most of these tools closely resemble those of Acheulian tradition of European prehistory.

The Narmada Valley of central India is also a very important source of Palaeolithic culture. After his experience from the Soan valley (characterized by the glaciation—inter-glaciation sequences) De Terra wanted to study central and peninsular India (characterized by the pluviation—inter-pluviation sequences) to have some idea of the effects of these two types of climatic fluctuations. Perhaps, Narmada region was the natural choice to study the effects of the different types of ecological conditions. The deposits, belonging to the Pleistocene, of Hoshangabad an Narshinghpur, have yielded good results. The whole of Narmada industry is characterized by large handaxes, cleavers, chopper/chopping tools and Clactonian flakes. In the same region at the place called Hathnora, a very important discovery has been made. It is a skeleton of *Homo erectus* that has now been designated as *Narmada Man.* This is the only skeletal remain from the Lower Palaeolithic in India. Though the deposits of Bhimbetka and Admagarh in Madhya Pradesh have also yielded Lower Palaeolithic remains but the basic character of these two sites is of later cultural phases. The eastern region has also yielded some Palaeolithic sites mainly along its hilly rivers and hill slopes. The archaeological research in this region is still in its infancy and nothing significant has come out except from 2-3 sites. From the Mayurbhanj district of Odisha, Kuliana

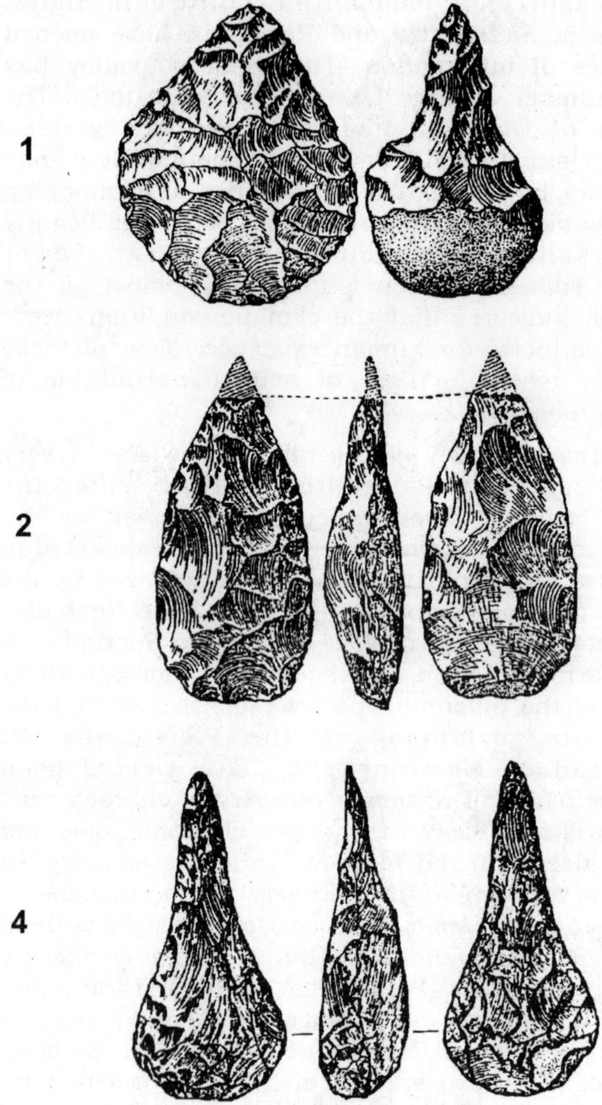

Lower Palaeolithic Tools

1, 2 & 4 Pear Shaped Handaxes

3

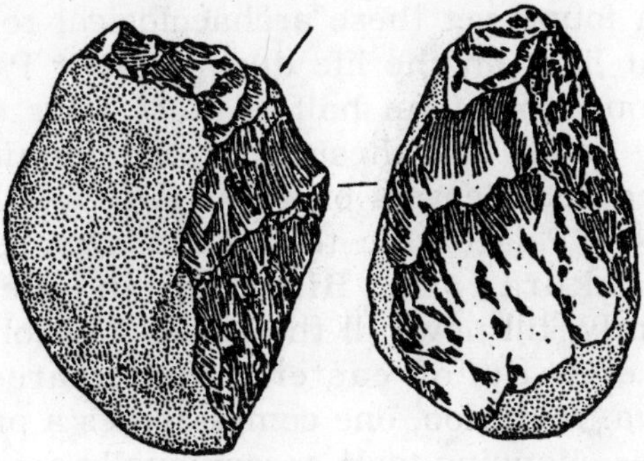

3

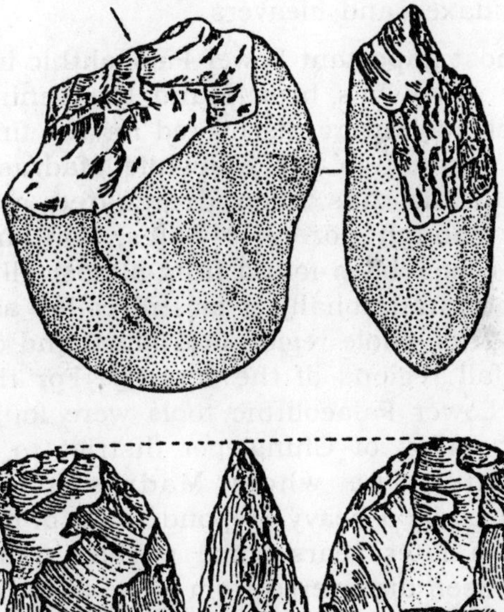

5

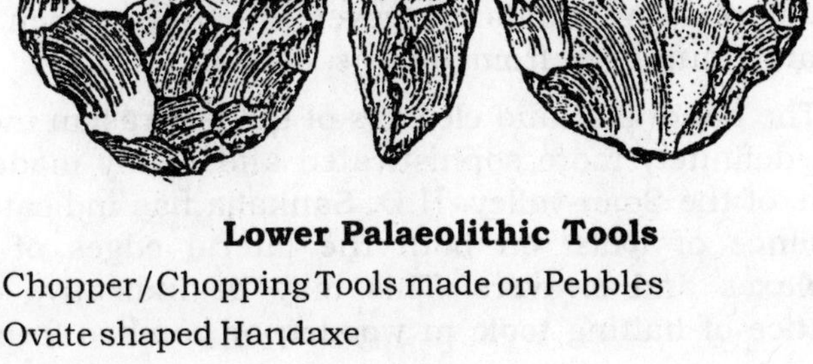

Lower Palaeolithic Tools

- 3. Chopper/Chopping Tools made on Pebbles
- 5. Ovate shaped Handaxe

and Kamarpada may be cited as such examples. These are large pits containing a rich collection of Lower Palaeolithic tools. Although no considerable stratigraphy has been found yet these archaeological remains throw important light on the life during Lower Palaeolithic in this region. More than half of these tools are chopper-chopping tools but these are accompanied by some hand-axes and cleavers of Acheulian type. Beside these sites Lower Palaeolithic tools have also been reported from Bankura and Birbhum in West Bengal. Significantly, till now, all the Lower Palaeolithic sites of the extreme tip of eastern region are located in Meghalaya. Here, too, one comes across a predominance of chopper-chopping tools occasnionally accompanied by some handaxes and cleavers.

The most important Lower Palaeolithic industry after the Soan valley has been found the peninsular India. Since such tools were discovered for the first time from the sites located in the erstwhile Madras estate, the whole industry has been designated as *Madrasian Industry*. Though dozens of sites, containing similar tools, have now been found from almost all parts of the country but traditionally it is still called as Madrasian industry. This whole region is tropical and comes under high rainfall regions of the country. For the first time in 1938, Lower Palaeolithic tools were found from the Kortaliyer valley of Chinglepet district in the present Tamil Nadu. The whole Madrasian industry is characterized by a heavy preponderence of handaxes and cleavers. In later years some pebbles and flake tools have also been discovered from some sites like Gudiyam caves but the character of the Madrasian industry still heavily remains handaxe-cleaver which have been found in large numbers from dozens of sites.

The hand axes and cleavers of the Madrasian industry look definitely more sophisticated and neatly made than those of the Soan valley. H.D. Sankalia has indicated the presence of *waist* on both the lateral edges of many handaxes and cleavers. This may be indicative of the practice of hafting tools in wooden or bamboo frames. It has opened new doors of research. If the presence of hafting is substantiated this will be, perhaps, the earliest instance of hafting from anywhere in the world. In recent times the sites of Nagarjunakonda and Kareumpudi have yielded such large deposits of tools that Andhra Pradesh may rightly be described as the 'treasure house' of Lower Palaeolithic in India. Beside these, Malprabha, Ghatprabha and Tungbhadra from the Karnataka have also yielded a number of Lower Paleolithic sites but here too the pebble tools are conspicous by their almost total absence like Kortaliyer valley's sites.

If summation is done of the Lower Palaeolithic culture on the basis of the well studied sites, one may conclude that the Lower Palaeolithic culture must have emerged during the earliest days of the Upper Pleistocene epoch. Even this antiquity does not tell the whole story of the sub-continent because of regional variations. The sites of this period tell us about various religions and their respective climatic conditions where man had made his earliest habitations. The Lower Palaeolithic man usually lived near the source of water because of several reasons. In the absence of containers and utensils of storage of any type, they could not afford to make their settlements far from the sources of water. That is why perhaps, most of the archaeological remains have been found from the river banks and valleys. The availability of raw material (mainly stone) must also have been an important determining factor in the location of settlements. They preferred to live near the deposits of pebbles and peripheries of forests (for the convenience in hunting). They never chose higher altitudes and dense forests for their habitations.

It is difficult to make any final comments on the use of tools fabricated by Palaeolithic man. Patterson has expressed the view with authority that the tools discovered from the Soan valley must have been meant for cutting and chopping, digging and skinning. Zeuner has opined that various types of handaxes of those times must have been used for digging out edible roots, cutting, boring and piercing, chopping and cleaving and skinning purposes. Man, during those times, used to live totally naked. He was food gather-hunter. Unfortunately we find tools of those times everywhere but no clues about the physical features of the tool maker. Perhaps, the highly acidic nature of Indian soil is responsible for this absence of fossil skeletal remains of that much antiquity. Chance or luck has also not favoured the prehistorians involved in the cultural construction of the past.

Middle Paleolithic

Lower Paleolithic gave way to Middle Palaeolithic all over the world. For quite some time it was not considered an independent cultural phase. The reason was the absence of any definite stratigraphy without which it was difficult to draw a line of demarcation between the Lower and the Middle Palaeolithic. The earliest date of this cultural phase is dated around 1,00,000 B.C. and it continued till around 36,000 B.C. Neanderthal man is believed to have dominated this stage of human evolution.

There was hardly any clue to the existence of Middle Palaeolithic in India till about 1960 after which only it was recognised as a separate cultural stage. Credit goes to H.D. Sankalia, for establishing the independent existence of this cultural phase, who through his excavations at Navasa in 1956, was able to achieve this breakthrough. During this excavation a number of flake tools, belonging to the Middle Palaeolithic, were discovered. Incidentally most of the important sites of Middle Palaeolithic happen to be in Maharashtra region and especially the river valleys of Godavari and its various tributaries. Among such sites are Nevasa, Suregaon, Bel Pandhari and Nandur Madhmeshwar. The recent excavations in West Bengal have added the names of Bankura ad Purulia in this list; Madhya Pradesh is yet another addition.

A striking feature of Indian Middle Palaeolithic that has drawn the attention of many archaeologists is the change is raw material for tool making when the Lower Palaeolithic gave way to Middle Palaeolithic. Earlier it was mostly quartzite stone but for the first time tools were made on such smooth and bright rocks as flint and to

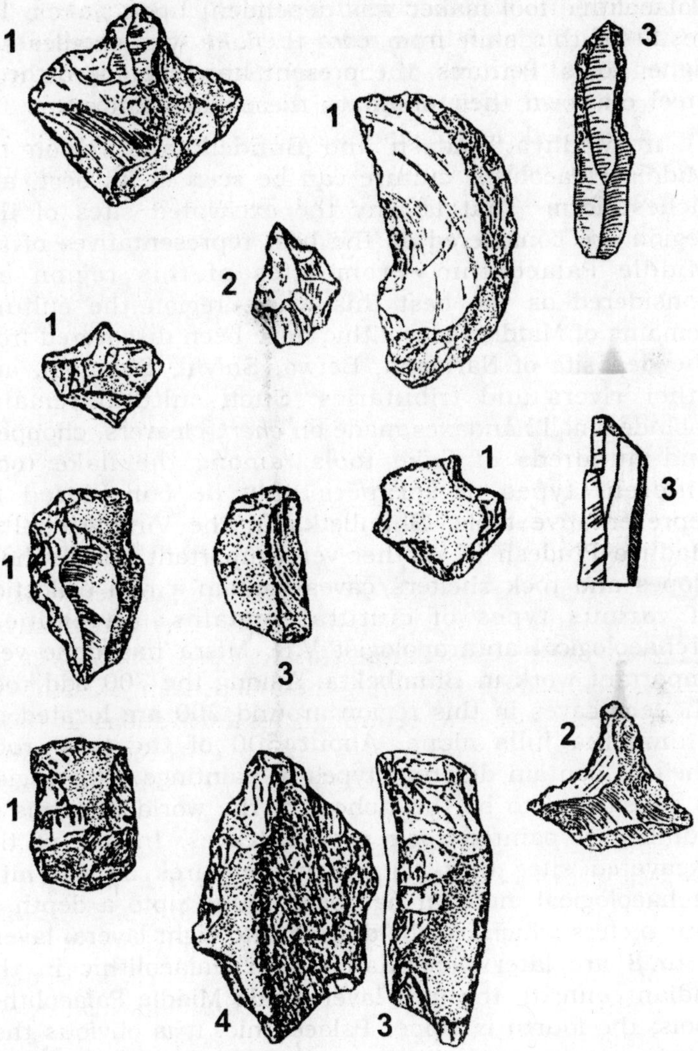

Middle Palaeolithic Tools

1. Different Types of Scrapers 2. Borer 3. Burin
4. Scraper-cum-Borer

a lesser extent on jasper and chalcedony. The Middle Palaeolithic tool maker was dependent upon *flakes*. The result of this shift from *core* to *flake* was smaller and ligher tools. Perhaps, the present knives made on iron, steel etc. own their origin to these flake knives.

In Madhya Pradesh and Bundelkhand region the Middle Palaeolithic culture can be seen in its best, and richest form. That is why the excavated sites of this region are considered as the best representatives of the Middle Palaeolithic. From sites of this region are considered as the best this whole region the cultural remains of Middle Palaeolithic have been discovered from the deposits of Narmada, Betwa, Shivni, Chambal, and other rivers and tributaries. Such cultural remains include small handaxes made on *chert*, cleavers, choppers and hundreds of flake tools; among the flake tools different types of scrapers may be considered as representative tools. Bhimbetka in the Vindhyachal of Madhya Pradesh is another very important name whose slopes and rock shelters/caves contain a rich collection of various types of cultural remains. An eminent archaeological anthropologist V.N. Misra has done very important work in Bhimbekta. Among the 700 odd rock shelters/caves in this region around 200 are located on Bhimbetka hills alone. About 500 of the total rock shelters contain different types of paintings. This region is considered to be the richest in the world in terms of number of painted rock shelters/caves. In one of the excavated sites (IIIF-23) which measures 52 sq. mts. archaeological material has been found upto a depth of four meters which can be divided into eight layers; layers 6 to 8 are later Acheulian (Lower Palaeolithic in the Indian context); the fifth layer yields Middle Palaeolithic tools; the fourth is Upper Palaeolithic. It is obvious that the tools were made in the rock shelter as evidenced by the presence of fabrication debris. The material used throughout was *orthoquartzite* for making handaxes and cleavers; the other tools were made on yellowish quartzite which withers faster. About five thousand tools were recovered from this site. Unfortunately, nothing has survived of the organic remains; no bones have been

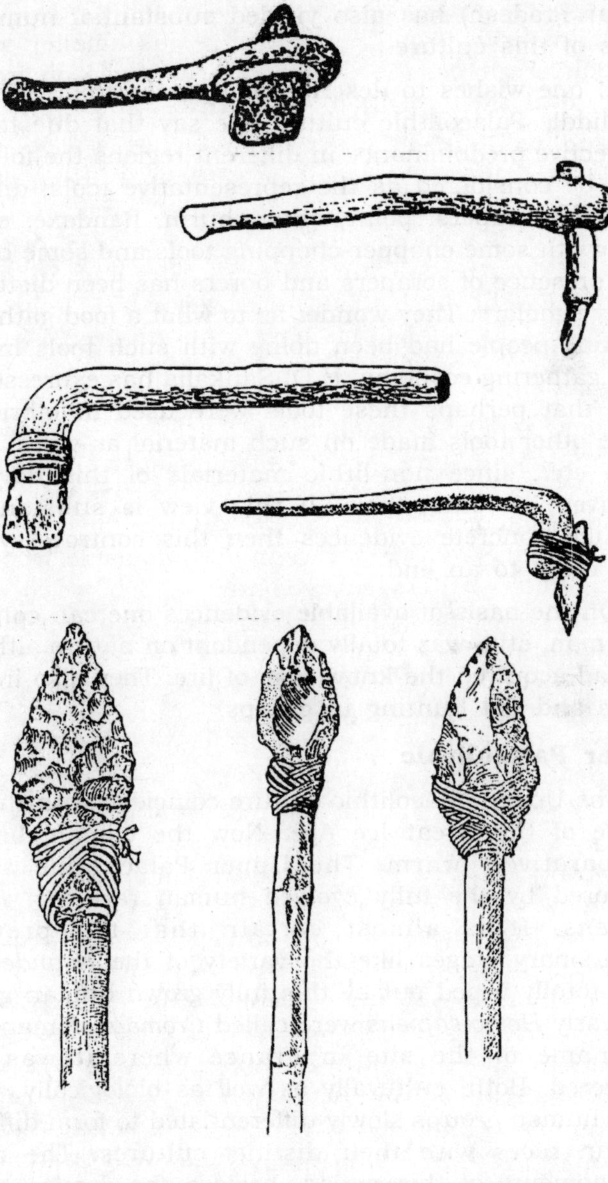

Hafting During Middle Palaeolithic

found yet. Lately, the Belan river valley in Allahabad (Uttar Pradesh) has also yielded substantial number of tools of this culture.

If one wishes to describe, in concise from, the tools of Middle Palaeolithic culture one say that due to their respective predominance in different regions the following may be considered as the representative tools; different types of scrapers, point, borer, burin, handaxe, cleaver alongwith some chopper-chopping tools and some blades. The presence of scrapers and borers has been disturbing many scholars. They wonder as to what a food gathering-hunting people had been doing with such tools in their food gathering economy. H.D. Sankalia has expressed the view that perhaps these tools were used in fabricating some other tools made on such material as wood, bone, horn etc., since non-lithic materials of this have not survived, so such tools. If this view is substantiated through concrete evidences then this controversy, too, may come to an end.

On the basis of available evidences one can conclude that man, still, was totally dependent on nature although he had acquired the knowledge of fire. They also lived in caves and did hunting in groups.

Upper Palaeolithic

The Upper Palaeolithic culture coincided with the last phase of the Great Ice Age. Now the climate became comparatively warm. The Upper Palaeolithic age is authored by the fully evolved human race viz. *Homo-sapiens*. It is almost certain that the previous evolutionary stages like the variety of the *Neanderthals* were totally wiped out by this fully grown human group. The early *Homo-sapiens* were called *Cromagnon* man after the name of the site in France where it was first recovered. Both, culturally as well as biologically, these early human groups slowly differentiated to form different human races with their distinct cultures. The major developments of this period, besides the demise of the Neanderthals and the appearance of modern man, can be summarised as follows:

1. The expansion of humans into most of the worlds' inhabited areas including the New world and Australia.
2. The relatively sudden and widespread appearance of *figurines* (especially female figurines) and other artifacts reflecting art and rituals.
3. The appearance of a wide range of bone tools including eye needles, harpoons, and other fishing tools.
4. There was a decided step towards organizing human groups in closely tied kinship organization," (D.K. Bhattacharya, ibid).

On the basis of above description (which is the portrayal of European Upper Palaeolithic of which we know a lot) it can be said that even today the Indian Upper Palaeolithic cannot be compared with its European counterpart as an independent and clearly distinct cultural stage. Obviously, sometimes scanty and some other times almost total absence of the above described cultural features is the main reason for this.

Among the not too many Upper Palaeolithic sites on which we base most of our knowledge of Indian Upper Palaeolithic, the sites of Renigunta (Chittor, Andhra Pradesh), Mutchtala Chintamani Gavi (Kurnool, Andhra pradesh), Bhimbetaka and Bagor (Madhya Pradesh) and Belan valley (Allahabad, Uttar Pradesh) may be considered very important. Renigunta has yielded a large number of blades that are often regarded as representative tools of the Upper Palaeolithic. Among such blade tools are burins, awls, scrapers, borers, point and small choppers. The cave site of Mutchtala Chintamani Gavai occupies a special place among the above mentioned sites.

The first bone tools have been discovered, from this site. Not only that, the richness of the site can be imagined by the fact that more than 90% of the tools found at this site consist of bone tools. Among such tools made on bone, horns and other non-lithic materials are scrapers, chisels, borers, barbs and spatula. The site at

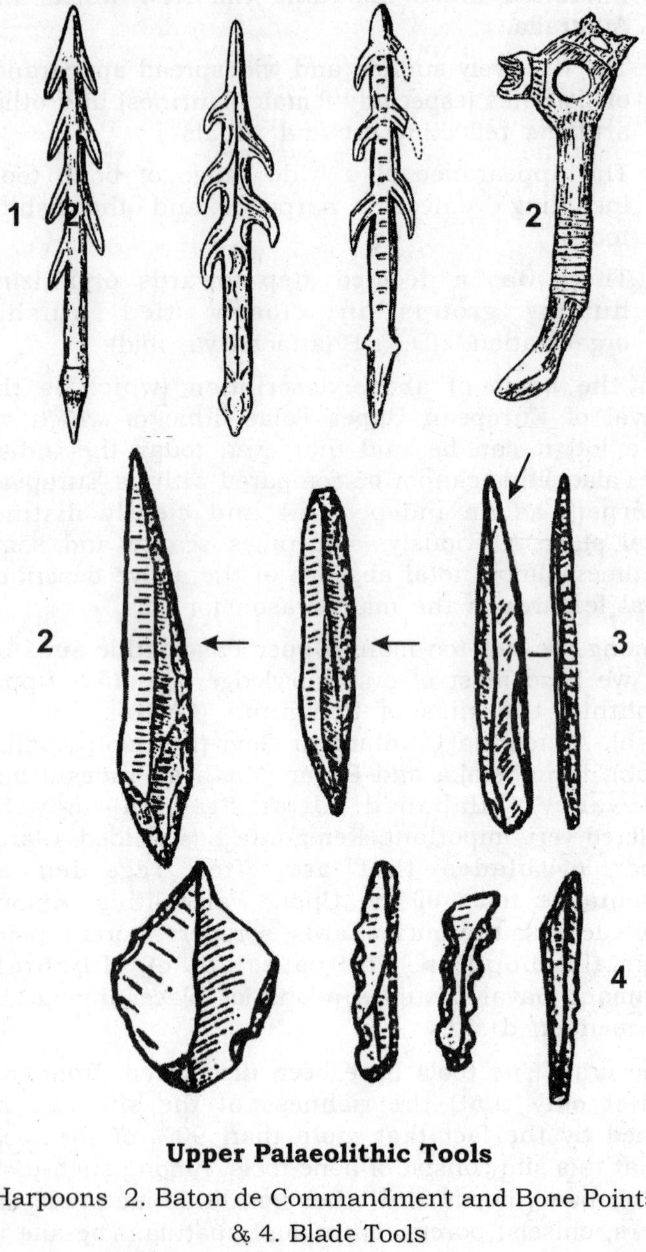

Upper Palaeolithic Tools

1. Harpoons 2. Baton de Commandment and Bone Points 3. & 4. Blade Tools

Beland valley, besides other artifacts, has also yielded a 'female figurine' made on bone. Similar figurines known as *venus* have been found in abundance from many European Upper Palaeolithic sites. But some scholars have created doubt over its nature by describing it as a fishing harpoon. If this is finally proved to be a venus like figurine, it will be the first object of this type from the Indian Upper Palaeolithic. Recently a site belonging to the Upper Palaeolithic has also been discovered from Bagor. The most striking feature of this site is that not only it is a habitation site, it also looks like a worshipping place.

This cultural phase world wide began around 36,000 B.C. and came to an end around 9,000 B.C. "It has a duration of barely 27,000 years or so which is less than 3% of the duration of the Lower Palaeolithic phase" (Bhattacharya, ibid). An important fact that can be drawn from it is that in this journey of cultural evolution the more man advanced, the less duration of the coming cultural phase of increasingly important and radical cultural achievements. Sadly, our knowledge of the Indian Upper Palaeolithic is till far from adequate.

Mesolithic Culture

With the folding up of the Great Ice Age some 10,000 B.C. the Palaeolithic age too came to an end. Upper Palaeolithic being the last phase. Thus, it may be said that this transitional period between Palaeolithic and Neolithic began around 10,000 B.C. and continued till approximately 4,000 B.C. The old glacial conditions had more or less disappeared throughout the world, and the dry period had started. With the drastic change in ecology man had to read just within the changed environment.

Though occupation of sites was more extensive and intensive than that of any of the two preceding stone age cultures, the knowledge we have of Indian Mesolithic period is based mainly on the few excavated and studied sites. The most important excavated sites are Birbhanpur in West Bengal, *Teri* sites in Tamil Nadu, Langhnaj in Gujarat, Bagor in Rajasthan, Bhimbetka and Adamgarh in Madhya Pradesh and Sarai Nahar Rai in Uttar Pradesh. Bhattacharya (ibid) has summarised the basic information gathered from these excavated sites as follows:

(i) Mesolithic people had not only achieved their special adaptation but also settled in artificially erected structures in as early as 8,000 B.C. This, in other words, can be taken to indicate that the time of onset of this culture agrees with the same in both Europe and Africa. So far we have only one site with such an early date from India (Sarai Nahar Rai). The rest of the sites ranges from 500 B.B. (Bagor) to 2000 B.C. (Langhnaj).

(ii) Most of these sites show total adaptation to microliths and do not contain any such heavy tools as picks and axes. Use of bones like the shoulder blade of a rhinoceros found at Langhnaj indicate the aspect of non-lithic (other than stone) environment used. Antlers or for that matter ivory are rarely used in Indian Mesolithic. Haematite with evidence of its having been rubbed, and spherical stone balls used as sling *bolas* are the other important features of the Mesolithic way of life and their hunting method. Some of the rock paintings discovered from Mirzapur district in Uttar Pradesh and Bhimbhetka from Madhya Pradesh would be isolated from the large number of art executions as being of Mesolithic antiquity. All these show animal forms with isolated hunting and fishing scehes. The hunting implements are spears with multiple barbs apparently obtained easily by attaching microliths.

(iii) At Bhimbetka there is evidence of a special structure erected outside the cave mouth to act as a wind break. At Bagor, natural concrete from river bed seems to have been specially transported to the living site to pave the living floor.

(vi) At Adamgarh, a large number of animal bones were found to be domesticated although associated finds were mainly suitable for hunting functions.

The domesticated animals could not have been taken to indicate pastoral economy because there are about six varieties of mammals found in this domesticated group. Further, Adamgarh is a cave for longer duration. Apparently our information about this site is not quite complete. It may be representing a younger industry.

(v) That inter group fight or warfare is not merely a conjecture for this period is proved by the skeleton found at Sarai Nahar Rai witha **Microlith** embedded into one of it's ribs. The characteristic tool of Mesolithic culture in India is microlith and microliths with the length ranging from 1 to 8 cm are the main industry of this period. It is obvious that such tools could have been used only as composite tools hafted in wood or bovine jaws, and not singly. We have evidence of such hafting from abroad but none from India. The first microliths were discovered by Carlyle in 1867 from the Vindhyan rock shelters and this was followed by more discoveries by Cockburn and Rivet Carnac in the nineteenth century. In the first half of this century, Cammiade, Todd, Hunter and Gordon reported microliths from different parts of the sub-continent (Agarwal, 1984). However, systematic and scientific work on the mesolithic was started only by Sankalia's excavations at Langhnaj in Gujarat in the early forties, Zeuner, Allchin, Krishnaswamy, Subbaro and Malik explored and excavated various sites. In recent years Verma has excavated sites in Mirzapur district, U.P., Joshi and Khare in Madhya Pradesh; and Sankalia in Karnataka. V.N. Misra excavated sites in Rajasthan and Madhya Pradesh and has published extensively on the Indian Mesolithic.

Langhnaj has yielded important objects. In the Mesolithic layer geometrical shaped microliths like lunates, semitriangles, crescents, trapezes, roundish, rectangular or square scrapers have been found. Most of these tools are crude though the material is chert, agate, carnelian and occasionally quartz. A huge rhinoceros shoulder blade discovered here was used as an anvil for manufacturing microliths. With the help of these tools Mesolithis people subsisted on cow, buffalo, sheep, goat, dog, fish, etc. Human skeletons from Langhnaj generated lot of controversy regarding their racial affinities. The crouchig posture in which the skeletons have been found indicates that they were deliberately buried along with some tools as part of burial ceremony.

Sarai Nahar Rai in Pratepgarh district of Uttar Pradesh was excavated by Sharma. Significantly hearths have also been discovered. A floor, of 5x4 was made of rammed, burnt clay lumps and four pot holes on the four corners suggesting some sort of communal cooking. Charred animal bones, recovered from hearths and floors give an idea of the fauna of that time-stag, bison, rhinoceros, fish and tortoise were roaming this part of the India. From other areas of the site thirteen burials were found; the head pointing west and the forearms diagonally placed across the abdomen. There were hearths nearby indicating that burials were inside the habitation. The microlithic culture of Sarai Nahar Rai is pre-pottery culture because pottery is completely absent in the burials, floors and hearths exposed in the excavations.

The rock sheltersand caves of Madhya Pradesh have yielded a lot of microliths and Sankalia has opined that the whole of Vindhya range from west to east is not only a prolific source of microliths but perhaps holds the key to the microlithic or mesolithic problem of Central India. The general sequence of the Mesolithic cultures in Bhimbhetka begins with a geometric microlithic horizon, devoid of pottery. At Adamgarh, near Hoshangabad, the sequence is similar to Bhimbhetka. The microlithic industry is geometric though a bit cruder in comparison. Pottery, too, occurs throughout the microlithic level.

Sangankallu, situated on the western fringe of the Karnataka plateau, was excavated by Subbarao, and later by Sankalia. The excavations produced an industry

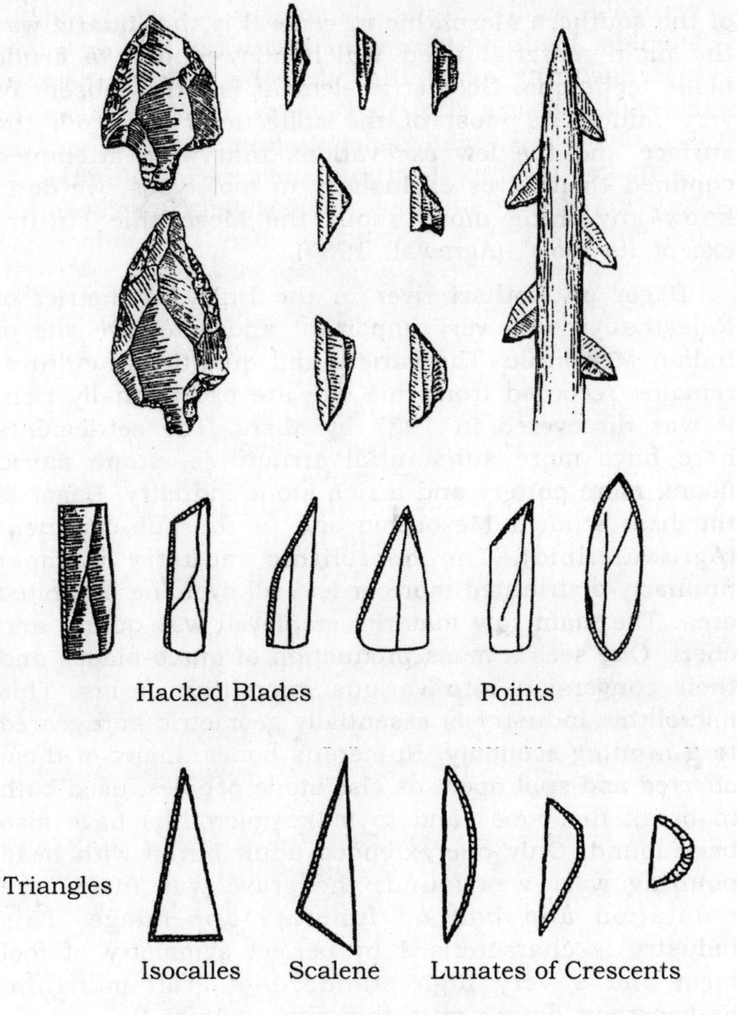

Tools of Mesolithic
(Different Types of Microlithis)

based on trap and quartz. "The characteristic features of the southern Mesolithic in general is that quartz was the main material used which allowed only a crude blade technique. Geometric element is either absent or very minor. As most of the collections are from the surface and the few excavations that were attempted confined themselves exclusively to tool types, we don't know any thing more about the Mesolithic culture except its tools" (Agrawal, 1984).

Bagor on Kothari river in the Bhilwara district of Rajasthan is still very important and extensive site of Indian Mesolithic. The variety and quantity of cultural remains recorded from this site are exceptionally rich. It was discovered in 1967 by Misra. The settlements here have more substantial structures, stone paved floors, more pottery and a rich stone industry. Bagor is the best studied Mesolithic site in the sub-continent (Agrawal, ibid). The microlithic industry is most profusely distributed more or less all over the inhabited area. The main raw material employed was quartz and chert. One sees a mass production of mirco-blades and their conversion into various microlithic forms. This microlithic industry is essentially geometric and geared to a hunting economy. Numerous bones, many of them charred and split open, as also stone pebbles, used both to break the bones and to make microliths have also been found. Only one extended adult burial with head pointing west was found; the grave was inside the habitation and had no funerary appendage. This industry is characterised by perfect symmetry of tool form and a very high standard of craftsmanship. Radiocarbon dating puts this site at 4600 B.C.

It is not clear whether microliths were the result of some external influence of developed out of the earlier stone industries. The prolific distribution of the industry not only in India, but all over the world in Europe, Africa and Asia points to some cultural link. It is also held by some scholars that probably a new race of people from Africa entered India with these implements.

Neolithic Culture

Neolithic culture marks great technological and economic changes in society. These changes are of such a far reaching importance that many scholars have termed this phase as '**Neolithic Revolution**'. Although the Neolithic age began much earlier, in 7,000 B.C., Neolithic settlement in the Indian Sub-continent are not older than 4,000B.C. Technologically speaking, it is marked by the grinding and polishing of stones; economically man became food producer. Domestication of animals like the cow or ox, sheep goat, pigs and dogs also contributed a lot towards his efforts for self-sufficiency. Later, he also made pottery. This new mode of life collectively implied that man started living at a definite place. His nomadism (mainly in quest for food), was replaced by settled life and a new relationship developed between him and a patih of cultivable and called 'field'. This relationship completely changed his life. He no longer remained a hunter moving from place to place in small groups. He developed an organized community or social life.

In spite of the common characteristics, there are regional peculiarities in Neolithic cultures becuase of local environmental conditions and diversity of influences. Thus a strict regional and chronological treatment is not possible. The probability of simultaneous or contemporary existence and overlapping of their cultures or certain cultural characteristics are noticed.

Among the zonal or regional Neolithic cultures the sites of Burzahom, Gofkral and Mar and in Kashmir; Brahamagri, Sangankallu, Piklihal, Maski, Nagarujana-Konda, Untur, Narispur and Tekkalkota from southern zone; Daojali Hading, Chirand and Barudith from eastern zone are important excavated sites. Most of the knowledge we have about Indian Neolithic is based on the these excavated sites specially Burzahom, Sangankallu, Brahmagri-Piklihal, Daojali, Handing and Chirand.

The northern Neolithic culture is represented by the site Burzahom situated at a distance of about 20 km.

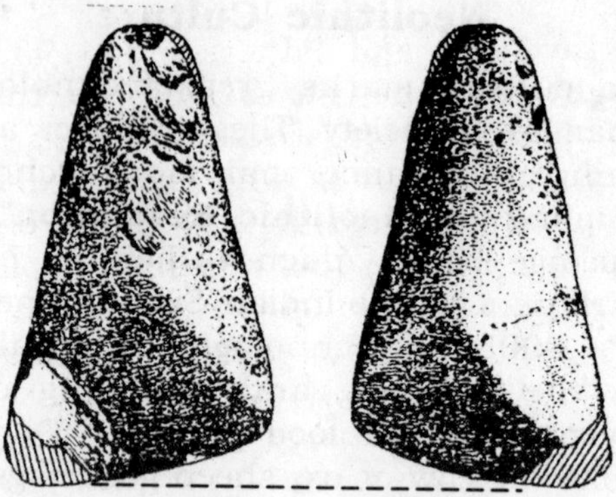

Fully Ground or Polished axe with a corner broken

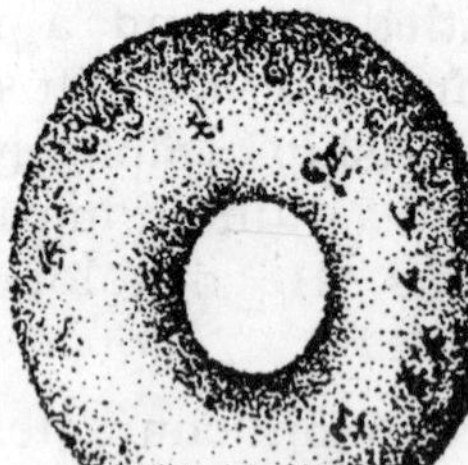

Ring-stone or Mace-head

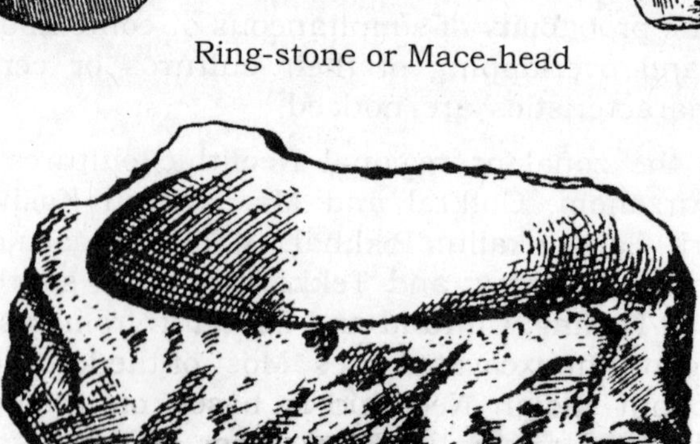

Saddle Quem or Mill-stone

from Srinagar, Kashmir. The first discovery of this site was made by De Terra and Patterson in 1935. They, however, thought that the site belongs to the Indus culture. The credit goes to Khazanchi of the Archaeological Survery of India who excavated this site during 1960-71 and established its Neolithic character. The Neolithic people lived in this region on a plateau in pits and probably had a fishing and hunting economy, of course having a faint clue of cultivation. The deposits at Burzahom may be divided into four periods, out of which the first two are Neolithic, the third Megalithic and the last, early historic. Pit dwelling is the most distinctive characteristic of Period I. The inhabitations lived in pit dwelling of irregular shapes, some resembling round, oval square or rectangular. Circular pits were bigger and deeper. One can even see the marks of long celts left during digging. A large pit had a mouth of 2.7 metre diameter expanding to 4.6 metre at the base with a depth of about 4 metre. The walls were plastered with mud. A variety of ground stone tools were used by these Neolithic people e.g., polished chisels and mace beads. Beside polished tools they used numerous tools and weapons made of bone. Agarwal (ibid) supports the view that the bone tool industry of Burzahom is unique and most developed of all the Neolithic cultures in India. It comprises of harpoons, needles, awis, spear points, arrowheads, daggers and scrapers. The Neolithic potters of Burzahom made graceful pots though the use of wheel was not known to them. Pant (1972) has shown through radiography of the pots that they were made off by a coiling technique. Pots were made over mats as is indicated by a variety of weaving patterns. These were occasionally decorated with incised and notched designs. Colour range varied from steel-grey to brown. Paintings depicting hunting scenes have also been discovered. Burial of both man and animal was practiced. The Carbon[14] method of dating indicates a time bracket for this culture of 2400-1400 B.C.

The earliest manifestation of Neolithic culture in south India is seen at Sanganakallu which was dug by Subbarao. Wheeler dug at Brahamagri. The pointed-butt polished axe seems to be the characteristic tool of southern Neolithic culture. The adze is another important type; a variety of chisels have also been discovered. Some pointed tools have been labelled as picks, borers or pointed tools. Besides these types, one gets hammer stone, sling stones, querns etc. Bone tools were also used. The ceramic is characterised by a dominant hand made dull greyware. At Maski the wheel made pottery seemed to be in larger numbers and it seems to be a later development. Terracota figurines of humped bull have also been obtained. These animals, might have played important role in their economy. These Neolithic people seem to have become acquinted with cattle rearing and agriculture. The remains of domestic animals such as buffalo, sheep and goat point towards it. Although, no grains or their impressions have been discovered, the discovery of concave shaped saddle querns and pounders suggests that some kind of grain was coarsely crushed before eating. This is also inferred from the worn out teeth of two intact skeletons. They lived in huts or houese remains fo which have been discovered from Brahmagiri and Pikhlihal. It is obvious that these peoples show mastery of pottery making and ground stone tools. The available C^{14} dating shows that the southern Neolithic time spread is confined to 2500-1000 B.C.

Except Deojali-Hading excavated by Sharma in North Cachar Hills of Assam, most of the collections in eastern India are from the surface. This small excavation has given for the first time stratigraphical occurrence of ground or polished stone axes and also pottery in a fairly deep deposit. The ground and polished celts are mostly shouldered at the butt end and had ground, sharp border. Assam Neolithic stands out as quite different from the rest of India. Numerous pot sherds were recovered from the excavations and significantly in association with stone axes. Pottery is hand made and decorated with cord impressions or basket impressions. Neolithic man here lived in mud walled houses. Unfortunately, this excavation could not yield any information towards habitation structure. Sankalia assigns - 4000-2000 B.C. to the Neolithic culture of Assam-Meghalaya.

The Gangetic plain has not yielded any other Neolithic site except Chirand, located on the confluence of the Ganga and the Ghaghra in district Saran of Bihar. Besides Burzahom, Chirand is the only site to have yielded so many varied types of bone tools-celts, scrapers, chisels, hammers, needles, points, borers, awls, shaft straighteners and arrowheads. Bone was also used to make ornaments such as pendents, earrings, bangles, discs and combs. Besides querns, balls and pestles, the ground stone axes were also recovered. The microliths made on chert, chalcedony and silicious stones also continued. The only effective weapons of offense reported are bows and arrows tipped with stone and bone points and terracotta sting balls. The pottery is extremely well made though the excavators insist that it is hand made or at best thrown on a turn table. It appears that pit dwellings with thatched roofs were initially used but later on only overground huts were made. It seems that these people had the know how of cultivation of grains because among the remains occur charred grains of paddy husk and wheat. Significantly terracotta figurines of snake have also been recovered yielding the first evidence of snake cult. The Neolithic culture of Chirand is dated around 100 B.C. but there is strong possibility that the beginning could be of an earlier date.

Although the people of Neolithic Age continued to hunt some of their food, they learned to produce much of it themselves. The Ox was used as beast of burden. Cattle used were raised in herds for their milk. The dog, which was the first animal to be domesticated, was not only a help in hunting, but also a companion and protector of the family and the cattle. While the men hunted and protected their families the women planted and tended flax, barley and wheat. In order to tend the grain and to harvest the crops, it was necessary for the family or group to stay in one place for longer periods of time. Over the centuries and millenia Nedlithic man learned other, arts. He found that the fiber of flax could be spun into thread and woven into linen cloth. The women used bone needles to sew cloth into simple garments. The men discovered that fire would harden

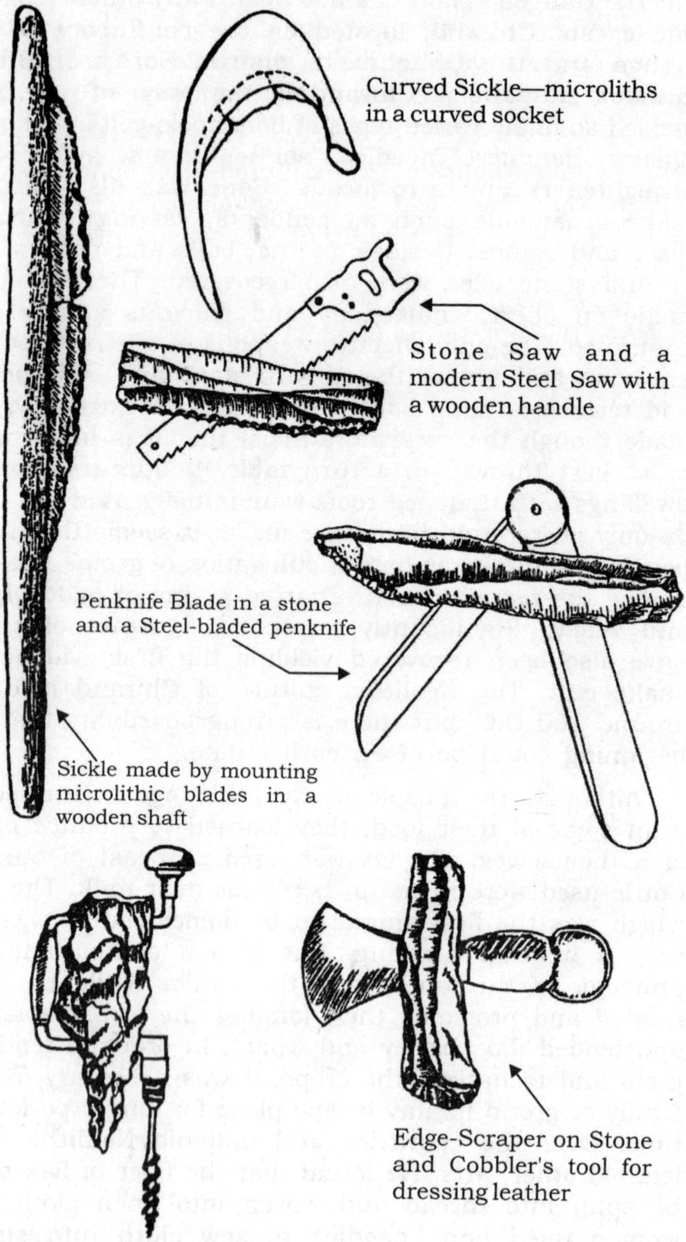
Curved Sickle—microliths in a curved socket
Stone Saw and a modern Steel Saw with a wooden handle
Penknife Blade in a stone and a Steel-bladed penknife
Sickle made by mounting microlithic blades in a wooden shaft
Edge-Scraper on Stone and Cobbler's tool for dressing leather
Stone Borer and Steel Drill 1:2

the pottery. They made dugouts by burning out the centre of long logs. Dug outs were the world's first boats and they enabled men to make more use of the rivers to get from place to place—another conquest of nature of serve man's needs.

The people Neolithic Age suffered from one great limitation, since they had to depend almost entirely on tools and weapons made of stone they could not found settlements far away from hilly areas. They could settle down mostly in the hilly river valleys. Further, even with great effort they could not produce more than what they needed for their bare subsistence. Still, settled life and cultivation gave man some leisure for the first time in his entire existence. The division of labour made it possible for various people to specialize. The settled community life needed rules to regulate the behaviour of its members. It is not possible to know exactly how regulations were established. It appears that the decisions regarding the community were taken by the people as a whole, or by a council of elders, as is the practice in all tribal societies of the present day. There were no kings or organized government; there were chiefs and chieftains. Archaeological excavations have not revealed anything which would indicate the prevalence of higher status for some members of the community. Thus, social inequalities do not seem to have emerged even in Neolithic times. Sources of production were socially or communally owned. There was no scheme of private property except perhaps some trivial things of individual use like ornaments, utensils, etc. Such a scheme of things in primitive economic system prompted Morgan to term this system as "**Primitive Communism.**" It was in the later stages, perhaps of Neolithic, that man invented wheel which brought about a technological revolution. From then onwards man never looked back. The pace of social progress and technological development gathered momentum with the beginning of Neolithic. The invention of script and several other achievements that followed paved the way for the development of civilization.

Prehistoric Art

The earliest evidence of the artistic capabilities of man goes back to Lower Palaeolithic. However the full flowering of this skill was visible only from Upper Palaeolithic onwards. But one may be reasonably sure that some crude form of art was being practised earlier which has not been preserved. "We can, indeed, imagine that long before man started topaint with colours or engrave with specially made engraving tools, he must often have made rough drawings in sand, in the earth and on clay with his finger tips or a piece of wood. Naturally, however, such examples of early art would hardly ever survive" (Leakey, 1960). Beautiful cave painting and objects of art of Upper Palaeolithic have been found from the caves and rock shelters of Spain, France and Italy. If we turn to a consideration of the places where Palaeolithic mural art can be found we notice that the sites fall into three main categories:

(a) Dark caves and passages where nothing can be seen without the aid of artificial light.

(b) Open rock shelters, with which we may include slightly over-handing rocks, which are not quite strictly 'shelters'.

(c) On flat slabs of rock and the tops of boulders.

The commonest explanation of the art, hidden away in dark corners and inaccessible places, is that it was the manifestation of the magico-religious. Many European and a few such paintings from India strongly endorse such a suggestions as most of these depict hunting scenes, bleeding animals arrow-stricken; the animal was captured in the painting and 'killed' before the actual hunt took place. Art for Man was part of the hunting process as is evidenced by numerous hunting scenes depicted by Palaeolithic man all over the world.

The first rock painting in India was reported by Carlyle, more than a century ago. Cockburn, Anderson, Mitra and Ghosh were the other early researchers who discovered a number of sites and published their

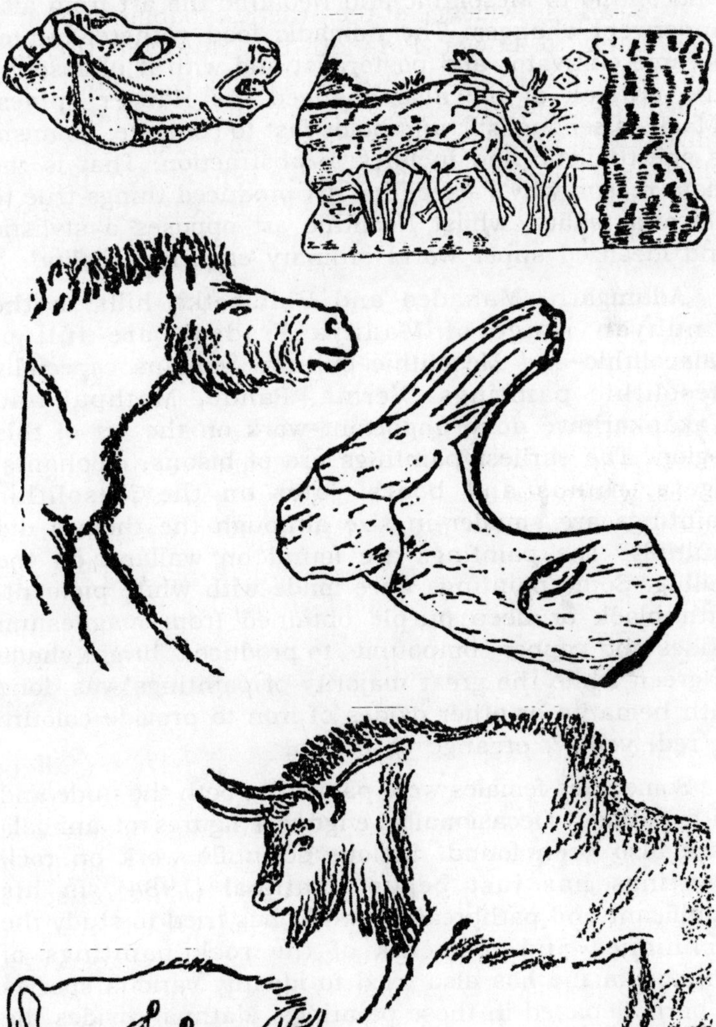

Some Specimen of Upper Palaeolithic Art

accounts. With the change in mode of life-from Palaeolithic to Mesolithic and Neolithic the art from also underwent changes. The nomadic food gatherer-hunter became cultivator and postoralist and with it philosophy and outlook of life also changed. As Hauser opines, "Magic is sensualistic and holds fast to concrete; animism is spiritualistic and inclines to abstraction. That is the main reason why Palaeolithic art produced things true to life and reality, whilst Neolithic art opposes a stylistic and idealized super world ordinary empirical reality".

Adamgarh, Mahadeo and Bhimbetka hills in the Vindhyan range of Madhya Pradesh are full of Palaeolithic and Mesolithic cultural remains especially Mesolithic paintings. Verma, Pande, Mathpal and Wakankarhave done important work on the art of this region. The earliest paintings are of bisons, elephants, tigers, rhinos and boars. later on the Mesolithic paintings are smaller in size although the themes did multiply. The paintings are found on walland on the ceiling. Some paintings were made with white pigment, with black or deep purple obtained from magnesium oxides and copper compounds to produce a bright shade of green while the great majority of paintings was done with hematite or other oxides of iron to provide colours in red, yellow, organge or brown.

Sometimes females were painted in both the nude and with clothes. Occasionally, engraved figures of animals have also been found. Serious scientific work on rock paintings has just begun. Mathpal (1984), in his significant and pathbreaking work, has tried to study the techniques and pigments of the rock paintings of Bhimbetka; he has also tried to identify various species of birds depicted in these paintings. Mathpal divides the paintings into four technical styles viz. dry colour or crayon painting; wet transparent colour painting; wet opaque or oil tempera painting; and spraycolour painting. He says that crayon painting is rare in India. Mineral and ochre colours were used with either vegetable juice or some kind of fat as solvent. He has found used hematite pieces fat as solvent. He has found used

Rock Paintings

hematite pieces throughout the Mesolithic occupation at Bhimbhetka. The attempt to identify various species of birds depicted in the paintings has revealed very interesting conclusions; perching birds are absent in the earliest group of paintings as these birds depended upon grain which was not available in the gathering-hunting society.

Granite rocks of north Karnataka and Andhra Pradesh provided suitable canvases to Neolithic man; Kupgallu, Piklihal and Tekkalakota are the three important sites. Apart from the depiction of various animals a site from Kupgallu presents a number of unique scenes where excited males with outsized organs are abducting females.

Under the category of Home Art is included any art executed on moveable objects. The Prehistoric man beautified his body with necklaces, pins and bracelets made of ivory bone, stone and shell. Various types of engraved designs on animal teeth and soft stones sculptured into exotic shapes have also been discovered from a number of sites of Mesolithic and Neolithic times.

The discovery of prehistoric art, though scanty, throws important light on a very significant aspect of the prehistoric man. Bhattacharya (1984) sums up the situation very appropriately when he says that "Palaeolithic art gives the earliest indication of the mind of Prehistoric man. Circumstantial evidences or arrangement of debris have all thrown indications about the Prehistoric society but his mind, by far, has remained unknown to the analyst. His agonies or, for that matter, his source of ecstacies will never be known to us. His art is the sole window we have to his mind, and hence its significance".

Indus Civilization

In many part of India, Neolithic phase was followed by the emergence of **Chalcolithic** (copper-stone) cultures in which stone continued to be used side by side with copper. Though most of these cultures belong to a period after that of the Harappan culture they were much less advanced than the Harappan culture. They neither had any cities nor script. Thus the Indus Civilization, the first known civilization in India, emerged earlier than other Chalcolithic cultures but had attained features hitherto unknown. It is also known as Harappan culture after the name of a major site of this civilization because some of its earliest excavated sites are located in the valley of the River Indus.

In the third millennium B.C. the Harappan culture appears in a fulfledged from suddenly in the Indus Valley. This culture, "like any other great revolution may best be visualised as a sudden offspring of opportunity and genius" (Wheeler, 1953). The creative geneius and environmental opportunity are said to be responsible for giving rise to this great culture. Though, the Indus civilization had long been accepted to have emerged suddenly on the scene yet some recent studies by Mughal (1970, 1974) indicate that several cultures contributed to the make up of the Indus civilization. He therefore calls the cultures immediately proceeding the Harappan culture as **Early Harappan**, instead of popular term **Pre-Harappan**.

The area occupied by the Pre-Harappan culture is quite vast stretching upto Indo-Iranian borderland. Some of the important excavated sites of this pre-Harappan culture are Kili Ghul Muhammad, Damb Saddat, Periano Ghundai and Kulli Mehli in Baluchistan; Amri, Kot Diji, Mohenjodaro and Gumla in Sind; Harappa in Punjab; Kalibangan in North Rajasthan; and Lothal in Gujarat. The common features of this culture as revealed by the excavated sites indicate that these people stood at the threshold of urbanisation. The skill of fortification, elaborate housing, pottery, cattle breeding and commerce are some of the striking features of Pre-Harappan Culture. It was in existence during 2700-2400-B.C.

The Harappa culture was discovered first in 1921 at the modern site of Harappa situated in the province of west Punjab, now in Pakistan. This discovery at once pushed back the history of India by at last a thousand years. After the discovery of Harappa in Punjab, a number of sites have been discovered showing the cultrual expanse of the Harappans from the foothills of the Himalayas at Ropar to the shores of Arabian Sea. It covered parts of Punjab, Sindh, Baluchistan, Gujarat, Rajasthan and the fringes of western Uttar Pradesh. "The Area formed a triangle and accounted for about 1,299,600 sq. kms. which is larger than Pakistan and certainly bigger than ancient Egypt and Mesopotamia. No other cultural zone in the third and second millennium B.C. in the world was as large as the Harappan zone" (Sharma,1977).

Of over 250 Harappan sites, only six can be regarded as cities. The two most important cities were Harappa in Punjab and Mohenjodaro in Sindh, both forming parts of Pakistan, situated at a distance of 483 kilometres they were linked together by the Indus. A third city lay at Chanudaro about 130 km. south of Mohenjodaro in Sindh, and a fourth at Lothal in Gujarat at the head of the Gulf of Cambay. A fifth city lay as Kalibangan in northern Rajasthan. A sixth called Banwali is situated in Hissar district in Haryana. "Harappa and Mohanjodaro standout like twin capitals in single empire among a number of sites" (Childe, 1952).

The Indus civilization is remarkable for its uniformity and standardization in weights, measures, ceramics, architecture, town planning and in other arts and crafts. As Allchin and Allchin (1968) rightly comment, this uniformity appears all the more imposing when one considers that culture extended over more than a million square kilometers. What this uniformity reflects, whether it was an empire or a trading zone, can only be a speculation. But such uniformity, almost amounting to monotony, in a third millennium B.C. context is indeed unique. Recent studies, however, are bringing out a good deal of regional variation.

Town Planning and Structure

The Harappan people built well planned cities. Among them, Mohanjodaro and Harappa were the metropolitan centres and the other secondary important towns are Chanudaro,, Kaligangan, Kot Diji, Lothal, Rangpur,

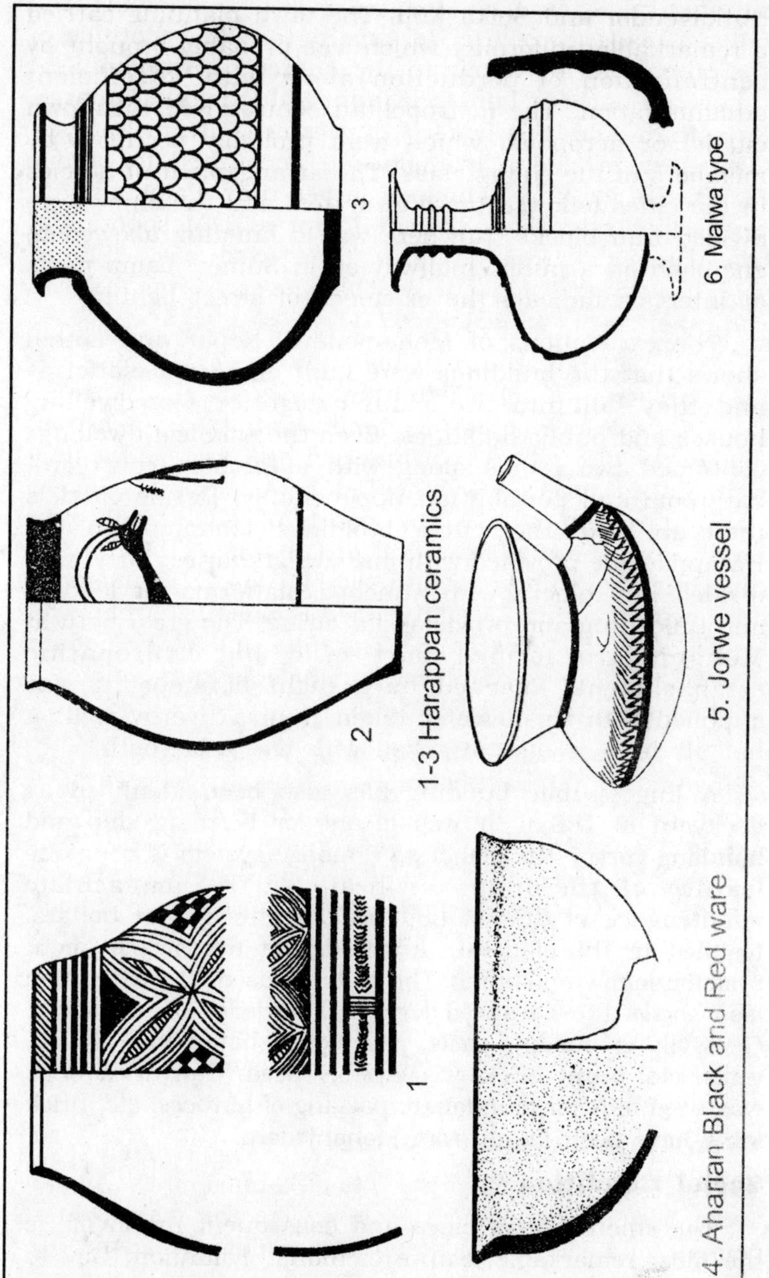

1-3 Harappan ceramics
4. Aharian Black and Red ware
5. Jorwe vessel
6. Malwa type

Sutkagendor and Solka Koh. The town planning carried a remarkable uniformity which was probably brought by centralization of porduction along with its efficient administration. The metropolitan centres had their own citadel or acropolis, which were probably occupied by members of the ruling class. The arrangement of houses in the cities followed the grid system and the cities were divided into blocks. Nowhere was a building allowed to encroach on a public highway as in Sumer. Lamp posts at intervals indicate the existence of street lighting.

The excavations of Mohanjodaro, Ropar and Lothal shows that the buildings were built on raised platforms and they fall into two main categories viz. dwelling houses and public buildings. Even the smallest dwellings contained two rooms along with a kitchen, courtyard, bathroom and possibly an upper storey. Beside citadels there are also other public buildings. Mohanjodaro and Harappa were provided with massive granaries. They were divided into blocks with attached platforms for loading and unloading and provision for airing. The great bath at Mohanjodaro formed part of a big hydropathic establishment. Reached by a flight of steps, it was supplied with fresh water taken from a nearby well. A hot air bath is also attached with the great bath.

A huge public building has also been identified as dockyard at Lothal. It was meant for berthing ship and handling cargo. The elaborate drainage system is a unique feature of the Indus civilizaiton. The immaculate maintenance of drains, both in the streets and houses, testified to the elaborate knowledge of the people about systematic town planning. The material used in construction also shows the advanced level of knowledge of mansonry. Generally in building wells, pavements, bathrooms, drains, wells, etc. burnt brick was lavishly used. Sun dried brick was used only for foundation, packing of terraces, etc. Brick kilns have been found from Mohanjodaro.

Social Condition

The emergence of cities and consequent urban life is the most remarkable feature of Indus civilization. Due to fast growth in the trend of specialization people were pursuing different occupations. yet, most of the people were farmers who lived beyond the walls of the cities. They grew wheat, barley, and peas. Cotton was also cultivated. Domestication of animals and cattle was also in vogue. Thus, we see that formation of different classes of people had started. The remains of Mohanjodaro demonstrate the existence of four main classes of people; the learned class of intellectual elite, warriors, traders and artisans; manual labourers constituted an altogether different class.

To reconstruct the religious life of a people on the basis of a few surviving material remains is a risky endeavour. A large number of seals depict the humped bull which may have been considered sacred. The impression of a god-like being on a seal is now believed to be an early form of the Hindu god, Shiva. Besides, figures of a goddess have also been discovered. Many scholars tend to believe that kings and the mother goddess were also worshipped. The Great Bath in Mohanjodaro may have been a place of ritual bathing. Dead bodies were buried as well as cremated. Some scholars are of the view tht these people also worshipped trees. Animals were also worshipped.

We have no definite idea about the political organization of the people. Unlike Egypt and Mesopotamia no temples have been discovered. No other religious structure of any kind except the Great Bath has been found. Hence, it cannot be concluded that priests ruled in Indus civilization. It was possibly ruled by a class of merchants.

Economic Activities

The abundance of fertile soil contributed to the progress of agriculture which was main occupation of the people. The farmers sowed seeds in the flood plains when the flood water receded and reaped their harvest of wheat and barley after maturity. No hoe or plough had been discovered but it is generally believed that they used wooden ploughshare. However, we do not know whether the plough was drawn by man or oxen.

These people belongs to the Bronze Age. They produced not only images and utensils but also various tools and weapons such as axes, saws, knives and spears. Weavers were weaving cloth of wool and cotton. The goldsmiths made jewellery of silver, gold and precious stones; the first two may have been obtained from Afghanistan and the last from south India. The potter's wheel was also in full use and they made their own characteristic pottery.

International trade of the Indus people has been a controversial subject. While Fairservice (1971) denies its existence, Rao (1973) supports it vehemently. Harappan cities did not possess the necessary raw materials and the early texts from Mesopotamia have references that indicate some interrelation with Indus people, hence the support in favour of international trade. They had commercial links with Rajasthan, Afghanistan and Iran.

The urban people of Indus region also needed and used weights and measures for trade and other transactions. Cubicle weights were the most common and they were made of different types of stones. They did not use metallic money and we have no idea about their currency.

Script

The Harappan seals, sealings and pots have legends in a pictographic script comprising some four hundred signs. Unlike the Egyptians and Mesopotamians, the Harappans did not write long inscriptions. Most inscriptions were recorded on seals and contain only a few words. These seals may have been used by the propertied people to mark and identify their private property. This script has still not been properly deciphered. Scholars generally agree that the script was written from right to left.

End

By about 1500 B.C. the Harappan culture came to an end. How and why it declined have been matters of great controversy among the scholars. Some ascribe its disappearance to the decreasing fertility on account of the increasing salinity of soil caused by the expansion of the neighbouring desert; others attribute it to some kind of depression in the land which caused floods while still others point out that Harappan culture was destroyed by the Aryans. So far, archaeological evidence of clear contact between the Aryans and the Harappans has been lacking. More geomorphological and archaeological evidences required to reach definite conclusions.

Recently, a Soviet scholar, M. Dmitriyev has stated that the sudden disappearance of Mohanjodaro about 3500 years ago might have been due to an atmospheric physico-chemical explosion. Discounting earlier hypotheses of a nuclear explosion or arson by extra-terrestrials, Dmitriyev propounded a new theory that the destruction could have been due to a natural phenomenon called "black lightening". Black lightening is an explosion with venomous power due to physico-chemical formations in the atmosphere, destroying all things in its frail. The temperature during the inferno was believed to be of the order of 15,000 degrees celsius. Even the epic Mahabharata refers to a powerful explosion at a site traceable to Mohanjodaro, which came in the wake of "a dazzling glow and fire without smoke". Referring to similar occurrences of black lightening in other parts of the earth, Dmitriyev said atmospheric conditions due to physico chemical reactions were believed to activate the formation of toxic agents which polluted the air. It seemed that in Mohanjodaro people were affected by poisionous gases followed by a powerful blast, completely destroying the city, he said. This was evident from the postures of skeletons and also melted stones found at the site, he added. Dmitriyev said calculations had shown that during the Mohanjodaro disaster, 3,000 black lightening discharges upto 30 centimetres in diameter and more than 1,000 chemiluminescent formations appeared in the atmosphere. New data for further corroboration of the hypothesis could be obtained from studies of material traces such as smalt and slag after the colossal fire there.

Chalcolithic Culture

The Chalcolithic cultures in India traditionally include non-urban, non-Harappan cultures characterized by the use of copper and stone. The Harappan culture is generally supposed to be followed by chalcolithic cultures. The urban traditions of the earlier Harappan culture disappeared and the subsequent traditions is marked by rural economy. The word 'chalcolithic' is formed from *Chekos*, meaning copper, and *lithos*, meaning stone. Towards the end of the Neolithic period began the use of metals, the metal to be used first was copper. For a long time stone tools continued to be in use along with copper tools. In this phase, people mostly founded rural settlements on river banks not far removed from the hills. They used microliths and other stone tools supplemented by a little use of copper tools. They were the first to use painted pottery.

The Chalcolithic communities founded the first fullflaged villages in India. They cultivated far more cereals than is known in the case of the Neolithic communities. Sharma (1977) points out the general weakness of Chalcolithic cultures on the basis of the burial of a large number of children. In spite of a good producing economy the lack rate of infant mortality was very high. It might be due to the lack of nutrition, absence of medical knowledge or outbreak of epidemics. At any rate the Chalcolithic social pattern did not promote longevity. This phase also exhibits the beginning of social inequalities. In the graves of Chandoli and Nevasa in western Maharashtra some children were buried along with copper bead necklaces around their necks; other children had grave goods consisting only of pots. Similar other features of inequality may be cited from a number of other sites. The inclusive time spread of this culture is from 1750 B.C. to 1000 B.C.

Except for the alluvial plains and the thickly forested areas, traces of Chalcolithic cultures have been discovered almost all over India. The Chalcolithic cultures of India may be divided into six regional groups: (1) The Ahar-Banas chalcolithic culture, (2) Chalcolithic culture of Madhya Pradesh, (3) Northern Deccan Chalcolithic culture, (4) The Neolithic-Chalcolithic culture of the Deccan, (5) Chalcolithic Culture of Gangetic doab, and (6) Eastern Chalcolithic culture. The bulk of knowledge we have about Chalcolithic culture in India is based on the excavated sites of Ahar, Bagor and Gilund of the Banas culture; Kayatha, Maheshwar, Navadatoli, Nagda, Avara, Manoti, and Evan of Madhya Pradesh; Prakash, Bahal, Chandoli, Jorwe, Nevasa, inamgaon and Nasik of Northern Deccan; Piklihal, Brahamagiri and Maski of the Deccan; Bahadurabad, Ambarkheri, Hastinapur and Atranjikhera in the Gangetic doab; Lothal, Rangpur, Somnath and Rajdi of Saurashtra, and Chirand and Pandin Rajan Dhibi of the east. Unlike Harappan culture which was marked by a striking uniformity despite its spread over a vast area, these cultures show a distinct regional identity probably determined by smaller ecological units. South eastern Rajasthan gives rise to the Banas culture, the Malwa region to the Kayatha culture and the mid-Gangetic valley to the Ochre Coloured Pottery (O.C.P.) culture. "The main differences among these cultures lie in their characteristic ceramics though economically they have a similar status. A limited amount of copper and an abundance of lithic blades mark most of these cultures" (Agrawal, 1984).

The ochre colour pottery is mostly known from the Gangetic doab. When Lal first discovered it from below the painted Greyware levels at Hastinapur he found that on rubbing off they left an ochreous colour on the fingers, hence the name. A variety of copper tools, mostly in catchas, were accidentally discovered from a number of sites in Uttar Pradesh, Bihar and Madhya Pradesh hence the name Copper Hoards. Copper was the main metal used by all the protohistoric cultures in India and therefore it is no surprise that a variety of tools cropped up from sites as far away from each other as Shalozan in north west Pakistan, Bhagrapir in Orissa and Kallur in the south. The tool types were equally varied: rings, flat and shouldered celts, anthropomorphs, swords, double edged axes, harpoons, socketed axes, etc. The eastern group of the copper implements coprises simple types like shouldered and flat axes and rings which are ubiquitous in most of the Chalcolithic cultures. Piggot saw in these Copper Hoards the remains of Harappan refugees on their eastward march.

The Banas culture is named after the River on whose banks the Banasian sites were found. Though more than fifty sites of the culture are known in the valleys of the rivers Banas and Berach in south east Rajasthan, excavations were conducted only at Ahar, Gilund and

Kayatha. The most characteristic of this culture is the black and red ware, painted in white on the exterior. Motifs are generally geometric: parallel or oblique lines, circles, and spirals. *Jawar* (a millet) is known from the pottery matrix of period II of this culture. There are also impressions of long grained rice. No other grains, charred or otherwise, have been found. Animal bones, however, are in plenty; turtle, fish, goat, deer, pig and cattle were eaten.

Kayatha, situated on the bank of the Kalisindh, an affluent of the Chambal, gives the culture its name. The most distinctive feature of this culture is its pottery in three fabrics. The most predominant is a thick, sturdy Brown Slipped Ware painted in violet or deep red. The designs are generally linear. The Kayathans, it seems were quite well off in copper as from one pot along twenty-eight copper bangles were recovered. They also had a developed blade industry comprising lunates, pen knives, parallel sided blades, etc. made on chalcedony. No complete house plans were uncovered by the excavations. The pot holes indicate the use of circular and rectangular huts made perhaps of split bamboo screens. No burrials have been reported.

Malwa is the main seat of the Malwa and Kayatha cultures and even and the Banas culture extended here. The Malwa culture is marked by the Malwa ware, a buff or orange slipped pottery painted in black or dark brown, use of copper and stone tools, and small settlement of wattle and daub huts. Sites of Malwa culture have been reported both from Madhya Pradesh and Maharashtra. The best known excavated sites are Eran, Nagda, and Navadatoli in Madhya Pradesh and Inamgaon in Maharashtra. Navadatoli is the site *par excellence* of Malwa culture. Being the richest site for paintings on pottery; the black and red ware has been used for more than six hundred motifs--both geometric and naturalistic. It has also revealed a lot of information about the food habits of the people. Charred grains of wheat, barely and rice, lin seed, black gram and lintel, *ber*, *amla* and grass pea were also consumed. There is also evidence that the people ate beef vension and pork (Agrawal, *ibid*).

Jorwe culture predominates the whole of Maharashtra excepting Konkan. The Jorwe people cultivating barley, wheat, lentil and rice. Artificial irrigation had also been discovered. Food was perhaps consumed in a semi liquid from as indicated by the absence of dishes. An earthen pan seems to have been used to bake *chapatis* (thin bread). Large saddle querns may have been used to make barley and wheat flour. It appears that five large pits were used to roast animals. The Jorwe ware is the hallmark of this culture. It has a red or orange matt surface painted with geometric designs in black. It has a find fabric and is well baked. Both adults and children were buried with the head facing north; the adults in extended positions and the children in coarse hand made red/grey ware urns. Female figurines, with or without head, both baked and unbaked have also been reported. Physical features are represented symbolically but reproductive organs have been shown in exaggerated form; indications are that these were used in their fertility cult. Settlement patterns also show important features in contrast to humble huts and pit silos of the craftsmen; the centre of the settlement was probably occupied by the elite.

The eastern Chalcolithic cultures included the present state of Bihar, Bengal and Orissa. Chirand, located on the confluence of the Ganga and Ghaghra in the district of Saran of Bihar, is a very important excavated site of this culture. Hand made thick grey ware, a wheel thrown red ware and black and red ware comprise the ceramic industry. Storage jars, dishes on stand, spouted vases, bowls on stand, *lota* etc. are the main pottery forms. A variety of terracota objects have also been found. Serpent figurines are quite common and here may be seen the origin of the *naga puja* (Serpent cult). It appears that pit dwellings with thatched roofs were used in the beginning but later on only overground huts were made.

The cultures that we have gone through in the preceding pages made use of copper, and in the later phases its alloy bronze, for making tools and implements. They emerged in regions where clearing of forests on a large scale for purpose of cultivation was not required and the soil could be easily exploited. The next major advance in the history of mankind was marked by the discovery and use of iron. It is harder than copper and bronze, cheap and available in plenty. The discovery of iron made it possible to make a variety of agricultural tools such as ploughshares, sickles, shovels and spades on a large scale. Iron axes facilitated the clearing of forests on a large scale for acquiring more land for cultivation. The use of Iron played a very important role in the growth of many of the civilizations. Since the discovery of Iron man never looked back in his endeavour for more and more technological development.

Megaliths and Megalithic Age

Megalithic monuments used as memorial stone for the dead are a worldwide feature. While megalithic culture in Europe is related with Neolithic, in India it is, by and large, a feature of Iron age specially in south India.

R.E.M. Wheeler (1956) describes megaliths as "those monuments which are built of rough, large, undressed blocks of stones, usually, though not invariably, of rudimentary character. Those monuments are connected with burials which fulfil funerary or commemorative or religious functions." The earliest evidences of megalithic graves and funerary appendages in India came to light in 1872 but concerted archaeological efforts began only in 1944 and since then hundreds of megaliths have been found especially in south India. Such monuments of similar type have been found near Madras, Chingelput, Akhor and Chittor. Probably these megaliths in the earliest stages were used in the funeral proceedings but later on these were erected as memorial stones. A number of such graves have yielded, beside skeletal remains of the dead, a number of other items as funerary appendages. Mainly, four types of Megaliths have been found in India:

1. Cairn circle
2. Cist
3. Menhir
4. Dolmen

Cairn Circle type of megaliths consist of several round shaped stones. It seems that at first the dead body used to be buried alongwith iron implements, clay pots or urns and bones of pets and then rounded stones were fixed all around the grave. Such megaliths have been found from Nayakund and Borgoan (Maharashtra) and Chingelput

1. Topikal - Capstone

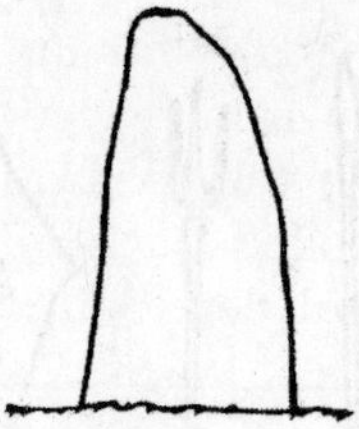

2. Menhir

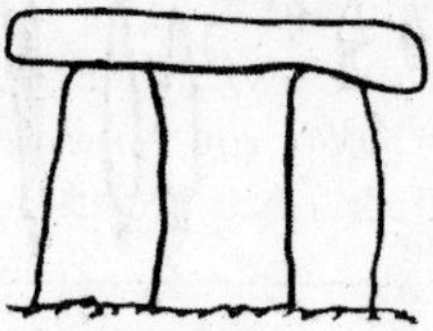

3. Dolmen

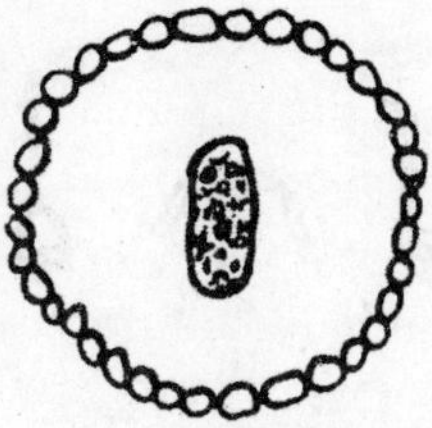

4. Stone Circle Pit Burial

5. Stone Circle Cist Burial

6. Sarcophaghus

(Tamil Nadu). Cist graves also follow a set pattern. The dead body was first buried and small stones erected all arount it. Then larger stone slabs were made to rest on the pillars, providing the grave some sort of a shade. Such megalithic graves have been found from Banda and Mirzapur of Uttar Pradesh. Menhirs are like large and tall memorial stones erected to give some clue to the presence of a grave at that place. These stone pillars varied in length between one and a half to about five and a half metres. Menhir graves have mostly been found in Maski and Gulbarga regions of Karnataka. In the category of Dolmen graves the dead body used to be placed on a slab of stone on a raised platform covered from all sides with a flat stone slab resting on the four legs of stone erected at the four corners of the dead body. Since it gives a table like look it has been designated as dolmen which loosely means a stone table. Such graves have been found from Bramhagiri in Karrnataka and Chingelput from Tamil Nadu.

The above described four types of megalithic graves may be cited as representative patterns of megalithic cult in India. But some more types have also been found though

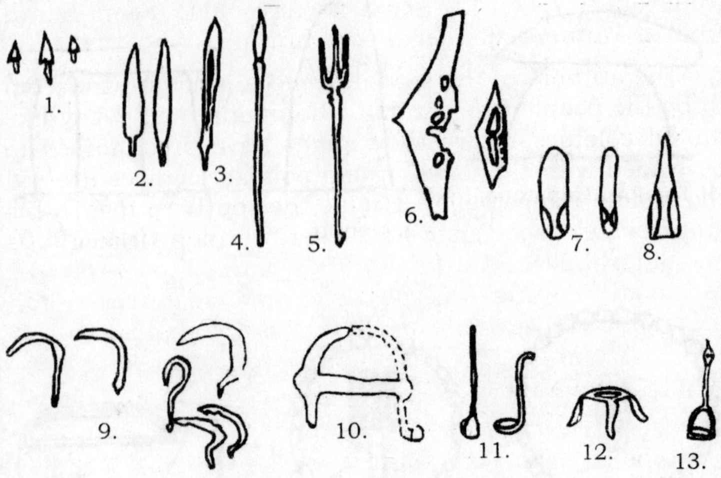

Iron Implements from South Indian Megalithic Graves —
1. Arrowhead; 2. Daggers; 3. Sword; 4. Spearhead; 5. Trident; 6. Battle axe; 7. Hoes; 8. Plough Share; 9. Sickles; 10. Stirrup; 11. Laddles; 12. Tripod; 13. Lamp.

scarcely. Among such lesser occurring graves come (i) umbrella stone, (ii) rock cut caves, and (iii) head and hood stone. Umbrella stone megaliths are those in which a round stone slab rests on pillars giving them the look of an umbrella. Such graves occur in Kerala specially in Ariyannur and Chermmanangal. In the second type called 'rockcut caves' the laterite deposits were cut to make a rectangular chamber in which the dead body was placed and covered. Such graves have been found from Kattkaumpal and Porkalam in Kerala. 'Head Stone' graves exhibit a simple burial; in this category the dead body alongwith the funerary appendage was used to be buried first and only a circular stone slab was placed over it. Such graves have been discovered from Andhra Pradesh and Kerala.

The iron implements which are common to all the megalithic graves are flat axes, sickles, tripods, tridents, spear heads, multiple lamp hangers, arrow heads and lamps. A number of ornaments used on the frontal region of a horse have also been found from a number of megalithic burials.

The authors of the southern megalithic culture seem to be the people from Arabia who maintained gypsy like tented colonies where they might have bred horses to be traded with the newly rising political centres around the middle Ganga valley. Beside the southern megalithic cultures, archaeologists have been working since 1950s on Vidarbha megalithic culture spread over Dhule, Amravati, Paunar, Nagpur etc. and a north Indian megalithic culture/cultures spread over Leh and Jhelum valley (Jammu & Kashmir), Dehradun, Mirzapur, Varanasi, Allahadad and Banda all from Uttar Pradesh and parts of Rajasthan and Madhya Pradesh.

Another important point to be kept in mind is that megalithic culture may not refer to as any prehistoric culture. Many tribal communities have been erecting similar memorial stones in the historic period. Megalithic monuments of Chotanagpur region are a case in point. But the fact remains that the practice of erecting megalithic monuments has been quite wide spread and megalithic burials have been found from certain places of the world between which potential geographical barriers always discouraged diffusion of this cultural practice.

ETHNOARCHAEOLOGY

Archaeology is understood as the cultural reconstruction of past and its' objective is to reconstruct the lifeways of the people who have left archaeological remains- artefacts, tools, or anything related with material culture. It is closely related with ethnography, a very important tool of cultural anthropology. It is related with the present based on direct observation of any people. Obviously, in order to have a holistic and authentic view of any society or culture, it has to be intensive and in-depth study of material culture and social-cultural institutions that also includes various types of customs and traditions. Moreover, participant observation has always been an important tool of field research in ethnography. As Lee Horne (1991) rightly says that in the traditional academic division of labour, ethnographers study the present, archaeologists study the past. Both aim to understand and explain human culture and society.

Thus, ethnoarchaeology is the name given to the study of the present in order to answer questions about the past. "It simply refers to ethnographic fieldwork by archaeologists, and has become a proper sub-discipline of anthropology." Sometimes ethnoarchaeology is also described as anthropological archaeology as it may provide insight into how people in the past may have lived, especially in regards to their social structures and beliefs.

Ethnoarchaeology is not a very old field of study. It is "since the 1960s, the field of ethnoarchaeology has emerged as a discipline explicitly concerned with examining the archaeological relevance of contemporary phenomena, including such topics as site formation and depositional processes: documentation of traditional technologies, community forms, and settlement pattern, the relations between humans and their environment and the study of the material implications of a variety of social systems and social strategies as well as of ideologies and belief systems " (Carla M. Sinopoli, 1991). In the South Asian (Indian) context the timelessness of Indian village and stability of social traditions and technologies and a vast range of human adaptations generate a wealth of data for the ethnoarchaeologists. Sinopoli (ibid) writes that South Asian ethnoarchaeological studies may be broadly divided into four main categories, covering:

- ⇨ traditional subsistence and settlement strategies among various populations
- ⇨ traditional technologies and the organization of craft production
- ⇨ social organization and belief systems
- ⇨ formation of archaeological sites

Some scholars have also described ethnoarchaeology as 'Archaeoethnography' and 'Living Archaeology'.

The ultimate objective of ethnoarchaeological research is to improve methods and procedures of archaeological inference, and particularly the use of analogical reasoning.

How Archaeologists Work

Only the later hominids can be studied from external evidence of their behaviour since, for the first time, this includes material culture which has so modified the environment as to leave a permanent record. The appearance of the earliest tools thus represents a great step forward, not just for the hominids, but for the investigation of human evolution.

The task of the archaeologist is to take the evidence and to 'squeeze' it so as to understand past life as much as possible. This is sometimes termed 'reconstructing the past', but this exaggerates what is feasible. We can certainly come to terms with the past, but it is in a simplified way because of the limited evidence and the vast spans of time involved.

Archaeologists, then, take those remaining aspects of human activity, which can be called material culture, and work with these to come to an understanding of past life. Occasionally, the picture can be remarkably complete as at the town of Pomeii, Itlay, which was buried by a volcanic eruption in AD 79. Almost complete buildings together with their contents are preserved in the most minute detail, and the catastrophe is described in contemporary historical accounts.

For the distant past, the archaeologist has much less to work with. Early people made little direct impression on their environment, often sleeping in the open, protected only by wind-breaks of branches, or at best flimsy huts. Their technology, too, was very simple, and consisted mainly of stone or wooden tools, probably supplemented by the use of animal products such as leather and sinews. Where the original events created such slight traces, even more careful and painstaking work is required to make the most of the surviving evidence.

We can ask what does enter the archaeological record? The greater part of human activity goes unrecorded, lost from the moment it happens. Nonetheless, some things are preserved. First, there are actual signs of activity, such as the Laetoli footprints, or even a fingerprint. Then there are objects which people make, ranging from the simplest stone tools to single artefacts as complex as carts or even ships. There is food refuse too, usually consisting of bones, but sometimes even plant remains. Finally, there are the more permanent surroundings which people create for themselves, at the simplest, a row of stones for supporting a wind-break, at the most elaborate, a complete city.

For the archaeologist, the individual object is of limited interest unless it comes from a well-documented archaeological site. Taken out of context, a find loses most of its value for telling us about human behaviour. The site, composed of a whole assemblage of objects in their context, remains much the most important unit of archaeological investigation.

The site is a place where human activity has led to the accumulation of the kinds of evidence mentioned above. Usually, sites survive because of the deposition of sediments, as in the "*Rift Valley*", but in some environments tools simply remain on the surface for quite long periods. Occasionally, in more recent times, human activity is responsible for the burial of earlier remains. The classic example of this is the Middle Eastern 'tell' or mound, where houses are built upon the debris of a previous settlement.

The individual site has the limitation of presenting a very local, perhaps idiosyncratic picture. Archaeologists therefore attempt to deal with number of sites, investigating patterns of settlement.

In this way we can attempt to come to a balanced understanding of any period in the past. Excavations cost so much to carry out that we never arrive at a complete picture, but fortunately much information can come from surveys. These are less expensive, cover wider areas, recover more general information, and often indicate which sites can most profitably be excavated.

Patterns of settlement can often be interpreted as a result of a survey, in which a whole area is examined systematically. Certain soils may have been favoured or avoided, highlands or lowlands preferred at a certain season, and so on. Maps are fundamental tools in the survey, especially geological maps, and ideally they are used together with aerial photographs.

In early periods, it is very unusual for whole landscapes to be preserved, so there is more emphasis on the individual site; but it has become abundantly clear that one site is not necessarily like another of the same age, so every effort is made to investigate this 'variability' - a very common word in the archaeological vocabulary.

In some areas these wider patterns can also be recovered from off-site archaeology. This method, developed by archaeologists *Glynn Isaac* and *Robert Foley*, involves mapping low-density archaeological traces over large areas. This provides a kind of average of those parts- perhaps ecological zones - which were most occupied by early man.

To understand such broad patterns, the archaeologist needs to put the sites in a framework of time. Here, stratigraphy, a concept borrowed originally from geology, is the most fundamental tool of archaeological interpretation. Sediments, both geological and archaeological, build up in layers, and naturally enough the higher levels are the younger ones. From the evidence we can establish a relative sequence, even when we do not know how old the layers are in an absolute sense.

In geology, sequences may become complex as a result of erosion, tilting, fresh deposition, or volcanic intrusion. In archaeology, it is very often the quirks of human activity - such as the digging of a pit - which make the record complicated, but archaeological and geological stratigraphy are not necessarily separate. In the early parts of the Old Stone Age, archaeological sites are found as fairly minor traces within a series of geological beds, so the stratigraphy is essentially geological. In the last few thousand years, on the other hand, man-made stratigraphy sometimes becomes dominant with, for example, the formation of city mounds which may be many metres thick.

Stone Tools: The Indelible Markers

The term, 'Old Stone Age', reflects the great durability of stone tools. No doubt, as the archaeologist Professor *Staurt Piggott* has pointed out, with different conditions of preservation we might have had an '*Old String Age*', but we have no idea how far back string was in use, because it always rots. Probably the great majority even of stone tools have perished, abraded by physical and chemical weathering - bouncing along in stream-beds, or breaking up through the action of sun, wind and frost. But those stone tools which are rapidly buried in accumulating sediments will survive for millions of years, sometimes as fresh and sharp as when they were made.

Stone tools gave early man an abundance of convenient working edges, suitable for altering other materials, such as wood, meat or bone. The sharp edge of a flint or even a fine-grained lava, can be as keen as the best steel. It lacks flexibility, it is true, and can quite easily be broken, but stone tools can usually be replaced, because most parts of the world abound with rocks suitable for their manufacture.

Flint is often thought of as the best material, for it is sharp and fine-grained, hence relatively easy for the knapper (stone-worker) to control. But it occurs only in some areas; it is rare in Africa where the earliest tool are found, though common in Europe. Other rocks suitable for stone-working, such as fine-grained lavas, volcanic glass (obsidian), quartz, or chert may have been used long before flint.

It is common to read of 'crude chipped stone tools', but for the most part the early stone tools were not 'chipped' and are less crude than might seem at the first glance. We know this because the techniques involved can be reproduced by archaeologists who specialise in technological studies. Further evidence is provided by the stone-tool making which has continued uninterrupted in various parts of the world up to the present day.

Most of the flaking was carried out through direct hard striking. The stone-worker would sit or squat, resting the piece to be worked on one thigh and strike it with another specially selected hammerstone. Smooth hard pebbles about 100g in weight were probably used as the hammers for much of the early stone-working, but later bone or antler was also used.

In Africa, and probably elsewhere, the commonest form of material used for early tool making would have been a large cobble picked out from a stream-bed. Even quite a gentle blow with the hammerstone will strike off a flake, provided that the angles are correct. If the cobble is struck at random nothing much will happen, because the force will be absorbed. A cobble broken in half is a much better starting point, because it offers acute angles, and a piece which projects, however slightly, can be struck off. Provided that the stone-worker selects an angle of the stone which is less than 90°, the force of the blow can be transmitted through and out; and a flake produced.

This process is greatly aided by the property of 'conchoidal fracture' possessed by the stones in common use. Conchoidal means shell-like and is applied because the stone ractures in smooth curves. Hence the experienced stone-worker can anticipate the shape of a flake with some accuracy.

Stone-working is vitally useful for the archaeologist because it displays a number of characteristic features. The flake is made by striking a particular surface - the platform - and a small area of this is usually detached with the flake, which remains recognisable. The fracture surface of the flake also has distinctive features. At the actual point of impact, there is a 'blip' or swelling, called the bulb or cone of percussion. The force transmitted from here leaves a series of concentric ripples, across the whole surface of the flake. The same features can be observed in negative form on the piece which was originally struck (the core).

Chipping is used when a flake, or core, is modified, not to create a sharp edge (for nothing is sharper than a fresh flake edge), but to have a strong, regular edge. Small flakes are struck or chipped, from the edge in a process which archaeologists term 'retouching'.

How can human stone-working be distinguished from the effects of nature? Essentially, by the way that the striking on the stone has been effected.

Frost, heat, and collisions between stones in a river-bed can cause flaking, but it occurs at random. In contrast, even the earliest stone tools show a systematic purposeful approach to the stone-working. A flake will often have negative impressions of previous flakes taken from the same core; retouch will be concentrated along a single edge; a core will show evidence that many flakes have been detached, often all from the same direction of striking. If a single flaked cobble is produced from a river-bed, there may be doubt about whether it was worked by man, but on an archaeological site there is no doubt.

Stone tools are invaluable markers of human activity and the great majority of early archaeological sites are found through their presence on the surface. Their similarities and differences form the basis for classifying the '*Old Stone Age*'. Similar tools were in use for long periods of time over huge areas. The name 'industry' is given to all the tools which are found within a limited area and timespan, and which might have been made by a single group of people. The tools belonging to an industry may have pronounced stylistic features in common-such as a particular form of scraper or point.

New industry names are usually given to each new area investigated, but there are also broader similarities which need to be recognised. Similar industries are conventionally grouped into an '*industrial tradition*'. Nearly all the very early industries consist of flakes and rather globular coreforms; these can be grouped into the industrial tradition called the 'Oldowan' after Olduvai Gorge.

A small collection of basalt tools from Hadar appear to be the oldest yet known, if their estimated date of about 2.6 million years is correct. This would make the tools several hundred thousand years older than those from any other early site. A number of the Hadar tools, including choppers, were found by the French archaeologist, *Héléne Roche* in 1976. Later, further artefacts, mainly flakes, were found in a trench excavated under the direction of Jack Harris. Although these tools are so old, they seem already to have the basic characteristics found in the Oldowan.

(Courtesy : *Ascent to Civilization* by John Gowlett. 1984)

❑

7 Contributions of Tribal Cultures to Indian Civilization

Despite debates and differences of opinion scholars have paid glowing tributes to the contribution of tribal cultures to Indian Civilization. A number of literary texts and archaeological and historical records provide us information about the contribution of several tribal communities to Indian Civilization. True to the word Adivasi, tribal people are the original inhabitants of the Indian sub-continent and they have been inhabiting this geographical region since the times immemorial. They are also considered as primary ethnic groups of this region maintaining their ethnic identities. The Aryans coming from outside were antagonistic to everything non-Aryan and sought to destroy everything of the original inhabitants of this land. Showing amazing resilience a number of tribal cultures not only survived but also contributed in the evolution of Indian Civilization.

The linguists and historians write that a number of tribal languages contributed and enriched Vedic language. A number of words from tribal languages such as

Dravidian, Mundari, Austro-asiatic etc. enriched Sanskrit language. Perhaps that is why Sanskrit acted and continue to act as a bridge between Dravidian and Indo-Aryan languages. Even today, writings in tribal languages, both prose and poetry, continue to enrich the repertoire of Indian literature.

The contribution of tribal communities to the social life may be seen at so many places. AL Basham says that the Hindu gotra system came from the tribes and Brahmins copied it from them. Moreover, tribal kinship system also had a deep influence on Vedic social structure. For instance, the social value of bride givers being superior to bride receivers was copied by Aryans. Same is the case with cross cousin marriage. Religious life in Indian civilization was also deeply influenced by the tribal communities. A number of tribal deities, customs, myths, rites and ceremonies, ancestor worship etc. may be taken as the impact of tribal cultures. Prominent historians and indologists such as D.D. Kosambi says that several Brahmin gotras such as Kashyap arose from tribal totems. Worship of Mahadeva/ shivaling, Sarpa, Vriksha (tree) may be traced back to its tribal origin. Further, a number of other little traditions of non-Aryan origin such as Jagannath, Balrama and Subhadra of Puri may be traced back to the Savara tribe.

Contribution of tribal cultures may also be seen in the field of techno-economic life. Smelting of iron, a major breakthrough, was borrowed from Asura tribe who kept this alive till the modern technology took over. The earliest agricultural implements such as hoe, seed driller, leveler etc. are the tribal inventions copied by the Aryans who were initially nomads or shifting cultivators. Even rice crop was borrowed by the Aryans from the indigenous communities as Aryans raised only wheat and barley. A number of majico-religious practices being performed for agricultural yields may be traced back to its tribal origin.

The indigenous tribal populations had an amazing Indigenous Knowledge System. They had profound knowledge of environment and forests. When the last tsunami hit the Indian Oceans in 2004 and the Andaman & Nicobar Islands were also badly hit, some of the most primitive tribes inhabiting these islands had an advance warning on the basis of changes in the behavior of marine life and they took shelter at suitable places and survived to the surprise of our scientists. As part of their Indigenous Knowledge System many tribes had their own native pharmacopeia in the form of their ethno-medicine system based on various types of herbs and medicinal plants. Acknowledging their knowledge of ethnomedicine Indian Council of Medical Research (ICMR) opened a research institute at Jabalpur, Madhya Pradesh where scientists have been doing documentation of the ethnomedicine systems of several tribal communities before it is lost to us. Thus, we see that the tribal communities have made tremendous contribution to Indian Civilization. The problem with the people of modern civilization is that they looked at the tribal communities from a higher pedestal of superiority. Instead of 'teaching' them all the time,we also have to learn from them in several spheres of life.

❑

8 Anthropological Museums and Museology in India

Museums today are no more a simple 'custody' or a passive safe keeping of collections. They have become complex institutions having, among others, two important functions. Firstly, museums are centres for research in various branches of knowledge, such as art, history, archaeology, and ethnology. They, therefore, provide classified research and reference material for scientists and scholars. Secondly, these are important places for mass education for which attractive exhibitions are arranged. Thus, museums stand for both specialized and general education.

As Michael Ames (1986) brilliantly puts it "the museum is where you would go to compare your own private perceptions of reality with what was the accepted and approved, therefore 'objective' view of reality, enhrined within the museum. The museum as a publicly owned civic temple is the culmination fo several centuries of development. Personal collections and private museums existed for centuries, and continue. Religiously oriented relic chambers, ornamented cathedrals and temples, and monuments also have long histories. But publicly owned and publicly accessible museums identifying with the state or the nation in a secular rather than religious sense, expressing and authenticating established views, are a new phenomenon probably no more than a hundred to two hundred years old".

A few hundred years ago museum collections were restricted to a few people, mostly the members of the ruling classes or gentry and access was granted only through the favour of the owner, and there was neither the necessity nor the means of communicating knowledge beyond the privileged few. As the collections grew in size and complexity, so did the need to house and care for them and therefore, also the need for people who specialized in the care and management of collections.

The museum movement in India started towards the close of the 18th century. "Since the very inception of this movement anthropology had found place in almost all the leading museums of the country" (Sachin Roy, 1976). It was to the credit of Sir William Jones, the founder of the *Asiatic Society of Bengal*, that ethnographic objective could take an important place in the society's acquisitions. The beginning was made by him in 1784. Since then ethnographic objective were continuously collected and added to the collection of Asiatic Society. N.C. Chowdhary (1976), while narrating the evolution of anthropological museums, tells that after the pioneering efforts of Asiatic Society, a number of Institutions of all over India started building their own collections of ethnographical exhibits. Mention may be made here of Madras Government Museum (1851), Natural History Museum, Trivandrum (1857), Central Museum, Nagpur (1863), Baroda Museum and Picture Gallery (1894), and Lady Wislon Museum, Dharampur (1928). In the post independent period a number of museums with ethnographical collections came into existence, a few of the most important ones being National Museum (1960), Central Museum, Arunachal Pradesh (1956), Nagaland

Museum (1964), Orissa State Museum (1963), and Punjab Government Museum (1959). The University Departmental museums of anthropology and the Tribal Research Institute museums are the two new categories of exclusive anthropological museums that have been set up in the post independence phase. The anthropology section as an independent unit exists in the majority of the composite museums like the National museum, Indian Museum and the State museums. These museums provide broad based knowledge of the physical and culture aspects of man. Chowdhary (ibid), summarizing the essential features of anthropological collections in the Indian museum, says that :

(i) Anthropological museums in India are essentially ethnographical in nature; very little attempt has been made to represent the biological aspect of man in these museums.

(ii) The collections are not only small but also not representative of the entire range of cultural variety in the country. Thematic display of objects is also lacking. The educative value of these objects has not been exploited.

(iii) The number of ethnographical museums is very small and there is ample scope for expansion.

(iv) In view of the state of affairs prevailing in the so called anthrpological museums in India today, it is an urgent need not only to develop and modernize these museums but also to open new ones which will give a clear idea about the bio-social aspects of man and his works.

One of the reasons for the poor performance of anthropology on the museum scene of India is due to lack of appreciation of its potentiality in the field of museum. The anthropologists are also partly responsible for this ignorance. We have not done much to explore the possibility of making full use of the discipline as a museum subject of considerable educational value. How right the eminent museologist Grace Morley (1967) sounds when he says that "probably no museum object in India needs more attention than anthropology. Few countries are richer that India in tribal and folk arts and artifacts, and all that goes with ancient traditional communities, which have developed and been protected in some isolation over a long period of time. Their disappearance without trace, or with only inadequate records, will represents a loss, not only for India but for the world". We are concerned to represent man in his entirety in the museums. Ethnography, physical anthropology and prehistoric archaeology and all other associate branches and sub-branches of anthropology should be represented in an ideal anthropological museum.

In the context of contemporary museological concept, the anthropological museum is not considered as a static institution serving only as the repository of cultural relics. "The scope of functioning of this class of museums is such that they can play positive role not only in disseminating visual education to non-literate and semi-literate sections of the population but can also contribute substantially in academic sphere both for higher studies and research" (Sachin Roy, Ibid).

In the applied field, the anthropological museum can be profitably utilized. The ethnographical museum has the scope of making significant contribution to emotional integration of the multi-ethnic, multi-lingual, multi-religious Indian society by countering ethnocentric streak among us. Most of the people are either not aware of others' way of life or consider their's as better than others. In our country there are numerous groups of people living in different ecological situations following totally divergent ways of life. An anthropology museum is perhaps the proper place where these various groups - tribal, folk and urban can find a place. To the museum audience such an exposition will not only enhance their knowledge, but it will also help to develop a healthy respect and tolerance for other fellow countrymen. The Indian culture is often described, to the extent of monotonous repetition, as an integrated pattern of culture in which all the varying forms of culture life fit like pieces in a mosaic. But for an average Indian it is difficult to visualise such a picture. It is only through proper display of ethnic and cultural diversities in an anthropological museum that we can focus and bring about the elements of unity in an apparently divergent cultural milieu, visiting such a museum will be education in itself.

With a little more specialization and expansion of scope, the ethnographical museums of many countries recently acquired a new and perhaps more accruable name viz. *The Museum of Man*, An outstanding example of such a museum is the Musee del '*Hamme Paris*. An ambitious project was undertaken recently by the Anthropological Survey of India to start regional anthropological museums and a central museum, *The Museum of Man*. It has been established at Bhopal and Jagdalpur in Madhya Pradesh. Many of the anthropological sections of the composite museums have been developed or are being developed under the active supervision and guidance of competent anthropological museologists. Clearly, revitalization of anthropology in the museum world of the country is not in progress.

Following is a selected list of important museums in India containing anthropological collections:-

1. **Indira Gandhi Rashtriya Manav Sangrahlaya** (Indira Gandhi National Museum of Man)

   This is a unique museum-one of it's kind in India. Any exploration of India's greatest museum is incomplete without a visit to the Indira Gandhi Rashtriya Manav Sangrahlaya, Bhopal. The Museum lies in a prehistoric landscape with evidences of prehistoric human settlement in its premises at Bhopal - the capital city of Madhya Pradesh. Covering an area of about 200 acres of undulating terrain in the Shamla Hills, it is one of the largest and leading Anthropological Museums in India. Aesthetically curated Open Air Exhibitions components with the most enduring Indoor Exhibitions, it promises to live up to the expectations of Museum visitors. This Museum depicts the story of mankind in time and space. It offers opportunity to explore the most subtle but artistic sensibilities of the rich Indian Culture and heritage through its appealing exhibitions. It has 8 (eight) open air exhibition and 12 indoor galleries. Impressive periodical and travelling exhibitions of the Museum on various topics are highly receptive and friendly to the visitors. Moreover, Museum activities of this Museum are designed to make informative, educative and entertaining. A visitor's friendly environment with improvised form of interactive displays offers a new taste to a Museum visit. Education Programmes, Workshops, Seminars, Symposia, Group discussions, Conferences, Cultural Programmes, Regional Cultural festivals, Lectures, Artists camps, etc. are some of the regular activities. Museum Outreach Activities ranging from artists camps and cultural exchange programmes to the organisation of grand community oriented cultural festivals are some of the community friendly activities of the Museum. The Reference Library of IGRMS provides abundant research opportunities for the students, researchers, designers, film makers etc. and it is an important source of documentation for the university community and Museum professionals.

Indira Gandhi Rashtriya Manav Sangrahlaya (IGRMS) / (National Museum of Mankind), an autonomous organisation of the Ministry of Culture, Government of India, began functioning since March, 1977 as a 'Subordinate Office' of the Department of Culture, at New Delhi. By early 1979, the establishment was shifted to Bhopal on allotment of a 200 acre campus by the State Government of Madhya Pradesh. The status of the Museum was converted from the 'Subordinate Office' into an Autonomous Organisation in March, 1985, and the 'Rashtriya Manav Sangrahlaya Samiti' was entrusted to control and supervise the programmes and activities of the Sangrahlaya. Subsequently as an extention of the Sangrahlaya, Southern Regional Centre at Mysore started functioning since October, 2001 from a heritage building 'Wellington House' allotted by the Government of Karnataka. The mandate of the Sangrahlaya include: presentation of an integrated story of bio-cultural evolution of humankind through outdoor and indoor exhibitions by highlighting the richness and diversity of cultural patterns of India and its underlying unity; to act as a centre of research and training in museology and generate a new museum movement in India and to present and preserve variety of cultural life. IGRMS is also working for national integration, and promote research & training and inter-organisational networking for salvage and revitalization of vanishing, but valuable cultural traditions. The innovative aspects of the organisation are its open -air and indoor exhibitions, built with active involvement of traditional artisans and experts drawn from different community groups, and the education, outreach & salvage activities in different parts of the country. Through its exhibitions, education programmes and salvage activities, IGRMS demonstrates the aesthetic qualities of India's traditional life styles, and the continued relevance of local traditional knowledge and mores of people to the modern society and cautions the people against unprecedented destruction of ecology and environment, local values and customs. The programmes and activities of the organisation are carried out under three sub-schemes namely: 1. Infrastructure Development: (Development of Museum Complex), 2. Education and Outreach Programme and 3. Operation Salvage.

2. ***Baroda Museum and Picture Gallery,*** **Baroda**

Established 1894. Composite Museum with a small ethnography section.,

3. *Bhuri Singh Museum*, Chamba, Himachal Pradesh

Established 1908. Composite regional museum with a small section on ethnography.

4. *Central Museum*, Shillong

Established 1956. Entirely ethnographical collection of material objects used by the tribes of Arunachal.

5. *Central Museum*, Nagpur

Established 1863. Composite museum with a small ethnographical section.

6. *Central Museum*, Jaipur

Established1876. Composite museum with a small ethnographical collection.

7. *Indian Museum*, Calcutta

Anthropology Section established in 1861 as a fulfledged Section.

8. *Junagarh Museum*, Junagarh, Gujarat

Established 1901. Small ethnographic Section.

9. *Kutch Museum*, Kutch, Gujarat

Established 1887. Contains collection of works of art and industry of Kutch and around.

10. *Lady Wilson Museum*, Dharampur, Gujarat

Established 1928. Composite museum with a small ethnographical collection.

11. Madras Government Museum, Madras (now Chennai)

Established 1851. Large composite state museum with a fairly large ethnography section and collection of stone age tools.

12. *Mahant Ghasidas Memorial Museum*, Raipur

Established 1875. Mainly a composite regional museum with a small ethnographical collection.

13. *Manipur State Museum*, Imphal

Established 1969. Regional composite museum with a good ethnographical collection.

14. *Museum of Cultural Research Institute*, Calcutta (now Kolkata)

Established 1955. Mainly an ethnographic museum.

15. *Museum of Tribal Research Institute*, Ranchi

Established 1954. Mainly an ethnographic museum.

16. *Museum of Tribal Research Institute*, Chhindwara, Madhya Pradesh

Established 1954. Mainly an ethnography museum.

17. *Mysore Government Museum*, Bangalore

Established 1866. A composite museum with a small ethnography section.

18. *National Museum*, Kohima

Established 1964. Entirely ethnography museum.

19. *National Museum*, New Delhi

Anthropological Section established in 1960.

20. *Natural History Museum*, Trivandrum

Established 1857. Composite museum with a small ethnographical collection.

21. *Orissa State Museum*, Bhubaneswar

Composite regional museum. Anthropology Section established in 1963.

22. *Sardar Ballabhbhai Patel Museum*, Surat

Formerly known as Winchester Museum, established in 1890 and contains a small ethnographical collection.

23. Sri Girdharibhai Children's Museum, Amreli, Gujarat

Established 1955. Contains a small ethnography section.

24. Sri Pratap Sinha Museum, Srinagar, Kashmir

Established 1898. A regional composite museum of art, archaeology, and ethnography.

25. Punjab Government Museum, Patiala

Established 1947. A regional composite museum with a small ethnography section.

26. State Museum, Lucknow

Established 1863. A composite regional museum with a small ethnography section.

27. D.N. Majumdar Museum, Lucknow

Established in 1977 under the auspices of Ethnographic & Folk Culture Society. Purely ethnographic museum with emphasis on Awadh region and it's culture.

❑

SECTION THREE

COLOURFUL MOSAIC OF INDIA'S POPULATION

9 Racial/Ethnic Elements in Indian Population

The identification and description of various racial elements in India has been a difficult task. India has always been a place of attraction for a variety of immigrants from various parts of the world. Whether it was religious persecution or harassment on other grounds or mere attraction towards India because of economic factors, waves after waves of people have been coming into the subcontinent. Most of them never went back to their original habitats. In this way people having different racial elements have been coming and setting down in India and the process of admixture has been taking place with the local populations. This has resulted in the colourful mosaic of human affairs that the Indian society is today.

Unfortunately, we have been getting only stone tools in the name of archaeological evidences; skeletal remains have rarely been found. Because of these constraints, it is very difficult to construct a racial history of India.

Even during historic times the paucity of skeletal remains is the major reason for the glaring gaps in our knowledge about the racial history of India. The last one hundred years have seen some spurt in archaeological researches leading to fossil finds. The situation is still hazy.

Risely may be considered as the first scholar to have attempted the racial classification of India on a scientific basis. He was a civil servant who in 1890 conducted this study on the basis of anthropometric techniques. He was appointed by the then government of India as Census Commissioner for 1901 Census. He presented his conclusions in the report of the Census and in 1915 in his path breaking work, **The Peoples of India**. He classified Indian population into seven racial types. Summarised description of his classifications is as follows :—

(i) The Turko-Iranian type: In this type he included the people of Baluchistan and frontier provinces (now in Pakistan)

(ii) The Indo-Aryan type: Punjabis, Rajputs, Jats and Kashmiri Khatris were the main groups in this type.

(iii) The scytho-Dravidian type: Best examples of this type are Maratha Brahamins and Coorgs.

(iv) The Aryo-Dravidian type: People of Uttar Pradesh, Rajasthan and Bihar are the main examples of this type.

(v) The Mongolo-Dravidian type: Bengali Brahmins and Kayasthas are considered to be the representatives of this type.

(vi) The Mongoloid type: The people of Assam, Nepal and Burma were included in this type.

(vii) The Dravidian type: The bulk of the population of the present Tamil Nadu, Andhra Pradesh, southern region of Madhya Pradesh and Chotanagpur was covered under this type.

The most glaring weakness and deficiency of Risley's classification is that many of his points are based on preconceived notions and arbitrary conclusions which have nothing to do with reality.

The second important attempt in this direction was made by Haddon. He divided India into three main geographical regions which, according to him, cover the entire racial groups present in Indian population. These three geographical regions are -

(i) The Himalayas,

(ii) The Northern plains of Hindustan, and

(iii) The Deccan

The major ethnic elements of these three respective geographical regions are (i) Indo-Aryan and Mongoloid, (ii) Indo-Afghan viz, the Jats and Rajputs and (iii) The Negrito, pre-Dravidian, southern Brachycephals and western Brachycephals.

Haddon's racial classification is based on physical traits, customs and traditions, language and the prevalent folk lore. He analysed the racial elements in Indian population with the help of these "evidences". This classification now carries only historical importance.

In this crowd of scholars B.S. Guha stands apart. He presented his racial classification basing it on scientific criteria. This classification is based on anthoropometric surveys conducted as past of the 1931 Census. It was for the first time that a study of racial types was done using the then developed anthropometric techniques. By virtue of being based on a sound scientific method, it is regarded as the most recognised and acceptable racial classification till date. It is invariably used in any study of Indian population. This classification is as follows:-

(i) The Negritio

(ii) The Proto-Australoid

(iii) The Mongoloid

  (a) Palaeo-Mongoloid

    (1) Long headed

    (2) Broad headed

(b) Tibeto-Mongoloid

(iv) The Mediterranean

(a) Paleo-Mediterranean

(b) Mediterranean

(c) Oriental type

(v) The Western Brachycephals

(a) Alpinoid

(b) Dinaric

(c) Armenoid

(vi) The Nordic

Among the conclusions of Guha's Survey the most important is that the Brachycephals (broad headed people) dominate the Indian population. This was not the general belief before Guha's classification. Guha's classification has received the maximum approval of the scholars in this field. Since no other study or survey based on scientific line of this magnitude has been conducted, this classification continues to be the most recognised and acceptable. The two points on which Guha has been criticised most are the undue importance to Negrito elements and that the sources of all racial groups in India have been traced outside India.

On the basis of intensive study of racial elements in Indian population three most important racial types may be described. These are: Negrito, Proto-Australoid and Mongoloid. It is the general belief that the people with mongoloid racial elements came last.

In fact the main difference of opinion is with regard to Proto-Australoid and Negrito. Guha, and before him De Quarterefages in 1877 had expressed the view that the people with Negrito racial elements are the earliest inhabitants of India. He expressed the view that a certain submerged Negrito race had come to India perhaps from Malaysia; this Negrito racial element seems to be present among the Veddas of Sri Lanka and Kadar, Irula, Kurumba etc. of South India.

Some proto-Australoid racial features have been noted from the skeletal remains found from Mohenjodaro. A number of scholars have expressed the view that the Australoid and Proto-Australoid racial elements are present throughout the Indian population. If the Negrito racial element had ever dominated the Indian population then some definite and clearly visible Negrito features should be there in the North Indian populations. The serological studies tell us that the Negrito features are almost absent even among the most primitive tribal communities of India. The primitive tribes of India have rarely demonstrated the predominance of B-blood group as is the case with Negroids. Australoid groups have a predominance of A-blood group; many primitive tribes of India have predominance of A-blood group. Another interesting and significant point in this discussion is that though the tribes like Bhil and Munda show a high frequency of B-blood groups like the Negrito but they lack other physical features of the Negritos. Even otherwise no final conclusion can be drawn on the basis of only serological facts specially under the conditions when not many serological studies have been conducted in India. There is a lot of scope for research in this direction. On the basis of the present status of knowledge we can conclude only that perhaps the proto-Australoids were the earliest inhabitants of India who experienced the admixture of African or Negrito blood in several parts of the subcontinent. Even this may not be the final conclusion but till the time some other evidences prove it otherwise it will continue to be the most acceptable conclusion.

❑

10 Linguistic Elements in India

India occupies a unique place in the world for its amazing linguistic heterogeneity; that is why she has been a subject of great interest among the linguists. The inhabitants of India speak so many language and dialects because of the fact that this subcontinent has been, for quite some time, the destination of diverse racial groups. Any linguistic group contains within it a number of features of social importance. One of the important features is the sentiments of social integration between the speakers of the same language or dialect. Common language also promotes emotional integration in the society. Diverse languages and dialects come into existence because of a prolonged geographical isolation of a group. In this way language plays an important role in the understanding and identification of a regional identity.

The magnitude of India's linguistic diversity can be estimated from the fact that here more than 200 languages are spoken by different groups. Half of these languages are spoken by less than ten thousand people each and the speakers of twenty three languages only constitute about 97% of the total population. Among these twenty three, twenty two (including English) are in the eighth schedule of the Constitutuion of independent India.

The languages spoken by Indian population many be divided into four language families.

(i) Austric family (Nishad)

(ii) Dravidian family (Dravid)

(iii) Sino-Tibetan family (Kirat), and

(iv) Indo-European family (Aryan)

The languages included in these four language families demonstrate a great diversity. The speakers of Aryan languages are around 73%, of Dravidian languages about 20%, of Austric languages 1.38% and the speakers of Sino-Tibetan languages are around 0.85% only.

In the Austric language family mainly the languages and dialects of central Indian tribal belt are included. The Santhals, Munda, Ho, Koraku etc. belong to this language family. The speakers of Sino-Tibetan language family are generally the tribal populations of North eastern region. Telugu, Tamil, Kannada, Malyalam, Gondi, etc. are prominent Dravidian languages. The largest number of speakers come from the Indo-Aryan language family. In this category come, on the one hand languages like Punjabi and Sindhi and on the other, there are such languages like Marathi, Konkani, Rajasthani, Gujarati, Marwari, Mewati, Hindi-Urdu, Chhatisgarhi, Bengali, Maithili, Kumayuni, and Garhwali etc.

In presence of such an amazing variety of languages and dialects one many conclude that such a great linguistic heterogeneity may prove to be disruptive for national integration. Such an apprehension may largely be deceptive. Side by side with this linguistic diversity one may also witness the pleasant development of an all India's common vocabulary, Sanskrit, Persian and English languages have been the state or administrative languages at one time or the other. Sanskrit has not only acted as a bridge between different Indo-Aryan languages but has also served as a communication link between Indo-Aryan and Dravidian languages. Within the medieval period of Indian history the Persian influenced a number of Indian languages like Marathi, Kannada, Telugu, Tamil and Bengali. The role of English language has been specially significant during modern times. During the last some decades Hindi-Urdu has contributed significantly to the linguistic unity of India, perhaps that is why Mahatma Gandhi promoted the idea of *Hindustani* language that contains words from different languages with the predominance of Hindi-Urdu. In this context we should not forget the role of movies in Hindi-Urdu (Hindustani) language. The mainstream cinema of Bombay may not deserve laurels because of generally poor quality but its immense contribution to the linguistic integration and the development of an all India vocabulary cannot be minimised. The amazing popularity of Hindi-Urdu movies in all the corners of the country bears testimony to the fact that the dialogue and the songs are being understood at least minimally and people are enjoying them. The growing influence of the neighbouring communities on the primitive tribes, who have been leading a life of relative geographical isolation till some time ago, reveal that the journey of linguistic unity in the country continues on an increased pace.

❑

11 Population of India and Indian Population Policy

India is the second largest country of the world, in terms of population, after China. Although India was one of the first countries of the world to have an explicit population policy the Indian performance so far is more of a failure than a success. India accounted for approximately 22% of the estimated population of developing countries. At present it has nearly 17% of the total world population, while it accounts for only 2.5% of the world's surface area. In any demographic miscellany growth of population occupies the most important place. The following table gives us a clear idea of growth in India's population over the years.

The first formal census enumeration was taken up in 1881 and since then the decennial census enumeration exercise has been a regular feature involving a high degree of expertise and substantial manpower. The offices of the Census Commissioner and the Registrar General of India have been responsible for providing the

Census Year	Population (in crores)	Average annual exponential growth rate %
1901	23.83	0.30
1911	25.20	0.56
1921	25.12	0.03
1931	27.89	1.04
1941	31.85	1.33
1951	36.10	1.25
1961	43.91	1.96
1971	54.82	2.20
1981	68.52	2.22
1991	84.63	2.16
2001	102.87	1.97
2011	121.01	1.64

demographic profile of the country. As per the 1991 census, the total population of India is about 85 crores, an increase of about 24% over the 1981 census. It rose to around 122 crores in 2011. According to the demographers the major cause for increase in population is the rapid fall in death rate. According to 1981 census, birth rate in the country was 33.3 per thousand and death rate 12.5 per thousand population while the figure for the same duration in the next decade is 30.0 and 10.0 per thousand population. In 2011 the birth rate and the death rate were registered 19 and 7 respectively while the life expectancy rose to 68.8 years. Thus, the birth rate as well as the death rate have registered fall, through marginally. But this marginal improvement is not enough because of the gigantic level of population India has achieved over the years. The following table gives us the idea of birth and death rates and help us to understand the population problem of the country.

When we take up the density of population in India we come across significant findings. Density of population means the number of people living per sq. km. Density of population of the present area (adjusted for partition of India in 1947), increased from 7 persons per sq. km. in 1901 to 267 persons per sq. km. in 1991 and then to

382 in 2011 census. Thus, it shows an increase of almost 3.5 times. The following table gives the density of population in India in different census years.

Year	Birth Rate per 1000 persons	Death Rate per 1000 persons
1901	—	—
1911	49.2	42.6
1921	48.1	47.6
1931	46.4	36.3
1941	45.2	31.2
1951	39.9	27.4
1961	40.9	22.8
1971	41.1	18.9
1981	33.3	12.5
1991	30.0	10.0
2001	25.4	08.4
2011	19.0	07.0

The table shows below that the rate of increase was faster in the later decades. However, it varies from the state to state depending on a number of factors: (1) The

Census Year	Density of Population per sq. km.
1901	77
1911	82
1921	81
1931	90
1941	103
1951	117
1961	142
1971	177
1981	216
1991	267
2001	325
2011	382

lowest density was found in Arunachal Pradesh where only 10 persons inhabit per sq.km. Other low density states are Mizoram, Andaman and Nicobar Islands, Sikkim, Jammu & Kashmir, Meghalaya, Nagaland, Manipur and Himachal Pradesh. All the eastern states except Assam and Tripura, have low density and so do the hilly states like Himachal Pradesh and Jammu & Kashmir. (2) Delhi, Chandigarh and Pondicherry have the highest density. (3) States which have population density of three times the national average are Daman and Diu, states which have two times or more are Kerala and West Bengal. (4) States which have population density above national average are Assam, Bihar, Goa, Haryana, Punjab, Tamil Nadu, Uttar Pradesh and Dadra & Nagar Haveli. (5) States which have population density lower than the national average are Andhra Pradesh, Gujarat, Karnataka, Maharashtra and Tripura.

Sex Ratio

In simple words, sex ratio in a population is the number of males per 1000 females and it affects various areas of social life. Availability of potential marriage partners and labour force are the most obvious areas affected by it.

In India's population sex ratio is becoming adverse to females as their numbers have been rapidly declining after every decade. In any population the sex composition is the most basic of all demographic features. As per 2011 census it is 943 against 933 in 2001. The States/UTs of very adverse sex ratio are Daman & Diu 618, Dadra & Nagar Haveli 775. Among the economically progressive states, surprising, Punjab and Haryana have a skewed sex ratio compared to other states. Among the reasons for this imbalance the following are most obvious:

- Pre-natal sex determination (despite a legal ban on it) and the consequent female foeticide and infanticide.
- Patriarchy's strong hold on gender inequality
- widespread son preference
- Marginalized role of women in the decision making process including reproductive matter

Census Year	Sex Ratio Males per 1000 females
1951	1057
1961	1063
1971	1075
1981	1069
1991	1076
2001	933
2011	943

The most glaring consequence of this skewed sex ratio is the purchase of girls from poverty stricken areas of Assam, West Bengal, Jharkhand, Chhattisgarh, Orissa etc and bring them to their homes where they serve as domestic and sex slave. Sharing such a 'wife' between brothers is not a rare phenomenon in those states. In several villages of Punjab, Haryana and western Uttar Pradesh one may come across women from several states speaking their native language till they learn the local language.

Various causes could be attributed to this phenomenon. Higher mortality rates at infancy and later relatively more neglect, higher mortality rates among women in the child-bearing age, female infanticide and foeticide may be some of the reasons for this increasing disparity. Sometimes female births are also not reported by the parents. As per 2011 Census, Kerala has the best sex ratio where there are 1084 females per one thousand males followed by Puducherry 1037, Tamil Nadu 996, Andhra Pradesh 993, and Chattisgarh 991. The worst sex ratio is reported from Haryana and Rajasthan.

The least explained fact in the issues involved with unequal sex ratio is related with the growing imbalance in the face of decreasing discrimination against females and decreasing rates of infant mortality. One probable reason is that many couples having a few sons do not want to have one or two daughters as well-they may go in for sterilization. Kerala is the only state where the sex ratio is higher for females. This may also be due to over-migration of males from the state in search of jobs.

LITERACY

Another feature of population is literacy rate. On the basis of the definition of literacy being the ability to "read and write a post card", 52.11% was the percentage of literacy in India according to 1991 census. The rate of literacy among males was 63.86% and for females 39.42% - a conspicuous gap. It has risen to 73% (2011 Census) — 80.9% for males and 64.6% for females. Kerala with 94% literacy enjoys the first position followed by Lakshdweep 91% while Bihar has the lowest (61%). And this is one of the factors accounting for economic backwardness of the country. Not withstanding the fact that literacy rate has gone up in the post - independence period, the number of illiterates has also gone up in absolute terms. Kerala became the first state of the country where almost 100% literacy has been achieved. But all literates did not get the education through school. Generally, Hindi speaking states are very unprogressive in terms of achieving literacy and female literacy specially. Madhya Pradesh, Chattisgarh, Uttar Pradesh, Bihar, Jharkhand and Rajasthan had very low female literacy rates. Literacy and education of children are to be taken care of more seriously. Studies have shown that even free education is of little help as long as children continue to contribute towards family economy. The phenomenon of child labour has to be overcome. Apparently, poverty of the parents is the root cause of the lack of education and high rate of drop-outs of children. Significantly wherever Christianity has been used as an agency of welfare, rate of literacy show an upward trend. This is apparent in case of states like Mizoram, Meghalaya, Nagaland and parts of Bihar.

SCHEDULED CASTES AND SCHEDULED TRIBES:

The scheduled castes constitute about 16% of the total population of India. This population may be divided into about one thousand castes with a number of names being synomymous. Some of the large scheduled castes are the Chamar (constituting about one fourth of the total population of the scheduled castes), Bhangi, Adi-Dravida, Pasi, Madiga, Dussadh, Mali, Parayan, Koli/Kori, Mahar, Adi Karnataka, Namsudra etc. Each state has it's own list of scheduled castes. Following is the tabular description of the states in terms of number of scheduled castes.

If one goes through the demography of the scheduled caste population, one comes across some important and interesting facts. For example, almost half of the total scheduled caste population inhabit five states of the Hindi

States	No. of Scheduled Castes
Karnataka	95
Orissa	88
Rajasthan	76
Tamil Nadu	74
Madhya Pradesh	60
Maharashtra	60
Uttar Pradesh	60
West Bengal	60
Andhra Pradesh	60

speaking belt namely Uttar Pradesh (23.5 million), Bihar (10 million), Madhya Pradesh (7.3 million), Rajasthan (5.8 million), and Haryana (2.5 million). Among the southern states they are concentrated mainly in Tamil Nadu (8.8 million), and Andhra Pradesh (7.9 million), and in East in West Bengal (12 million). Interestingly the highest ratio of the scheduled caste population in the total population is in Punjab (31.9%), closely followed by Himachal Pradesh (25%), West Bengal (22%), Uttar Pradesh (21%), and Haryana (19%). In terms of absolute population Uttar Pradesh has the highest numbers (166.63 millions). The bulk of the scheduled caste population (84%) live in rural areas as agricultural workers, share croppers, marginal farmers and atisans.

Thc Schedule Tribes constitute a little above 8% of the total population and they are among the weakest sections of the society. They speak different languages and dialects and inhabit virtually all the geo-climatic regions of the country. About 55% of the scheduled tribe population is concentrated in the eastern and central tribal belt including West Bengal, Bihar, Madhya Pradesh, Orissa and part of Andhra Pradesh; about 28% are in the Western tribal belt consisting of Gujarat, Maharashtra, Rajasthan, Dadra and Nagar Haveli and Goa, Daman and Diu; only about 6% of the scheduled tribe population are found in the south consisting of parts of Andhra Pradesh, Karnataka, Kerala and Tamil Nadu, about 10% are in the north-east, 0.83% are in Himachal Pradesh and 0.10% are in Lakshdweep and Andaman & Nicobar Islands. There are four states, Meghalaya (80.58%), Nagaland (83.99%), Arunachal Pradesh (69.82%), Mizoram (93.55%), and two Union Territories namely Dadra & Nagar Haveli (78.82%) and Lakshdweep (93.82%) where 70% or more of the population belong to scheduled tribes category. There are also five states where more than 20% of the population are tribals. These are Madhya Pradesh (22.97%), Manipur (27.30%), Orissa (22.43%), Sikkim (23.22%) and Tripura (28.44%).

Among the major tribes the population of Bhils is about six million followed by the Gonds (about 5 million) the Santhals (about 4 million) and the Oraon (about 2 million). Among the minor tribes the Great Anadmanes have been reduced to just 30 souls because of severe depopulation. The Sentinelese, the Jarwa and the Onge of Andaman & Nicober Islands are within 200 number in terms of population. It is estimated that the tribal areas comprise about 17% of the total geographical area of the country but these areas contain about 70% of the forest and mineral wealth of the country. A number of tribes are polyanderous such as Toda of Niligiri Hills and Khasa or Jounsari of Jounsar Bawar (UP) while some tribes like the Khasi of Meghalaya are matrilineal. There are about 70 tribes who are still food-gatherers/hunters and are concentrated mainly in Andhra Pradesh, Tamil Nadu and Kerala. The tribes practicing shifting cultivation mainly inhabit the north-eastern region while about 70% of the tribal population depend upon settled/plough cultivation. A few tribes still earn their livelihood as artisans. The percentage of literacy among the scheduled tribes is around 19%. However inter-state variations are quite considerable ranging from 8% in Andhra Pradesh to about 60% in Mizoram.

Religious Composition:

India has always been a multi-religious and multi-ethnic society. Followers of almost all the major religions of the world inhabit this great land. They are Hindus, Muslims, Christians, Sikhs, Buddhists, Jains, Zoroastrians (Parsees) and Jews. The Hindus are the majority community comprising about 80% of the total population of the country followed by Muslims (about 14%), Christians (about 3%), Sikhs (about 2%), Buddhists (about 1%), and Jains (about 0.5%). The Parsees and Jews are microscopic minorities. Among the major religious communities, Hindus Muslims and Christians inhabit virtually all the geo-climatic regions of the country and speak local languages and dialects.

In terms of ratio, Muslims are in majority in Lakshadweep and Jammu & Kashmir, whereas Christians are in majority in Nagaland and Meghalya, Sikhs are in majority in Punjab and Buddhists in Arunachal Pradesh.

It has been reported that the religious minorities show a greater percentage of literacy and education than the majority community. Parsis, Jains, Jews and Christians have shown this pattern. Among the Muslims, the Shias, an important minority within a minority, may be cited as a case in point. They show a very high rate of literacy, comparable only with the Parsees and Christians. The most plausible explanation of this phenomenon is that in a multi-religious democratic society every intelligent minority knows that it cannot influence the society or enjoy leverage through its sheer number. That is why it goes for excellence to have its due place in the society and through their contributions they tend to command influence and respect.

Population Policy:

India was the first country to launch a national programme of family planning in 1952: It emphasised the necessity of reducing birth rates to stabilize the population. The National Health Policy, 1983 stated the replacement levels of Total Fertility Rate (TFR) should be achieved by the year 2000. Stabilizing population is an essential requirement for promoting sustainable development with more equitable distribution. In pursuance of this goal the National Population Policy 2000 (NPP2000) was launched. It affirmed the commitment of government towards voluntary and informed choice and consent of citizens while availing reproductive health care services. The immediate objective of the NPP 2000 is to address the unmet needs for contraception, healthcare infrastructure and health personnel, and to provide integrated service delivery for basic reproductive and child health care. In pursuance of this objective the following National Socio-demographic goals to be achieved by 2010:

- Address the unmet needs for basic reproductive and Child Health Services, supplies and infrastructure.
- Make school education free and compulsory up to age 14, and reduce dropouts at the primary and secondary levels below 20 percent both for boys and girls.
- Reduce infant mortality rate below 30 per 1000 births.
- Reduce maternal mortality ratio to below 100 per 10,000 live births.
- Achieve universal immunization of children against all vaccine preventable diseases.
- Promote delayed marriage for girls, not earlier than age 18 and preferably after 20 years of age.
- Achieve 80 percent institutional deliveries and 100 percent deliveries by trained persons.
- Achieve universal access to information/counseling, and services for fertility regulation and contraception with a wide basket of choices.
- Achieve 100 percent registration of births, deaths, marriage and pregnancy.
- Contain the spread of AIDS and promote greater integration between the management of reproductive

tact infection (RTI) and sexually transmitted infections (STI) and the National AIDs Control Organization.

- Prevent and control communicable diseases.
- Integrate Indian System of Medicine (ISM) in the provision of reproductive and child health services and in reaching out to households.
- Promote vigorously the small family norm to achieve replacement levels of TFR
- Bring about convergence in implementation of related social sector programmes so that family welfare becomes a people-centered programme.

If the NPP 2000 is fully implemented, we anticipate a population of 1107 millon (110 crores) in 2010, instead of 1162 million (116 crores) projected by the Technical Group on Population Projection.

Factors Influencing the structure and Growth of Indian Population

- High fertility due to unmet need for contraception: Urgent steps are required to make contraception more widely available, access and affordable. The accessibility of contraceptives is still relatively more difficult in remote rural and tribal areas.
- High infant mortality rate (IMR): Because of high infant mortality rate in the rural areas of Hindi belt people are not sure about the survival of their infants and hence go for more children.
- Early Marriage of Girls: Over 50% of girls marry below the age of 18 leading to "too early, too frequently, too many". High percentage of births occur at intervals of less than 24 months which also results in high infant mortality rate.
- widespread son preference: Across all religious Communities there is widespread son preference because of social economic and religious factors. With increased empowerment of women-educational, social, economic and political — this may be curbed to a great

extent. The social evil of dowry is also a contributing factor behind son preference.

- Poverty and educational backwardness: It is now universally accepted that in the conditions of poverty and deprivation children are considered asset and not liability because from a younger age they start contributing to the family economy. Wherever, children contribute to the family economy, they may not be sent to schools or it may result in higher rate of dropouts. Moreover, it is also now proved that higher rate of female literacy and education lead to better management of small family norm.
- Religious beliefs and traditions: India is a strongly religious and traditional society. Among large sections of people across religious lives, it is believed that the children are a gift of god and their birth should not be curbed. But the same society also resorts to female foeticide and infanticide. The same people are comfortable with this contradiction and hypocrisy.

Migration

Migration factor in population studies is also important. In the simplest terms migration is the physical movement of people from one geographical area to another or movement of people within or between social systems. Population shifts were a central feature of pre- modern history. Robin Cohen in Social Science Encyclopedia (2009) writes that "the DNA 'architecture' revealed by the human genome project conclusively situates the common origin of human kind in Africa. Humans were thus subsequently dispersed by the disintegration of the continents or by relocation." Migration is not only about the movements of people. It can also generate enormous shifts at the subjective social and cultural levels. As a consequence of population mobility, cultural and linguistic diversity is always there and the capacity to communicate with others and to understand their cultures is available to many.

When we look at the Indian scenario we are confronted by a fact contrary to general perception. Myron Weiner (2003) says that only a small proportion of Indians people live outside their place of birth or that of their spouses. Rural to urban migration is modest. The majority of urban dwellers are locally born, not migrants.

Movement of people from one place the other may be voluntary or involuntary. This may be explained through 'Pushed out' factors and 'Pulled into' factors. Under the push factors people migrate because of threat to their life and property, persecution-religious, linguistic or any other ground - exploitation, low wages, lack of employment opportunity, poor standard of living natural calamities such as earthquake, flood, epidemic etc. Under pull factors one may include better wages, better educational facilities, peace and security, over all, promise of a better quality of life and future. It may be seasonal migration or short term migration or permanent relocation to another area. It also contributes to the population growth of a region. Perhaps, the largest migration after India's partition in 1947was witnessed recently when because of Covid-19 pandemic millions of people returned to their villages from big urban centres. After some time, on a smaller scale, reverse migration is also being witnessed when a number of people started going back to the respective cities.

❑

SECTION FOUR

UNDERSTANDING INDIAN SOCIETY AND CULTURE

12 Approaches to the Study of Indian Society

There has been several approaches to the study of Indian society ranging from Indological approach to Subaltern approach. Some of these have been used by different scholars over a period of time while some others are new additions. Taken together the following approaches may be enumerated to understand and study the Indian society. However, there is a certain degree of overlapping between two or more approaches:

1. Indological Approach
2. Structural – Functionalist Approach
3. Historical Approach
4. Culturological Approach
5. Marxist Approach
6. Subaltern Approach

Indological Approach has been quite popular among the scholars of Indian Society. Indology is the academic study of history, culture, languages etc. of the Indian sub-continent which may include the modern day states of India, Pakistan, Bangladesh, Sri Lanka and Nepal-all coming under the Indian or South Asian Civilization. Thus, Indology may be understood as a systematic study of Indian society and culture. The justification behind the Indological approach is that the Indian civilization is too unique to be fitted into the framework of western sociology and the Indian society can be understood only through the concepts, theories and frameworks of Indian civilization.

The major drawback or weakness of Indological approach is its reliance on texts or textual/book view of Indian society rather than the empirical/field view. Thus, it presents a stereotyped and static image of Indian society and culture. It is also to be noted that the Indological approach is deeply influenced by Indology but should not be taken as co-terminus with Indology. Most of the Indologists were the products of different schools of Indological tradition such as Indological Research Centre of Pune, Lucknow, and Asiatic Society of Bengal founded by Sir William Jones. Significantly, the founding fathers of Indian Sociology were influenced by Indological approach and they Included G S Ghurye, B K Sarkar, Radhakamal Mukherjee, K M Kapadia, P H Prabhu and Iravati Karve. G S Ghurye was more influenced by the works of the Indologists of Bhandarkar Institute, Pune. Being a student of Sanskrit, Ghurye primarily used Sanskrit texts to understand Indian society and culture. His understanding of Caste, Tribe, Indian Muslims, Indian Values and Knowledge was hotly contested by other sociologists and anthropologists on the ground that it was biased and unidimensional. The critics of Ghurye are of the view that he failed to recognize the rise of modern India and the contribution of Islam and British rule. Moreover, his approach romanticizes that India which lived within inequality and exploitation. Thus, other approaches arose as a reaction to the book view promoted by the Indological approach. **Structural – functionalist Approach** is, perhaps, the most popular of all approaches to the understanding of Indian society. Significantly, it gives more importance to the empirical structure than to the normative framework of culture. Inspired by A R Radcliff-Brown this approach promotes a very systematic and rigorous fieldwork.

The followers of structural functionalist approach never take 'truth' for granted. They believe that it happens in social context that requires empirical investigation as opposed to the textual view followed by the Indological approach. Thus, one must go to field for first hand information. It rules out the glorification of the past on the basis of available texts. For a structural functionalist, social structure is an empirical reality present at a given point of time. Radcliff-Brown was of the view that any scientific study of culture should be undertaken as a dimension of social structure. Thus, social structure is the central concept of this approach. This approach became very popular after India's independence spearheaded by M. N. Srinivas. It was used for the study and analysis of rural community, caste structure, family structure, kinship structure, religious structure, and political structure.

M N Srinivas not only used structural-functionalist approach himself but also inspired his colleagues and students to apply it in understanding Indian society. His classic study of '*Religion and Society among the Coorgs*', Rampura Village and '*Social Change in Modern India*' are important examples of application of structural-functionalist approach. S C Dubes' study of 'Indian Village' is another important example. All of these and similar studies used field study approach to the understanding of Indian society. Though the major strength of this approach is its strong empirical foundation, its critics are of the view that it suffers from its limitation of neglecting the cultural and historical dimensions.

Historical Approach is another important approach to study Indian society. Its' uniqueness lies in the fact that gives more importance to the historical process of development than to the synchronic structures of the social phenomenon. Like Marxists and Weberian, it is primarily concerned with the process of social development. It focuses on the historical processes of Industrialization, urbanization, democratization, modernization etc. thus aiming to understand various processes of development within the historical framework. Though G. G. Ghurye and R. K. Mukherjee also used historical approaches yet their works are classified under Indological approach.

Culturological Approach is a relatively minor and 'non- standardized' approach because of the reason that it encompasses a variety of view points. However, what is common to all these viewpoints is the emphasis on primacy of culture as the object of study relegating social relationships and social structures as the secondary manifestation of culture. It looks person as a cultural being. This approach evolved mainly under the influence of cultural anthropologists rather than sociologists. This emphasis on culture may bear similarity with Indological approach but unlike this, it takes the field view, rather than the book view as practiced by the Indologists. Moreover, the method of cultural analysis and theories of culture have played important role in this approach. The works of such important anthropologists as Clifford Geertz, McKim Marriot, David Schnider and Milton Singer and others bear testimony to this fact.

Marxist Approach to study Indian society has had a profound impact. It came out of historical approach being used in historical sociology. Marxist approach helps to understand the social reality through the means of production, the techno-economic division of labour involved in operating the instruments of production and social relations of productions or what was more precisely characterized as property relations. The Marxist approach gives central importance to property structure in analyzing society. It recognizes the dialectics of evolutionary as well as revolutionary changes of the breaks in historical continuity in the transition from one socio-economic formation to another.

D. D. Koshambi, A. R. Desai and D. P. Mukherji are considered as exponents of the Marxist analysis of Indian society. Desai made an attempt to develop a historic sociological model to understand Indian society. As a Marxian scholar he considers that the foundation of Indian history is based upon the modes of production that evolved during different points of time pre-colonial stage, colonial stage and post-colonial stage. Among his seminal contributions the study and analysis of social economic and cultural structure of rural India and the changes coming into it has given as new insight. His 'Social Background of Indian Nationalism', 'Rural Sociology in India' and "Rural India in Transition' are invaluable contributions to Indian sociology.

Subaltern Approach to the understanding of Indian society is perhaps the youngest of all these approaches. It is often seen as post-Marxist movement because many of its protagonists combine Marxist theory with a variety of other influences. The subaltern school of historiography emerged in 1980s in the study of South Asian Societies, especially India. Influenced by the Marxist philosopher Antonio Gramci, the concept of subaltern includes all the marginalized people in a society. This approach was prompted by the fact that the Marxists were reluctant to accept the ideology of caste and religion as crucial factors in Indian history. They were thus, according to the subaltern scholars, totally unable to gather and use vital historical data for the lived experiences of various oppressed classes, which were submerged in religious and social customs.

A galaxy of eminent scholars such as Ranjit Guha, Partha Chatterji, Gyan Prakash, Shail Mayaram, and Shahid Amin did pioneering work using subaltern approach. The subaltern concept is now being used regularly in various disciplines such as history, literature, anthropology, sociology, etc. This is largely used in post-colonial theory. Though the subaltern studies emerged in 1980s in India, it now has a global presence as an area of academic specialization. With reference to Indian society this approach documents the lives of all the marginalized, deprived and oppressed people such as the exploited peasants, workers, tribals and dalits whose voices were rarely heard in history.

❑

SECTION FIVE

INDIAN CIVILIZATION AND IT'S CULTURAL PROCESS

Introductory Note

The role and importance of tradition in the study of culture is well known. Culture has two aspects the realities and the phenomena of the present which have not passed into oblivion and the other aspect which has been persisting over a period of time. The totality of culture cannot be understood without taking into consideration both these aspects. Thus, traditions occupy an important place in the study of culture. Since civilization consists of traditions and the study of traditions has not been the usual field of study in anthropology, the study of civilization in this discipline is comparatively new phenomenon.

The most familiar and usual field of study in social/ cultural anthropology has been the small scale, localized, relatively isolated primitive or simple societies; this has been their favourite 'hunting ground'. The social/cultural anthropologists have been doing comparative study of such human groups. Compared to any other field, anthropologists have studied such groups over about 150 years of anthropology's history. Through such cross-cultural comparisons, the anthropologists have been able to compile a treasure of data which reveal a wide range of cultural variations and similarities. But the result of this endeavor has been that they could not develop an insight and expertise to study and analyse a social system when it gets complex. They did not have the experience, aptitude, or academic training of studying complex societies. Thus, as we see, the study of civilizations was beyond the pale of anthropological investigations.

The trend described above continued till about nineteen forties. Around this time emerged Robert Redfield on the horizon of world anthropology. Credit goes to Redfield for providing a new direction to social-cultural anthropologists. Not only did he provide a better and more logical-scientific definition of civilization, he also inspired a whole generation of anthropologists to study various aspects of Civilization. Because of his path-breaking and trend-setting contribution he is sometimes described as the founder and propounder of the '*Civilizational School of Anthropological Thought.*' With the help of his illustrious students and followers like Mckim Marriot, Milton Singer, Oscar Lewis, etc he succeeded in firmly establishing the study of civilization in anthropology.

Redfield and Singer (1954) have differentiated between two types of Civilizations-Primary and Secondary Civilizations. Primary Cililizations may be understood through orthogenetic evolution while Secondary Civilizations in terms of heterogenetic evolution. Primary Civilizations evolve through their indigenous, folk cultures while Secondary Civilizations are the products of external influences over the respective primary or indigenous cultural patterns. Indian and Chinese Civilizations qualify to be good examples of primary civilizations as propounded by Redfield and Milton Singer while Puerto Rico (South America) civilisation, a product of intermingling of Spanish Indian and African cultural influences, as studied by Steward may be described as a secondary civilizations. This type of differentiation has given us a new approach to the 'National Character' studies. Such an approach strives to look at civilization as a process. M.N. Srinivas is the first Indian anthropologist to have applied this approach to analyse and understand sanskritised and non-sanskritised cultural elements in the field of rituals in Indian society. Redfield studies civilization in terms of folk and urban aspects and their extensions. He studied folk and urban cultures and tried to understand and analyse the nature of interaction between these two types of cultures. The resultant concept is 'Folk-Urban Continuum'. It would be in the fitness of things to throw a glance on 'folk society' and 'urban society' before trying to understand and explain folk-urban continuum.

A **folk society** may be explained in terms of a small, homogeneous, non-literate and isolated human group which demonstrates a strong sense of solidarity. Describing folk societies Redfield says:

"The ways of living are conventionalized into that coherent system which we call a 'culture'. Behaviour is traditional, spontaneous, uncrticial and personal; there is no legislation or habit or experiment and reflection for intellectual ends. Kinship, its relationship and institutions is the unit of action. The sacred prevails over the secular; the economy is one of status rather than of the market."

The economy of the folk societies is self-sufficient and is different from the food gathering-hunting economy of the primitive societies. The folk societies maintain contacts with the centres of intellectual ideas and their evolution known as civilization. Briefly speaking a folk society is any small, unlettered society with homogeneous cultural traditions and which is religions-oriented rather than secular in it's outlook. Such a society is found exhibiting a high degree of unity and group solidarity.

The concept of **urban** has been utilized by sociologists-anthropologists for quite some time yet the confusion prevails vis-a-vis the differentiations between 'industrial' and 'pre-industrial' cities or urban centres. Here, we are more concerned with the pre-industrial city and it's communities. Communities from pre-industrial cities have usually been minimally influenced by such forms and patterns of production as those we usually associate with the European industrial revolution. Perhaps, that is why, we find lot of closeness between such pre-industrial regions and rural peasants. This fact reveals the reality that the peasant communities and the pre-industrial urban communities have been an integral part of 'pre-industrial civilization.' The pre-industrial cities have been dependent on the folk communities for their requirements of food and raw-materials and perhaps that is why such cities have also been centres of handicrafts and their products. Such cities have also been serving useful purposes in the fields of political, religious and educational activities. As for the working of social systems goes, the 'literate elite' always enjoyed dominance over such cities but this dominance always depended upon peasant/folk communities. The legitimacy of this elite class was always drawn from the fact that they were the 'keepers' of sacred texts. While talking about the peasant-urban relationship. Redfield says that the 'market', beside being the centre of trade and commerce, also represents a '*state of mind*'. It weaves a network of behaviour and relationship 'which binds a city with another city' a village with another village, and urban communities with rural/folk communities. In the Indian context the Jatis, interwoven with the texture of caste relationship, function as the bridge between the urban-folk cultures. Briefly stated, an urban community is such a community which has a higher populaiton as well as population density and which is characterized by a functional specialization in the fields of industry, occupations and services and presence of agriculture related jobs. It shows a highly complex scheme of division of labour and it is managed by a formal apparatus of local bodies.

Another type of society that comes between folk and urban communities is peasant society. Redfield, in his landmark workes *Peasant Society and Culture* (1956) has described the following three as the most important features of a peasant culture:

(a) highly reverent attitude towards land

(b) acceptance of agriculture as the noblest, best and ideal job and

(c) a pronounced, industrious attitude of the people demonstrating a fiem belief in the dignity of labour.

Among the important features of **peasant society**, are (i) family is the primary unit of multilateral social organization, (ii) the main source of livelihood is land and agriculture which fulfil almost all the requirements of life, (iii) they maintain a distinctive, traditional culture in terms of day today life and it's schedule and, (iv) usually, they are dominated by outsiders. For the peasant societies, agriculture is not an enterprise but a way of life which cannot be given up in favour of any other activity promising more money or profit (for detail discussion on peasnatry and peasant society like Redfield, Eric Wolf, Theodre Shanin and others, Nadeem Hasnain's General Anthropology may be referred to). On the basis of the above described features, a peasant community comes inbetween the fold and the urban community and it also acts as link between these two types of communities.

The concept of '***folk-urban continuum***' is explained and understood through one of Redfield's landmark studies, Folk Culture of Yucatan, Redfield did his fieldwork in Yucatan, a province in Mexico. During his fieldwork he came across four types of communities which were subjected to a rigourous cross-cultural comparison. These four types of communities are Marida, Diztas, Chankom and Taski. The people of Marida were represented by city society and Taski by folk or simple society. Redfield observed a pronounced continuum between the cultures of these four communities. He put Marida on the one end of the contunuum and Taski on the other extreme end. On the basis of the study of culture traits of these four societies it was observed that

Taski and Marida displayed a high degree of cultural variations but Marida society and Diztas society on the one hand and Chankom and Taski on the other shared lot of similarities. However, some commonness or similarities, though on a lesser scale, was also there between Diztas and Chankom especially in terms of presence of market, shops and middlemen. Since the city community shared a lot with town community on the one hand and the peasant community and folk community also show resemblance accordingly, Redfield described Marida and Diztas as Urban community and Chankom and Taski as Folk community. On the basis of

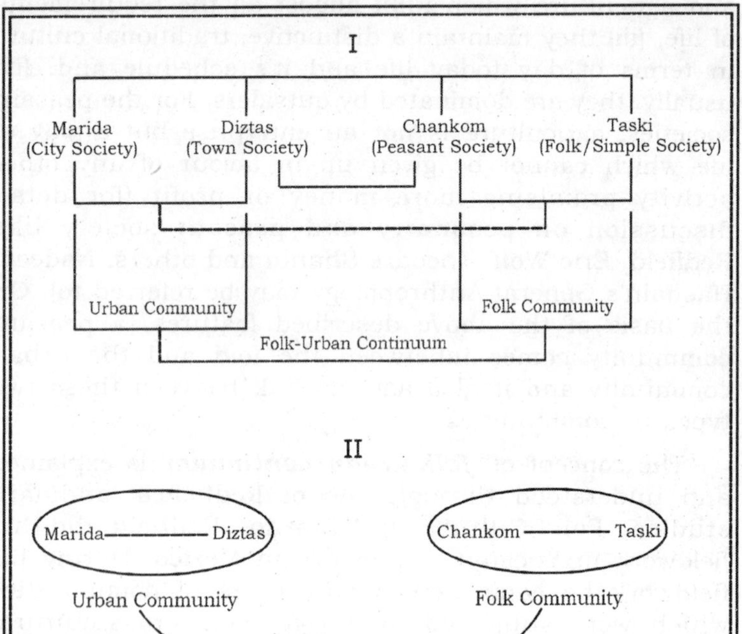

Diagrams I & II showing various aspects and stages of *Folk-Urban Continuum* based on the study, *Folk Culture of Yucatan* by Robert Redfield.

this highly significant empirical study Redfield concluded that no known society should be exactly the same as the societies on these two poles. However, different societies may share some cultural features of these two extreme poles and hence may be put between these two poles. Thus, we find a continuum between these two cultural poles. The simple conclusion one can draw of this situation is that it is impossible to tell as to where folk culture comes to an end and peasant culture begins; as well as at which point a line of demarcation may be drawn between peasant culture and town culture and town culture and city culture. These cultural overlappings between folk society and peasant society, peasant society and town society, and town society and city society is largely due to the phenomenon we known as continuum.

Redfield is of the view that folk-urban continuum also explains as to how a folk community comes into contact with an urban community and how the mutual adoption of each other's cultural traits takes place in this interaction. Further, he has also tried to understand and explain the conceptualization of relationship between simple and complex societies. This also provides us insight to look at a community in terms of an ecological system or social structure or a point of view of social existence. Oscar Lewis, a fellow American anthropologist, is a prominant critic of this concept. Among other points of criticism, Oscar Lewis remarks that Redfields concept seems to be indicative of ideal patterns and situations which may be at variance with the empirical or ground realities. Morever, the extent or degree or culture contacts between folk and urban cannot be measured in any precise terms and culture change may not be a matter of folk-urban progression, but rather of increasing or decreasing heterogeneity of cultural elements. Despite it's limited theoretical applicablility the concept of folk-urban continuum helps us a lot in understanding the cultural process in a civilization.

❑

13

Little and Great Traditions

The concepts of 'little' and 'great' traditions were first used by Robert Redfield. These concepts were proposed in his book "Peasant Society and Culture" (1956) and were used in his studies of the Mexican communities. Primarily meant to analyse social change in distant region, Milton Singer and Mckim Marriot have applied this conceptual framework on the Indian Cultural Setting as an approach to analyse culture change in Indian Society.

Redfield holds that every civilization is composed of traditions. On the one end are the tradtions of 'elite' and 'thinking class' while on the other there are traditions of unlettered peasants. The former emanate from urban centres and their temples, educational institutions and so on and are called as **Great Traditions**. The concept may be understood from another angle. Every society consists of a Great Community and Little Communities. The traditions, behavioural patterns, customs and rites, rituals and festivals of these communities may also be termed as Great and Little. In the Indian society, in the traditional sense, the urban Hindu community is the Great Community and it carries a 'great culture' and social structure. The source of its Great Traditions may be traced back to its ancient thinkers and philosophers and the scholarly works and epics and treatises composed by them. Such Great Traditions are found not only among the Hindus of India but also among those who have settled elsewhere in the world. Within the boundaries of this Great Community and Great Traditions come a number of Little Communities and their **Little Traditions**. These communities are found in the rural and tribal segments of the society. Thus, such a rural-urban dichotomy adds variety in an otherwise monotonous existence.

It would be prudent if we have some idea about the meaning and implications of the two terms-Tradition and Little Community.

TRADITION: The term tradition owes' it's origin to the word '*tradere*' which means 'to transmit'. Thus, we see that tradition is the transmitted value and behaviour of any community which has been persisting over a period of time. Traditions are respected, exemplified and referred to frequently. In the process of socialization members of a community are taught to appreciate, revere and respect the traditions. Traditions do not remain static; they are not like stagnant water. Old or previous traditions fade away and become extinct and new ones continue to evolve and be adopted by a community. external as well as internal factors, both contribute to the changes in tradition. In order to understand the comprehensive meaning of tradition and to capture it's spirit one has to go beyond it usual explanation of 'transmission'. The spirit of tradition lies in it's value. If the element of 'value' is removed from tradition, it would be difficult to differentiate between tradition and custom. A number of customs may continue to be alive and practised even without the element to be alive and practised even without the element of value, pushed and maintained by negative forces like inertia. In order to

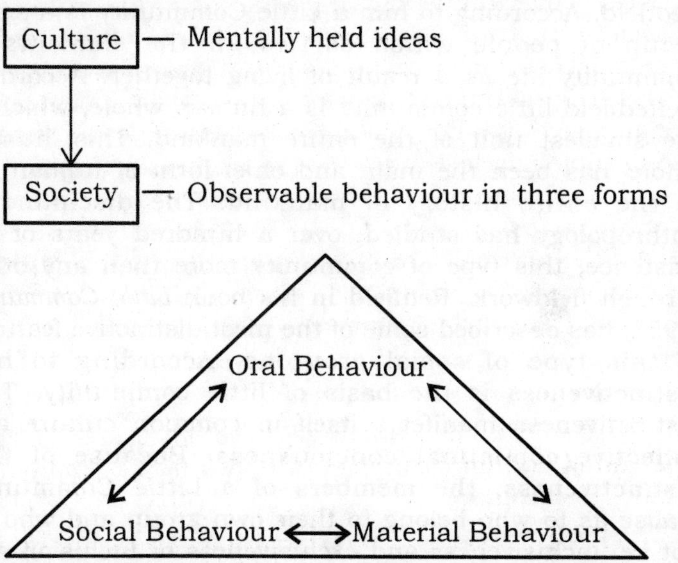

Tradition is the transmitted value and behaviour of any society persisting over a period of time. Tradition as part of culture, is revered by a society and may be, observable through Oral Behaviour, Social Behaviour and Material Behaviour.

understand the full implications of this explanation let us refer to Max Radin in *Encyclopaedia of Social Sciences.*

"Strictly and properly speaking ....a tradition is not a mere observed fact like an existing custom; it is an idea which expresses a value judgement. A certain order or arrangement is held desirable. The maintenance of the tradition is the assertion of this judgement. It produces in a nation or in a group an exalted group conciousness and is therefore most effective in creating groups or in re-establishing them."

LITTLE COMMUNITY: The concept of Little Community is an important contribution by Robert Redfield. According to him a Little Community is a small group of people which carries all the elements of community life as a result of living together. According to Redfield little community is a human whole, which is the smallest unit of the entire mankind. This 'human whole' has been the main and chief form of human life in the entire history of mankind. The discipline of anthropology has studied, over a hundred years of it's existence, this type of community more than any other through fieldwork. Redfield in his book *Little Community* (1955) has described some of the most distinctive features of this type of social grouping. According to him distinctiveness is the basis of little community. This distinctiveness manifests itself in common culture and collective/communal conciousness. Because of this distinctiveness, the members of a Little Community realise as to who belong to their own group and who do not i.e. inclusiveness and exclusiveness or inclusion and exclusion. Little Communities are small sized in terms of population. If the population of a little community increases to an extent where every member is not able to identify and recognise every other, and where personal relationships are difficult to maintain, a Little Community shall cease to be such in the pure and classical sense of the term the most distinctive feature of a Little Community is it's cultural homogeneity. The members of a Little Community share the cultural features in terms of language, dress pattern, food and food habits, lifestyle and world view. Since the members of a Little Community have got a strong tendency of cultural emulation, every succeeding generation maintains almost the same culture patterns which minimizes the scope and possibilities of social-cultural changes and this, in turn, is largely responsible for the maintenance of cultural homogeneity. Since most of the Little Communities live in relative isolation they are able to maintain a self sufficient economy. A number of social-cultural anthropologists have utilized and applied this approach of Redfield in studying folk and tribal communities.

The little and the great traditions, though existing independently to a certain extent, also interact with each other and maintain a certain level of relationship. In the Indian context the pantheon, festivals, rituals, literature, dance, music, etc. whose sources are religious epics like Mahabharata, Gita, Ramayana and Upanishads are based on Great Traditions. The folklore, religio-magical practices, customs and rituals whose references are not found in religious epics and which are transmitted orally constitute Little Traditions as *Shastriya* traditions. In the contemporary Indian society, Islamic and Christian communities too may be considered as great communities.

Civilization or social structure or tradition grows in two stages—Orthogenetic and Heterogenetic.

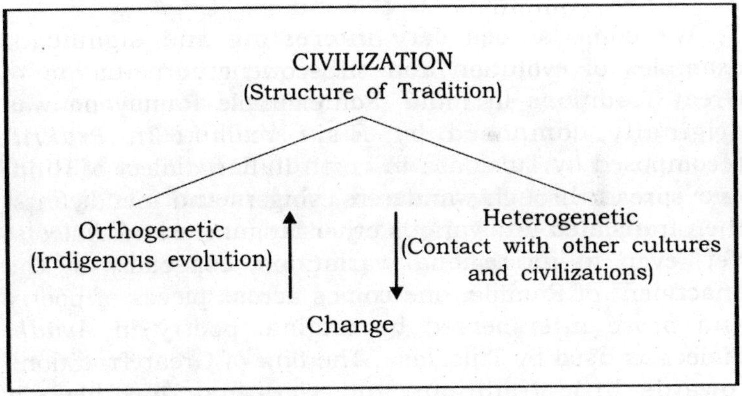

Thus, it is assumed that all civilizations start from a primary or orthogenetic level of cultural organization and, in course of time, are diversified not only through internal growth, but more important, through contact with other civilizations— a heterogenetic process. The direction of this change presumably is from folk or peasant to urban cultural structure and social organization. Usually the urban elite consider their traditions as 'beliefs' and little traditions as 'superstitions'. Redfield has also taken the stand that the worldview of India's little traditions is polytheistic, magic oriented and unphilosophical.

Following are some salient points of differentiation between great tradition and the little tradition.

Great traditions are usually mentioned in original religious epics. Their range is very wide, usually national in nature. These are related with elite, thinking, reflective few of urban class. Moreover, they are usually organized and norms, rituals, etc. are largely clearcut and unambiguous. The great traditions are transmitted from one generation to the other through texts; sometimes these are referred to as 'elite' tradition.

Little traditions are mostly oral and are followed as mere beliefs not necessarily based on rationality: these are mostly localised and related with rural, unlettered, folk, tribal or peasantry. These are believed to be usually unorganized, haphazard and ambiguous, transmitted orally, through oral literature.

We come across very interesting and significant examples of evolution and subsequent perpetuation of Great Traditions in India. For example Ramayana was originally composed by *Rishi Valmiki* in *Prakrit*, recomposed by Tulsidasa in north Indian dialect of Hindi and spread through wanderers, singers and mendicants, then translated into various other languages and dialects. Yet, even in its regional variations, especially in the enactment of Ramlila, one comes across pieces of poetry and prose interspersed by original poetry in *Avadhi* dialect as used by Tulsidasa. The flow of Great Traditions towards little traditions and vice-versa has been a familiar process in Indian civilization. Yet, it is also true that the extent or degree of this flow, from great to little has always been much greater than the vice-versa.

← Great to Little
(more)

Little to Great →
(much less)

Despite this unevenness of 'exchange' the periodic revival of interest in things 'folk' even among the most sophisticated urban elite is not without significance. Rural dress patterns, popularlity of folk songs and folk theatre (*nautanki*, etc.), religio-magical practices like hanging painted earthen pots on the exterior of the newly constructed houses (to avoid evil eye) etc. may be taken as the examples of flow of little traditions towards great traditions.

However, Little Tradition and Great Traditions are not neatly differentiated along a rural-urban axis. Both kinds of traditions may be found in villages and in the cities in different forms. The inspiration for the great traditions is found partially in the existing little traditions from which the elite has sprung. There is no *precise* definition of great tradition and Little tradition. Both traditions are incomplete by themselves and there is no clash of fundamental interests between them.

Mandelbaum, speaking about the nature of participation in the Indian tradition makes a very important comment:

".......the 'great tradition' is essentially a convenient abstraction. It is not followed in it's pure literary form in the village or for that matter among city folk either. There is ..... the vast corpus of scripture and literature, a reservoir from which elements may be selected for prominent notice during a particular period or among a special group."

Supplementing the view of Mandelbaum (ibid), S.C. Dube raises an important point. "Is it proper to use such a static definition of 'great tradition' when, as the concepts have been formulated by Redfield, the process of interchange between the two traditions is a continuous and dynamic one?" The 'great tradition', according to Redfield himself, is always changing, expanding, taking in new elements, and loosing old ones. How then can it be described in terms of books which were completed hundreds and thousands of years ago? Redfield apparently realizes the difficulties involved

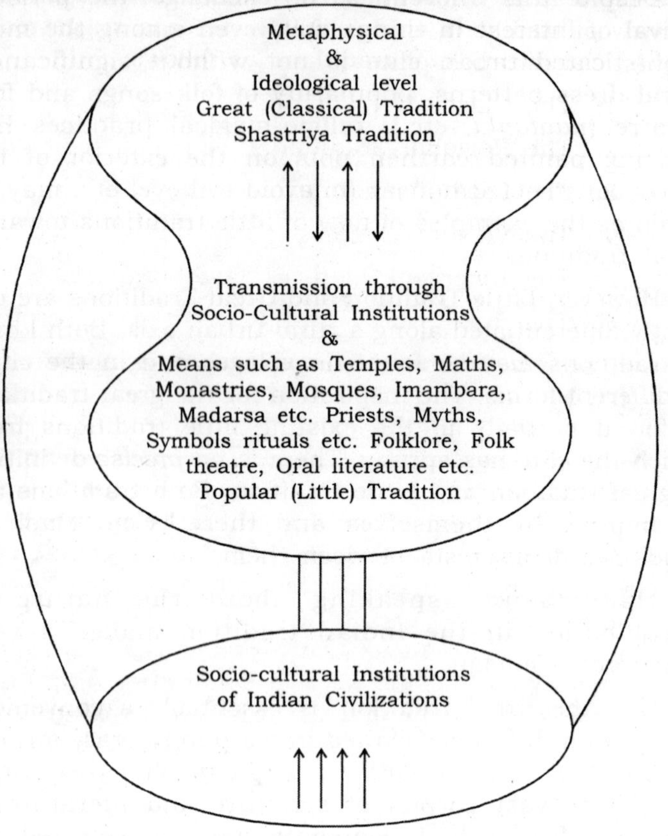

Cultural Process in Indian Civilization
(Great and Little Traditions)

in such a specific definition of the 'great tradition'. For this reason he makes no clearcut statement as to what kind of things should be judged to constitute the great tradition, but prefers to speak in generalized, abstract terms. But, if one is going to use these concepts in the analysis of data with any kind of scientific accuracy, one needs to know their meaning more precisely. And here lites it's main weakness.

SC Dube (1965) has expressed the view that Indian cultural realities are too complex to be understood through a mere 'bioplar model' of Great and Little Traditions. His view of traditions is 'multipolar'. He has suggested a six fold classification of traditions as follows:

1. The Classical Tradition;
2. The Regional Tradition;
3. The Local Tradition;
4. The Western Tradition;
5. The Emergent National Tradition; and
6. The Subcultural Traditions of special groups;

The classical traditions are rooted in mythology, religious lore and historical past. Most of these are derived from sanskritic texts but they are by no means the only source. **The regional traditions** refer to the territorial spread of certain culture traits and complexes. It refers to spatial sharing of cultural elements that give a distinctiveness and identity to the regional culture. Many of the regional traditions may be found to be shared by all the people irrespective of religious differences. **The local traditions** are confined to local groups and are confined to a smaller territory. Many of the traditions of small scale primitive tribal groups may be put under this category. **The western traditions** are the result of the impact of westernization on Indian society. It should be understood in terms of idological spheres as well as technological spheres. **The emergent national traditions** are related with the emergence of a strong national consciousness. It has given rise to nativistic, revivalistic, reinterpretational and vitalistic trends. **The sub-cultural traditions** of special groups refer to the 'special' traditions of such groups as the ruling families, the bureaucracy, and the landed aristocracy. These groups have been partly governed by other traditions, but partly they have always had separate norms and traditions of their own.

Yogendra Singh (1973) rightly comments that the various levels of traditions no doubt offer a wide scope for the study of change but the principle on which they have been classified is again ad hoc and a few other attempts, beside Dube's, too towards a multiple classification of traditions or cultural patterns in India also suffer from similar limitations.

These traditions do not function in isolation; each one significantly influences the others. A study of the dynamic aspects of their interaction is necessary to understand adequately the contemporary cultural scene in India. Moreover, maintenance of cultural continuity through mutual existence of different types of traditions has been the hallmark of the cultural process in the Indian civilization. Millions of Hindus pay respect and worship at the '*mazaar*' of *sufi* saints but this does not dilute their 'Hindutva'. Similarly, the presence of numerous Muslim musicians, vocalists as well as instrumentalists, in our great *Shastriya Sangeet* may be taken as a good example of continuity in our civilization. Music, one of the most hated things in the orthodox interpretation of Islam, along with *Saraswati Aradhna* has always been a pleasantly striking feature with hundreds of our deeply religious Muslim musicians of *Shastriya Sangeet.* Likewise magic and medicine have coexisted. Magic, or more precisely religio-magical beliefs and practices, have largely been a part of 'little traditions' whereas formal medicine or pharmacoepia is a textual thing like the Ayurveda system of medicine or modern allopathy. Even in highly modernized families, when medicine fails, recourse is taken to magic and religion. They are used alternatively by some people to meet different situations at different times. The great tradition of the urban world has not displaced the little traditions of the village. "Interaction between the two has led to a fusion and interpenetration. The modernizing processes and the traditional forms do not necessarily clash." (Sachchidananda, 1976). Instead, what we come across is 'modernization of tradition.'

❑

14 Universalization and Parochialization

In an interesting study of a north Indian village in terms of Great and Little traditions, Mckim Marriot, a disciple of Redfield and an eminent American anthropologist, has further refined this concept of interaction between the two traditions. Marriot conducted a notable study in a village called Kishangarhi in western Uttar Pradesh and found that there was a constant interaction going on between the cultural elements of Little and Great traditions. The whole approach of Marriot is historical and cultural and he has studied the structure of rural communities and societies through this approach.

Mckim Marriot speaks of the twin processes of **Universalization**, and **Parochialization**.

One may regard universalization as the process of Redfield's Great traditions and Parochialization as the process of Little traditions. The concept of universalization refers to the "carrying forward of materials which are already present in the Little tradition" (in other words upward journey of Little traditions to become a part of Great traditions). While Parochialisation is the "downward devolution of Great traditional elements and their integration with Little traditional elements. It is a process of localisation".

Thus, we see that there is a constant interation between Little and Great traditional elements.

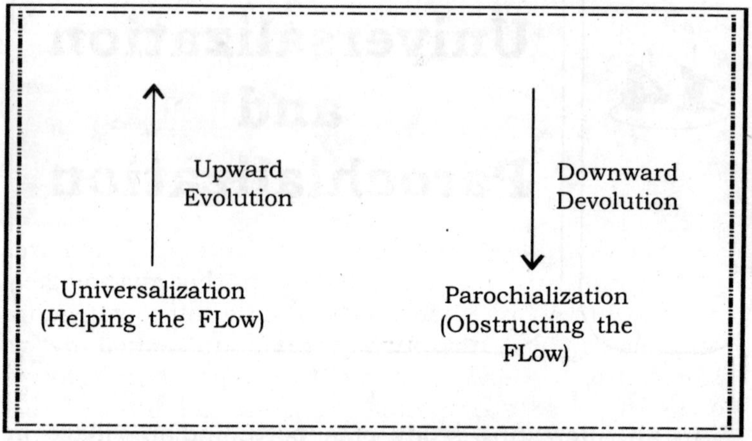

When the elements of Great traditionn. In order to perpetuate themselves, go downward and mix with the elements of Little traditions, they parochialize themselves. It shows that despite their limited range the local rural or folk traditions have a lot of cultural resilience because instead of being over-awed or completely submerged, they add up to the Great traditions and change their (Great traditions) from and content. It is a very interesting way of assimilation.

It may be said that Parochialization does not give much importance to rationality and deep thinking. Therefore, it cannot necessarily be explained rationally. There are many Little traditional elements which cannot stand the scrutiny of reason and rationale, yet they continue to be accepted generations after generations. It may also be remarked that through the process of Parochialization importance is given to the views, experiences and beliefs of a small group. As a result of 'dilution' or 'distortion' of Great traditional cultural forms, Parochialization takes traditions away from their original forms. As far as the structural aspect is concerned it may be concluded that one comes across comparatively less organisation in traditions vis-a-vis Parochialization.

Giving examples from his field work in Kishangarhi, marriot tries to prove his point. Takaing up '*Govardhan Puja*' and '*Nauratha Puja*' he cities the parochialization of two great traditions. In and around Kishangarhi *Govardhan Puja* has been a very popular ritual among the rural folks in which mounds of cowdung (Gobardhan literally means cowdung wealth) are decorated with corns and *puja* performed. Marriot is of the view that this *Govardhan puja* is nothing but parochialized form of *Govardhan Puja* (worship of the 'possessor of cows' i.e. Krishna). *Govardhan* hill which is about 40 kilometres from Kishangarhi is associated with the mythological story in which Lord Krishna had lifted a hill to safeguard his followers from the fury of rains unleashed by an angry Indra. It goes to show that during a journey of 40 kilometres or so the mythological foundation of a Great tradition was altered by the process of Parochialization and when a Great tradition of *Govardhan's* worship reached Kishangarhi after encountering a number of Little traditional elements it had been parochialized. Same is the case with *Nauratha Devi's* worship. *Nauratri* festival has been quite popular throughout the country in which Puja of Durga, Amba and Kali is performed during the days of Dussehra. People of Kishangarhi do perform *puja* and other rituals during these days but a little differently. Hence *Nauratha*— a local or parochial goddess— occupies the place of pride. *Nauratha* does not enjoy any mention in Great traditional Hindu scriptures. Obviously it is an example of Parochialization of a Great tradition.

The concept of Universalization was first introduced by Redfield and Milton Singer. Marriot clarified and applied it to explain the mutual relationship and interaction between Great traditions and Little traditions. Culture has got the characteristic of diffiusion. When local or Little traditions while moving upwards (i.e. diffusing to larger areas) interact with Great traditions and in course of time are accepted and incorporated in religious texts and epics of Great traditions such a process of diffusion may be called as Universalization. Evidently in this process a local cultural form of traditional elements gets wider acceptability and hence 'universalized'. It is a great expansion of Little traditions. Citing the examples of the worship of goddess *Saurati* and celebration of *Saluno* festival from Kishangarhi, Mckim Marriot has demonstrated the universalization of parochial cultural elements. He says that the practice of Lakshmi's worship during Diwali — a very popular religious practice in many parts of India— is nothing but universalization of little traditions like a worship of goddess *Saurati.* During Diwali the people of Kishangarhi carve the image of *Saurati* on the walls with rice flour to invoke her blessings for health and wealth. He contends that such practices did not originate in Great traditions of the Hindus but such Little traditions as *Saurati's* worship during *Diwali* travelled upwards, were accepted incorporated in the religious texts and epics of Great traditions and became part of it in the course of time. Like *Lakshmi Puja*, the celebration of *Raksha Bandhan* (in which sisters tie *Rakhi* on the wrists of their brothers for their security and well being) a popular festival in the length and breadth of India also has it's origin in Little tradition. The corresponding celebration of *Saluno* festival in Kishangarhi and other such festivals of Little traditions popular in other parts of the country are said to have been universalized into *Raksha Bandhan.* In Kishangarhi the married daughters, on the day of Saluno apply *tilak* of barley on the foreheads of their unmarried sisters and brothers and get money or gifts in return. Likewise Brahmin priests tie *rakhi* on their patrons' (*Jajman*) and get something in return. Marriot contends that the festival or *Raksha Bandhan* came into being as a result of universalization of festivals like *Saluno.*

The most glaring drawback of these concepts is that if we regret Universalization and Parochialization as *the* explanation of this cultural process, it is like stopping in the middle of what should be considered as the *circular flow*. The dynamics of the Great and Little traditions is not two directional but is rather circular and continuous in operation; parts of the elite from the *great community* emerging from the *little community*, little traditions becoming part of the great traditions maintains a circular flow and journeying again to the little communities and thus goes on the process. The following diagram explains this arguments:

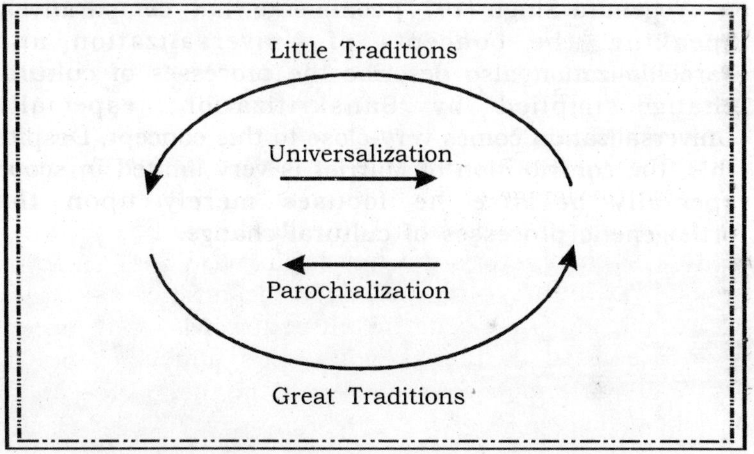

Marriot's twin concepts of Universalization and Parochialization may be sound in so far as they refer to the process of give and take between the 'elite' and the 'folk' traditions *but* they are substantially erroneous when it is implied that if an element passes down from the Great to the Little tradition it is bound to be localised or parochialized. Folk culture is confined to no single village not even a small region. Hence, these concepts have limited validity and often fail to explain a number of cultural facts of comples Indian civilization. Due to lack of comprehensive study what may, at first glance, appear to be 'parochial may be essentially pan-Indian and vice-versa. Moreover, without history even the dicotomy of Universalization and Parochialization may have no meaning.'

This is largely because of the inability to trace back the origins of many cultural phenamena in the centuries long process of development that makes the task of assigning them to one or the other tradition a difficult one. A detailed historical knowledge of the area alongwith social history might be of some help in tracing the starting point of many rituals and beliefs, but it would not reveal the origins of all. And it is seldom possible, particularly when dealing with semi-literate sub-groups in a society, to learn enough this aspect of their history.

Yogendra Singh (1977) comments that, comparatively speaking, the concepts of Universalization and Parochialization also describe the processes of cultural change implied by Sanskritization; especially Universalization comes very-close to this concept. Despite this, the contribution of Marriot is very limited in scope specially because he focuses merely upon the orthogenetic processes of cultural change.

❑

15 Sacred Complex

Before discussing the concept of Sacred Complex it would be better to go into the historical background of studying Indian civilization by social anthropologists. The 1950s and early 60s witnessed a major impact of Chicago School of Anthropology on Indian social anthropologists. Through their path breaking studies Redfield (1955, 56 & 57). Singer (1955, 58) and Marriot (1955, 59, 60 & 61) gave theoretical and methodological leads in the study of folk and peasant communities in India as dimensions of Indian civilization. Redfield's concept of Great and Little traditions provided a new insight in understanding Indian civilization. In a significant essay, (1955) he says that in a civilization are found "an organization of specialists, kinds of role occupiers in characteristic relations to one another and to lay people and performing characteristic functions concerned with the transmission of tradition". Hypothesising about Indian civilization he says, beside other things, that the cultural continuity was maintained because its Great traditions were culturally continuous with the Little traditions. A common cultural consciousness was responsible for this cultural continuity and this consciousness, in turn, has been formed in India by certain factors common to all primary civilizations like sacred texts and objects, a special class of literate practitioners who have the traditional authority to recite and interpret the sacred scriptures, sacred centres of pilgrimage and so on.

Utilizing these theoretical propositions Vidyarthi who was, in a way, a product of Chicago School of Anthropology (he did his Ph. D. from Chicago and studied under Redfield) studied the sacred city of Gaya located in the ancient cultural zone of Magadh. In this study, he developed a set of analytical concepts and descriptive terms to describe a sacred city as a part of Indian civilization. The city has been described in terms of three analytical concepts namely sacred geography, sacred performances, and sacred specialists. These three concepts conceived collectively, are termed a Sacred Complex.

In his landmark study the (The Sacred Complex) of Hindu Gaya (1961) Vidyarthi came out with his three constituents of a sacred complex with the help of some hypotheses formulated by him. He says that the sacred comples of a Hindu place of pilgrimage reflects a level of continuity, compromise and combination between Great and Little traditions. The sacred specialists of place of pilgrimage maintain a distinct style of life and transmit certain elements of the Great tradition to the rural population of India by popularising certain texts, by organising pilgrimage and by officiating as the ritual and temple priests. The sacred specialists in particular have been in the process of modification and transformation as a result of general development in the large universe of Hindu civilization of which they are a part.

The classification of the sacred phenomena i.e. sacred geography, sacred performances and sacred specialists is applicable not only to Gaya but, indeed, to all the sacred places of Hindu pilgrimage. Both Vidyarthi (1961) and Cohn & Marriot (1958) have considered these places and the network of pilgrimages functionally important in the integration of Indian civilization.

Among the three basic components, the sacred geography has been further classified into zones, segments, and clusters of sacred centres. Gaya contains a complex of hundreds of sacred objects and places located within this sacred *Kshetra* (region) revered by all Hindus. Both in space and time the sacred geography demonstrates the continuity of India's Great and Little traditions. It also exhibits several kinds of combinations between Hindu and Buddhist traditions at different levels. However, due to drastic changes in modern times the secular zone of Gaya has been expanding at the cost of the shrinking sacred zone. This is discernible at the sight of many old and dilapidated sacred objects where rest houses, parks, restaurants, etc. have come up. Besides so many sacred performances the main one for which Gaya is revered in the Hindu world is an elaborate form of sacrifices to ancestral spirits. This is known as Gaya Shraddha. All the sacred performances are led by the Gayawal Brahmins —an orthodox priestly caste following a highly ceremonialized and sanskritic life style greatly influenced by the Hindu Great tradition. The relationship of this sacred complex with the outside world is not one sided. The sacred complex survives mainly on the sustenance derived from the latter. The Gayawal priests have *jajmani* relationships with well to do patrons located in various parts of the Hindu universe. The construction of sacred buildings was financed mainly by rich persons from all over the country. The same persons provide a livelihood to the sacred specialists by holding elaborate sacred performances and giving them valuable gifts.

The sacred complexes are the centres of civilization where pilgrims from different regions of India, from different levels of culture interact; Saraswati (1982) raising a pertinent question asks whether these heterogeneous pilgrims who interact in a sacred complex share in common the Brahminic concept of sacred which has laid the foundation of these centres, and do all of them interact fully and equally with the sacred phenomena operating at the sacred centre? In semitic religions, all those who interact at a place of pilgrimage, say Mecca or Jerusalam, may belong to diverse linguistic regions and cultural strata, but they hold a common concept of sacred and participate equally in sacred performances. This does not seem to be true with the Hindu places of pilgrimage, and yet they serve importantly to integrate diverse cultural traditions into a common bond of civilization.

Taking lead from Vidyarthi a group of younger social anthropologists was attracted towards this new field of research. Saraswati has made prominent contribution to this field through his studies like *The Holy Circuit of Nimsar* (1965), *The Temple Organization in Goa* (1962), and Kashi: *Myth and Reality of a Classical Cultural Tradition (1975).* Saraswati is of the view that the concept of 'sacred' is essentially based on man's desire to communicate with the spiritual world, usually, in order to attain *moksa*. In his significant study of Kashi, Saraswati has concluded that although the sacred complex of Kashi may appear as predominantly a Brahmin complex, it is indeed a complex of a much bigger organization of traditions, known as Indian civilization, which makes the Brahminic temple of Viseshwara and the non-Brahminic shrine of Agryabeer to co-exist, the textually learned *Karmakandi*, and illiterate untouchable *Domto* conduct sacred performances together and Nasik Brahmin touch the feet of an *Awadhoot* who eats carcasses. This kind of arrangement at sacred placed of pilgrimage demonstrates and reminds the pilgrims coming from different cultural traditions again and again that they must not be too egoistic in upholding their own traditions as the superior most.

Among other contributions are Jha's, *The Sacred Complex of Ratanpur* (1978), *Mohapatra's Lingaraj Temple: Its Structure and Change*, Morab & Goswami's Chamundeshwari Temple (1974). Apart from his intensive study of Janakpur, following the theoretical model of Gaya, Jha also tested certain hypotheses raised by Redfield, Singer, Vidyarthi and others. While Vidyarthi developed the concept of Sacred Complex for studying the places of pilgrimage as a dimension of Indian civilization, Marriot and Cohn developed the concepts of 'Network and Centres' (1958) to study the channels of integration of Indian civilization. Thus, in Indian social anthropology, the concepts of Sacred complex' and 'Networks and Centres' have become very popular theoretical models for studying the traditional cities and places of pilgrimage as dimensions of Indian civilization.

❑

16 Tribe-Caste Continuum

It is while working in Mexican villages that Robert Redfield attention was drawn to a number of cultural similarities and overlappings in rural and urban life. He gave serious thought to the demarcating factors but found that it was very difficult to draw a neat and clear line of demarcation between 'folk' and 'urban'. Hence the concept of continuum through which Redfield explained that it was not always prudent to view the two segments of the society as completely disjunctive entities. Continuity of even some cultural traits observed in such a dichotomous scheme should be viewed in terms of 'continuum' or continua. The concept of continuum was first explained by Redfield in *The Folk Culture of Ycatan* (1941).

Much before Redfield pinpointed the areas of continuity between folk and urban cultures, Indian ethnographers were grapping with the problem of discriminating between 'tribe' and 'caste'. The ethnographers along with Census officials confronted this problem, for the first time, during the last decade of the nineteenth century when the census operations began under the supervision of British administrators. The decennial census operations of those times included not only counting of heads but also the classification of populations into such categories as tribes, castes, sects and occupations. Initially, they used the term 'tribe' in a rather loose sense, describing even such groups as the *Jats* and *Ahirs* as tribes. However, when J.H. Hutton took over the charge of census operations, more academic rigour was applied. That is why we see that the discussion on the points of distinction between 'tribe' and 'caste' became an academic issue of importance from 1931 onwards. If a group could be shown to be clearly Hindu in its religious beliefs and practices, it was a caste; if it was 'animist', it had to be treated as a tribe. Economic, political and ecological factors were of secondary importance.

Ethnographers, sociologists, social anthrpologists, social workers and other have been grapping with the problem of developing one way of defining a tribe or tribal society— a definition that should command total acceptance. Unfortunately, these definitions have been either very broad and loose or very narrow and restricted. Sometimes it becomes so wide that it also included peasantry. Nadeem Hasnain in Tribal India (1988) has dealt in detail with this problem presenting all the possible view points. Andre Beteille (1974), presenting a sociologist's point of view enumerates "certain commonly observed differences between tribes and castes". There is first the relative isolation of tribes as compared with castes. This has two facts. It means, first, that the tribes are geographically isolated, being concentrated in areas which are or have been more or less inaccessible. It also means — and this is for the sociologists more important — that a tribe is a world within itself having few external social ties, whereas a caste is by its nature a part of a larger whole, being linked by multifarious ties with other castes. The second criterion is lanaugae or dialect. The tribes speak a variety of dialects which can be shown to differ, on a number of important count, from the major Indian languages. Then, there is religion. Even if we regard the contrast between 'Animism' and 'Hinduism' as too crude, we might concede that there are numerous elements of 'religious belief' and practice common to many tribes which do not find a place in what is commonly accepted as Hinduism. But religion, unlike language, is a loose criterion, for what we encounter is continuum without sharp breaks and where we draw the line between 'tribal' and 'non-tribal' must remain arbitrary.

Among a vast crowd of scholars working in tribal India, F.G. Bailey stands apart. His major concern was to creat a definition for certain characteristic of tribal society which would be appropriate to the Indian context. The problem of delineating and defining a tribe or a tribal society in other countries did not create much of a problem because cultural proximity of tribe with any other related segment of the society did not assume the dimensions of great similarities. Here these are 'too close to comfort'. In his very important paper "Tribe" and "Caste" in India' (1961). Bailey took all the points, raised by various sociologists and social anthropologists, into account and presented a scheme to discriminate between tribe and case in structural terms. He suggests that we should curb the tendency to view 'tribe' and 'caste' disjunctively. Instead, they should be viewed in terms of continuum. Bailey further argued that a caste society is 'organic' and hierarchical while a tribal society is 'segmentary' and egalitarian. Thus, he seeks to make the distinction not it terms of the totality of behaviour but, in a more limited way, in relation to the politico-economic system. Yet, Bailey is also aware of the change occurring in Indian society. He clearly sees that both caste and tribe are becoming transformed. He declares that "both caste and tribe are being merged into a different system which is neither one nor the other". In such a social scenario where caste and tribe are ceasing to be such, according to their classical points of distinction, the practical value of even Bailey's scheme is limited.

Surajit Sinha, a disciple of Redfield, tried to understand the tribe-caste continuum on the basis of his field work among the tribes of Bastar. After Bailey's efforts to reach some kind of conclusion of academic durability, this was the most serious attempt to understand Indian society in terms of tribe-caste continuum. Citting certain cultural characteristics as the basis of continuum, Sinha opines that many of the lower castes in India seem to share with the tribals emphasis on equality in social behaviour within one's own ethnic group, considerable freedom of cultural participation for the women, and a value system burdened by puritanical asceticism. Further, the supernaturalism of these lowest castes has some similarities with that of tribes.

Until 19th century, when some of the tribal areas were thrown open, most tribal groups had little contacts with the Hindu society and civilizational centres. Yet the remotest and the most isolated of tribal groups in India had certain cultural traits in common with the *Jati* people. The case of Jaunsari tribe inhabiting the cis-Himalayan region of Uttar Pradesh and some other tribes may be cites as examples. Like other *Jati* people, the Jaunsari people, too, had an elaborate caste hierarchy and the notion of purity and pollution has been working in their society with all the accompanying social evils. They have been supporting the social inequality rather than minimizing it.

The tribe-caste continuum may be understood on another level viz. on the interactional level of Little and Great traditions. The presence of references of tribes like *Khasa* and *Bhils* in the epics and texts of the Great traditions such as Ramayana, Mahabharata, etc. go to prove that despite their general isolation the tribes did maintain, through occasionally, cultural contacts with the larger Hindu society. The absorption, into Great tradition, of several traits from Little traditions because of occasional contacts, is also responsible for the tribe-caste continuum. N.K. Bose in his *Hindu Methods of Tribal Absorption* (1941) showed the mode of absorption of *Jati* influence by the primitive tribes of Orissa, Martin

Orans', study, *Santhal: A Tribe of Search of Great Tradition* (1965) goes on to show, how on a different plane, many tribes in India are being attracted towards the complex belief of high Hinduism. In certain cases the process of Hinsuisation of tribes, due to intimate cultural contacts, has been so rapid that such tribes remain 'tribes' for the namesake only. However, the concept of tribe-caste continuum has gained currency in writings of social analysis.

❑

17 Nature-Man-Spirit Complex

The concepts of Nature-Man-Spirit Complex is an important contribution by L.P. Vidyarthi for applied anthropologists in the formulation and implementation of development programmes in tribal India. This concept is based on cultural ecological approach in anthropology which explains the constant interaction between man and nature.

Culture may also be viewed as the human response to the local environmental conditions. In other words culture may also be described as the man made part of the environment. In this arrangement some external or outside factors are also very relevant. This arrangement between man and his environment helps him on individual as well as collective level to fulfil all the practical requirements of life. Man has got an amazing capacity to adapt himself with his ecology. But the adaptation model is not uniform throughout the world. It varies from region to region because of environmental and other factors. That is why cultural ecologists are always in search of cultural adaptation models or patterns. In fact the distinctiveness of the culture of various human groups lies in the variations in the cultural ecological models.

The concept of Nature-Man-Spirit Complex is an attempt to understand the adaptation of the socio-cultural institutions with the local environmental conditions. it has been observed that constant interaction goes on between the social organization, ecological conditions and religious complex in the whole of tribal India. It's results and adaptation process has been studied by L.P. Vidyarthi with special reference to the Maler (Mal Pahariya)- a primitive tribe of shifting cultivators inhabiting the Rangmahal Hills of Bihar. The Malers believe in different types of spirits. The influence of these spirits is all pervading in various spheres of life of the Malers. The spirits they behave in may broadly be categorised into two; the benevolent spirits are responsible for health, wealth, increased productivity in agriculture and so on while the malevolent spirits cause sickness, abortions, death and natural calamities with the presiding spirit *Gosain or Gosaiyyan* governing over all the spirits. Thus, propitiation of various types of spirits becomes one of their pre-occupations. To achieve this objective they resort to various types of rites and rituals. Since the presiding spirit *Gosain* serves as the bridge between the Malers and their concept of super human and supernatural, it is held in highest esteem. They do not do anything worthwhile without the 'approval' of the *Gosain.*

In this way the spirits, the social institutions and their principal economic activity viz. shifting cultivation known as *Khallu* in the local dialect from a complex. This complex may be explained through the following line diagram (on the next page).

Thus, the 'nature' and 'spirits' exert profound influence over Maler life and these three interrelated factors are in constant interaction with each other.

The utility of this concept may be observed when it serves as an important aid or tool for an applied

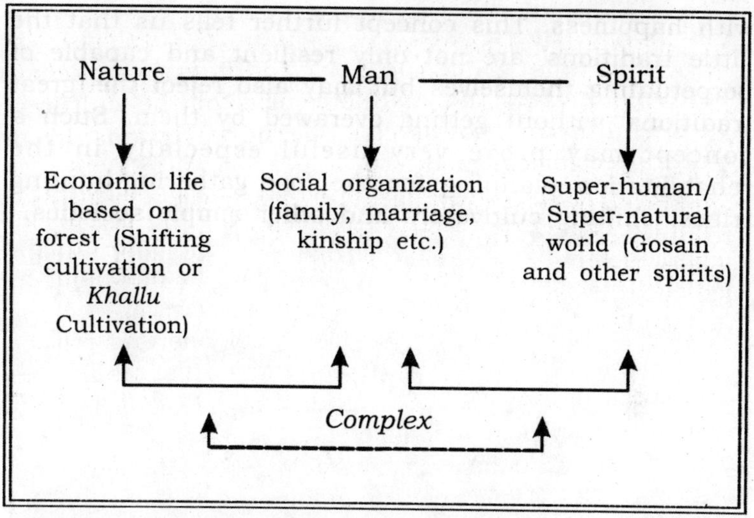

anthropologist, during the formulation or implementation of developmental programmes among the primitive tribal communities. It has been seen several times that the primitive tribal groups resist or reject totally any attempt on the part of the development administration to rehabititiate them anywhere else or introduce radical changes in their life. This resistance or rejection may be explained in terms of their despair or anger at the disturbance in the equilibrium of nature, man and spirit. This Complex highlights that these tribals can be disturbed radically and abruptly by introducing innovations in their life without preparing them sufficiently for this change.

This concept tells an applied anthropologist to be very sensitive and receptive to any such change that threatens to disturb this equilibrium otherwise the target group or the potential beneficiary of any programme may not accept it and the scarce resources may go down the drain. This hardly means that the primitive tribal groups or simple peasant groups should be left to their fate with all the vistages of status quoism. The purpose and objective of this caution is to ensure that the schemes for their welfare and development help such groups achieve 'development' with happiness. This concept further tells us that the 'little traditions' are not only resilient and capable of perpetuating themselves but may also reject the 'great traditions' without getting overawed by them. Such a concept may prove very useful especially in the rehabilitation planning for the food-gathering-hunting tribes, shifting cultivators and other simple societies.

❑

SECTION SIX

INDIAN SOCIAL SYSTEM

18

Traditional Bases of Indian Social System

India is inhabited by the followers of the three most important religious ideologies of the world- Hinduism, Islam and Christianity. Beside these, followers of other major religions such as Judiaism and Zoarostrianism also live in the sub-continent alongwith those who had branched out from the popular mainstream of Hinduism such as Budhism, Jainism and Sikhism. During the last five thousand years or so, the Indian sub-continent has witnessed a unique synthesis of these and several other schools of thought. The contempory Indian Society and it's social organization is the result of this unique experiment in mutual existence. Yet, when we talk of the bases of Indian social system in the traditional sense of the term it is invariably the concepts in Hindu social system which still dominates the thought and action of crores of Indian masses.

Hinduism is the name given by the Europeans to the religious, socio-cultural, political and philosophical beliefs which make up the totality of the Hindu way of life.

Hindus themselves call their religious tradition 'the eternal law' (*Sanatan Dharma*). The most important bases of the Hindu (Indian) social system are *Varna, Ashrama, Purushartha, Karma, Rina, Punarjanm (rebirth),* Joint Family and the Caste System.

PURUSHARTHA :

Purushartha refers to four goals or rather goal orientation or aims of life namely *dharma, Artha, Kama* and *Moksha.* The wish for a long span of life on this earth is the immediate desire of a person but the ultimate goal is *Moksha* (Liberation or Salvation). The theory or doctrine of *Purushartha* explains the desired harmony between these two aims. The theory of *purushartha* provides the basic principle of Indian ethical system. These comprehend "the whole man".

Of these four *purushartha* (also referred to as *purushartha chatushtham*), dharma is central to all human activities. It is derived from the root *dhr* which means "to uphold", "to support", "to nourish". In his *History of the Dharmashastra,* V.P.Kane, in very lucid terms, explains *dharma* as :

(i) the rights and duties of man as man;

(ii) his duties and privileges as a member of the Aryan community;

(iii) his special duties, rights and functions as a member of the social group or "caste", - *varna-dharma*; and

(iv) the rights and obligations of every man in the changing of stations of life as a student, householder, etc- *ashrama-dharma.*

Dharma is like a centripetal force in nature which keeps things to the centre; *dharma* is a centripetal force in man, society, and the universe. It is *dharma* that enables us to have right satisfaction of desire. *Dharma* is regulative principle which regulates the enjoyment of *artha* and *kama.* Is *dharma* a means to an end or is it an end in itself? Both views are present in Indian ethics. "The view which says that *dharma* is an end in itself resembles Kant's theory that what is good is the goodwill itself which will shine like the starry heavens even if it accomplishes nothing. If *dharma* is an end in itself, then, the philosophy of values in Indian Culture will not be four fold but three fold. But the view that *dharma* is a means to an end, that *dharma* is only an "instrumental" value is interesting" (N.A. Nikam, 1973). It is also a law of all moral action.

Artha refers to all the means for acquiring worldly prosperity, such as wealth or power. It means a righteous and honest pursuit of economic activities. Thus, all economic activities are oriented towards (i) acquisition of wealth, (ii) *aparigraha* (non-appropriation), and (iii) *asteya* (non-stealing). Though *artha* refers to security and materialistic aspect of life but at the same time a parallel stream of non-acquisition and renunciation also runs side by side. Accumulation of wealth is only a means to an end and not an end in itself. It is necessary only to the extent that the individual can fulfil other social obligations as enjoined by *dharma*. One has to guard against the undue involvement with material things.

Kama refers to all desires in man, seeking pleasure through satisfaction of senses including sexual satisfaction. It includes all impulses, instincts and desires of man though in popular connotation undue emphasis has been laid on the needs of the flesh only. It definitely includes aesthetic satisfaction. Inspite of an emphasis on exercising control over senses, man always crave for indulgence in sexual pleasures. Hence, a corrective balance has to be struck between the needs of the body and mind. The inclusion of *Kama* as one of the essential elements of purushartha is the sign of its recognition. That is why love has been adored in Indian life throughout the ages. As Raghvan states : "In the wider context *Kama* provides the source from which all activities spring. It supplies energy to innovate, to create something. It provides *rasas* which give birth to architecture, painting, music, poetry". Thus, apart from satisfying sexual needs of man which is essential for perpetuation of *Kula* (family & lineage), *Kama* fulfils the craving of man to substitute his feelings for aesthetic development.

Moksha is salvation, liberation from the endless cycle of births and deaths. It also refers to absorption of the self into eternal bliss. *Moksha* also implies self realisation or realisation of the identity. As N.A. Nikam (ibid) rightly points out that "although many similes are used in the *Upanishad* to convey it, the simile of the rivers joining the ocean, and the simile of the ultimate return to the source of Being are the most important; *moksha* is the realization in which the knower becomes what he knows, *brahmavid brahmaive bhavati*, "the knower of the Brahma become Brahma" which means that the knower becomes *aware* that in his real nature he is Brahma; it becomes the affirmation of a realized experience, *aham brahmasmi*, "I am *Brahma*" in self realization." It is the state of mind and does not mean the total negation of worldly existence. It is not the privilege of everyone. A true *sanyasi* could only attain it.

Thus, we find that the *Purushartha* are value themes, goals of life arranged in an hierarchical order to be pursued by all individuals and social categories. *Dharma*, *Artha* and *Kama* are three principal motivating forces or urges/drives around which the whole life conduct of man is comprehended. Management and conduct of individual and social life is conceived and formulated in terms of these three with reference to the ultimate end/goal of life i.e. *moksha*'. Louis Dumont(1960) has given a correct perspective to this triology of human functions in society. The three values in this critical triology are *dharma*, *artha* and *kama*. While *Dharma* implies duty and leads to moral universalism, *artha* is profit that implies rational action in our economic theory extended to politics, *Kama* refers to pleasures of life. Manu says that the management and conduct of life should be conceived and formulated in terms of harmonious coordination of these three *Trivarga* (classes of needs).

ASHRAM :

The theory of *Purushartha* has been given concrete expression in the scheme of *Ashrams*. Ideally speaking, the life of a Hindu is divisible into four stages. This fourfold division of the total life span is known as *Ashram* system. It connotes life stages and its value obligations. These four stages are :

(a) Brahmacharya Ashram

(b) Grihastha Ashram

(c) Vanaprastha Ashram

(d) Sanyasa Ashram

The first Ashram is Brahmacharya which implies the life of a student or learner. It constitutes the learning stage. Here, an individual is to be trained by a *Guru* to enable him to fulfil his obligations in the later Ashrams. A *Brahmchari*, person passing through brahmcharya, is supposed to lead a life of piety, self-denial, discipline and non-indulgence in *artha* and *Kama*. His sole concern should be with the fulfilment of *dharma*. The brahmacharya ashram used to begin with an initiation ceremony known as *Upnayan Sanskara* (sacred thread ceremony). In this scheme of things total celebacy is prescribed till marriage.

When the *guru* certified that the boy was now a man and fit to enter the second stage, he was supposed to come back to his parent's household. In this ashrama, a person is initiated into a new role through the *vivah* (marriage ceremony). This is considered to be the most critically important ashram because the basic triology of *dharma*, *artha*, and *kama* are to be translated into action. Manu is of the view that it is the stage full of bliss and blessings. All the remaining three *ashrams* acquire totality through this *ashram*. Among the duties of a *grihastha* (household) is reproduction, acquisition of wealth, to feed the family, to provide education to the family, to help other members of the society, to practice selflessness, sacrifice, piety and sympathy towards fellow beings and to fulfill his own wants and desires, of course within the lines drawn by the *dharma*. Besides these, the *grihastha* (householder) is also required to repay all the *rina* (debts). It is believed that every Hindu is born with certain debts such as *Dev rina*, *rishi rina*, *pitra rina* etc.

He has to repay all these debts through a variety of means such as recitation of *Veda*, performance of certain rituals, *Yagna* etc.

The third stage is preparatory to the ultimate retirement. This is *Vanaprastha Ashram*. During this stage the householder relinquishes his duties in the household and devotes his time to religious pursuits. His links with his family are weakened. A *Vanaprasthi* is expected to retire into the nearest forest where he has to lead a life of meditation with minimal needs. The wife could accompany the husband but there should be total abstinance from sex. The significant point to be noted here is that a *Vanaprasthi* is still *not* totally detached from this world.

Finally, an individual is enjoined to take to *Sanyas* which involves total detachment from the social life. Thus, in the *Sanyasa* stage an individual ceases to be a member of the society and is to concern himself with purely personal goal. Now the individual transformed into *Sanyasi* is to preach truth, teach the people and becomes oblivious of sorrows and sufferings. Kautilya suggested punishment for those who tried to adopt Sanyasa without fully undergoing his responsibilities for his family and society. And significantly Gita does not say that *Sanyasa* is necessary for *moksha*. It says that since a *Karmayogi* (man of action) is also a *Sanyasi*; he is not required to adopt *Sanyasa* formally.

Thus, we find that *Purushartha* and *Ashrama* are regulators of life. In sociological-anthropological parlance the four hierarchies of *Varna*, *Guna*, *Purushartha* and *Ashram* may be described in terms of 'role institutionalization', 'charismatic endowments; 'goal orientation', and 'life stages and its value obligations respectively. And all these elements of social order reveal that the foundation of Hindu Social Organization is both *material* as well as *spiritual*. It has been organized into such a way that man is supposed to move from material to spiritual life. Another point to be noted is that the *Varna-Ashram Vyvastha* presents only the textual view of

Hindu Social Life, which was never fully replicated in reality. Most of these values were ideological-motivational phenomena. A great deal of flexibility was also allowed in the expectation of conformity to the prescribed values and obligations. The obligations were relative to *Desha* (space), *Kaala* (time), *Shrama* (efforts), and *Guna* (innate qualities). Thus, Hinduism is more a way of life than a religion or religious order in the formal sense of the term.

RINA :

The concept of *rina* is also a very important component of Hindu Social System. In order to bring about a healthy social order every individual of the society is to be 'socialized' in such a way that he finds himself under obligation to fulfil responsibilities not only for his sake but for his family, kith and kin and the society at large. All these obligations are *rina*(debts). Every Hindu is born with certain debts(*rina*) which he has to repay in his life time for his salvation. The underlying idea of this theory is to make the members of the society aware of their vast array of responsibilities and obligations. Following are different types of *rina* one has to repay in ones' life time.

(i) *Deva Rina* : Its a debt one owes to gods and godesses. This may be repaid through recitation of *Vedas*, offering sacrifices, performing *Yagna* and showing devotion in a variety of ways.

(ii) *Rishi Rina* : One is always indebted to the *rishis* and *gurus* through whom one acquires knowledge and thus removes darkness of mind and soul. One repays this debt by giving *guru dakshina*, and study and perpetuation of knowledge contained in various *shastras*.

(iii) Pitra Rina : One owes one's existence to one's parents. Thus, this debt can be repaid by reproducing *santana*(progeny), making the children good human beings and useful members of the society and by performing *pind daan.*

(iv) Atithi Rina : Man does not live in isolation. There is constant inter-action between different members of the society. People visit each other and strengthen social ties. That is why, perhaps, *atithi*(guests) have been equated with gods whose service is an important element of the Hindu Social Order. Thus, the *atithi rina* can be repaid through showing reverence, and serving the guests in the best possible way.

***KARMA* :**

The concept of *Karma* is one of the hallmarks of Hindu Social Order. It refers to a belief in the efficacy of actions of a person, either good or bad. The concepts of *dharma, artha, kama* and *moksha* are related to tenets of *Karma* and *Sansara.* The term *Sansara* is used for the arena or place where the cycle of birth and re-birth continues to operate until one attains *moksha.*

Karma is action and the consequence of action. It is one of the social values stressing the individual responsibility for one's action. The doctrine of *Karma* enunciates the principle of the moral responsibility of man for his own deeds. His actions lead to certain consequences and so he should be aware of this when he acts. It assumes that one's present condition is not the result of his present deeds but is also the consequence of his past life. Thus, it is closely linked to *punarjanm* (re-birth).

There is a long history of the interpretations of the 'doctrine of Karma' right from the time when it was spelt out in the *Upanishads.* In recent years, contemporary thinkers have tried to re-examine and reinterpret it in a variety of ways. N.A.Nikam (ibid) in a lucid interpretation talks of the 'causal efficacy', *artha-kriya-karitva* which implies that good actions produce good effects instantaniously and bad actions produce bad effects instantaniously. While the natural science says that man is a product of natural evolution, the doctrine of Karma asks man to take concious charge of the greater adventure of his own evolution, the evolution of his moral and spiritual conciousness, which is greater than the physico-biological evolution of "structure and function" that has taken place so far; for, whatever might have been the past the future is *new* and the future could be left to take care of itself if we take care of the present. In another interpretation, one finds an individual driven by his *Karma*, moves from one existence to another, since individual life is only a span out of a series. This series is called a round of transmigration. S. Radhakrishnana, an eminent philosopher of this century, observes that there is no doctrine that is so valuable in life and conduct as the *Karma* theory, it implies hope for the future and resignation of the past.

In the *Bhagvad Gita*, Krishna tells us that *Karma* is ubiquitous and eternal, and it is not possible for any one not to perform some *Karma* at every moment of his life. There are five factors involved in its make-up: (1) *adhisthana*, the basis or centre from which one is to work, (2) *Karta* or doer, (3) *Karma* or the instrumentation of the doer, (4) *Chesta* or effort, and (5) *daiva* or fate. The last is the "power of powers other than human". Radhakrishnan giving greater importance to the path of action in his translation of the great epic *Bhagvad gita* says : "*To action alone thou hast a right and never at all to its fruits; let no fruits be thy motive; neither let there be any attachment to inaction*".

The doctrine of Karma is sometime misunderstood as fate and faith in fatalism. Those who accepts such an interpretation as this comment that it retards moral progress and hence contains 'anti-social' implications. They further comment that it does not take into account the influence of the social forces regarding one's present predicament. Consequently, this outlook induces a lack of concern for the suffering of other people, because the suffering of each one, whether of oneself or the other, is interpreted in terms of the actions in the past life. But several other modern interpreters reveal that the belief in *Karma* is not fatalism since it is a rational concept and devoid of any mysterious or divine force which is a pre-condition of fatalism. On the contrary it preaches *purushartha* and inculcates a sense of morality and encourages everyone to do good in the present life as well as in the life to come.

RE-BIRTH :

The concept of Karma is fully developed and woven into the belief in rebirth (punarjanm) which in turn is related to the belief concerning heaven, hell and *moksha.* The concept of rebirth or transmigration of soul is based on the belief that the *atma* (soul) is immortal or imperishable. It is part of the Brahma and survives even after the destruction of the mortal body. In the event of *moksha,* it again reunites with the *Paramatma.*

The earliest mention of belief in rebirth on the earth is found in the *Satpatha Brahmna,* when the idea of reincarnation, implying repeated deaths, was viewed as a cursed evil, a nightmare imposed on those who failed to perform sacrifices. "The linkage of the belief in reincarnation with the doctrine of *Karma* was a post-vedic development. In the Samakhya tradition the final goal of Yoga is for the disciple to reach *moksha*, the ultimate liberation of the life-monad, *purusa* "(R.N. Saxena, year not cited). Two stages are clearly marked in this ultimate goal, according to whether the disciple wishes to remain in this world or not. In the first context, he remains content with the *savikalpa-samadhi,* the super-concious ecstacy in which the dualism, object-subject, still exists; in the second, he escapes from life altogether through the *nirvikalpa samadhi,* the final liberation of soul.

It is therefore evident that moksha did not mean the total negation of worldly existence of purusa. It was the *state of mind,* before this stage was reached, that is of real significance. It was not the privilege of everyone to attain *moksha.* It was the true *sanyasi* who could claim it.

In the popular connotation rebirth is in accordance with deeds or *Karma.* This principle assures that those who live a life in conformity with *dharma* i.e. whose actions are governed by *dharma* should expect a better and more prosperous life. Thus, it exercised a deterring effect on the individuals and tries to mould his conduct in such a way that it is good for himself, for his kith and kin and for the larger society.

JOINT FAMILY :

Family based on blood relations extending over three or more generations - known as extended family- acquires a slightly different form of a joint family when this structural form is subject to certain cultural norms converting it into a corporate group. A joint family has vertical as well as horizontal extensions and has a bigger size than only vertically extended family. The main characteristic feature of the joint family is the indivisibility and common sharing of the property. The property belongs to the family. The family members have the obligations to maintain it and share the benefits of property commonly. Since this requires proper management and someone to be responsible for it, traditionally it is the eldest male member who has the right to manage the property and the responsibility to see that none is deprived of the benefits of the property. As the manager or the 'Karta' of the joint family, he also wields authority and enjoys the respect and the confidence of the other family members. A characteristic pattern of Hindus in India, it has developed as a philosophy of life where individualistic motives have to be suppressed in favour of the family interest. A joint family may also some times include distant kins. Not all members may have similar capacity and skill to work. This, at times, develops bickerings among the more active and therefore more productive members. It is here that the judicious role of the manager becomes important. The rule of distribution of work according to capacity and skill and disbursement of benefits according to the needs has made it as a source of social insurance for such members who are physically disabled, mentally abnormal or the victims of protracted illness. Their wives and children have not to suffer because of the disability of the bread winner. It is also characterised by a common kitchen and a common code of conduct for all the members. This family system has been compatible with agrarian background of Indian economy with predominantly male preference for many privileges, women enjoyed little of status or freedom in such a system.

With the advent of British rule in India, there have been certain changes which had a long term influence on this institution. The first and the foremost has been the western education which has brought in a value system in which individualism acquires the prime motive for all the behaviours and which also opened up the opportunities for the women in education and right in property etc. This was a severe blow on the prevailing philosophy of life which sustained the institution for a long time. Britishers also gradually started establishing industries which suited their economic interest. A number of urban centers were created around these industrial centers. There was mass scale exodus of people from rural joint families to grab these opportunities. Thus, industrialization and urbanization made erosions in the structure of the joint family so that the system is on the verge of collapse if not totally broken and set apart.

CASTE :

The term caste has been derived from the Portuguse *casta*, meaning race, lineage or pure stock, which is in turn derived from the Latin *castus*, meaning clean, pure or pious. It has been coined to refer to the traditional Hindu-based system of social organization in and around India. Thus 'caste' refers to the basic idea or notion or ideology of social stratification in Indian society. This is believed to have originated in the 2nd or 1st millenium B.C. and was largely in place by about 500 A.D.

In precise terms caste may be described as a "form of social stratification which involves a system of hierarchically ranked, closed, endogamous strata, the membership of which is ascribed, and between which contact is restricted and mobility is theoretically impossible. Although it reflects economic inequalities, by virtue of the occupations typically followed by, or permitted to, members, caste stratification is ultimately rooted in non-economic criteria. In it's purest form, in Hindu India, the caste principle is religious : Castes are ranked in accordance with the degree of 'ritual purity' ascribed to it's members and to their activities" (David Jary and Julia Jary in *Dictionary of Sociology*). Caste may be properly understood through two models viz. *Varna* model and *Jati* model.

Varna Model

The origin of caste (*Varna*) cannot be traced to an exact point of time or source. There are various theories which deal with the origin of caste system. The *Divine Origin Theory* explains the divine origin of caste system. It involves a certain amount of sacrament and thus it is believed that it is an arrangement made not by human beings, but by divinity. The *Purush Sukta* hymn of *Rigveda* tells us of the emergence of four *varnas* after the *Purusha* (Brahma) resorted to self-destruction so that a proper social order could come into existence. Thus, the Brahmins came out of the mouth, the Kshatriyas from the arms, the Vaishyas from the thighs and finally the Shudras from the feet of the primordial being, the *Mahapurush*. The *Racial Theory of Varna* has clear racial connotations. As the very term, *Varna* means skin colour, an important criterion of racial classification, this classificatory scheme suggests segregation of people according to their social affiliations. Several scholars like H.H. Risley agreed with this theory. But in the virtual absence of any scientific data or evidence like fossil record the racial theory suffers from several lacunae and unexplained areas. However, another view, the *guna* theory of the origin of *varna* makes some anthropological sense. It is based on the view that there are three basic gunas (charismatic endowments) found in the personality of each person. These are the *Sattva guna*, the *Rajguna* and the *Tamaguna*. The *Sattva guna* refers to the purity, lack of attraction towards worldly things and devotion to knowledge, the *rajguna* represents the steadfastness to truth, duty, justice and self-sacrifice for the larger interests of the society; the *tam guna* refers to obsession with worldly things, satisfaction of biological needs and hence beastly tendencies. It is believed that all these *guna* are present in each person but one of these predominates and hence becomes the chief marker of one's personality. Thus, the predominance of *Sattvik guna* entitles one to be a Brahmin, the *rajvik* a kshatriya and the *tamsik* a vaishya. Those who possess only *tamsik guna* were Shudras. Thus a Brahmin's duty was to acquire knowledge and preaching, a Kshatriya was entrusted with the job of administration and protecting and defending the land, the Vaishya was supposed to do cultivation, trade and commerce and a Shudra was obliged to serve the above three varnas. In hierarchical order the Brahmins occupied the highest place followed by the Kshatriyas, Vaishyas and the Shudras. Significantly, these groupings did not enjoy any ascribed status and as the *Vishnu Purana* tells us everyone is born as a Shudra and it is only one's *Karma* that entitles one to be a Brahmin or Vaishya or Shudra. It further implies that the *varna* system was not closed and inter-*varna* mobility was possible. During vedic times Shudras were not untouchables but they were merely a conglomeration or a multiplicity of artisan castes.

The work of Manu throws lot of light on the state of society of his times as well as the desired and ideal social order. It relates both to secular and sacredotal spheres of life. He prescribed, in well defined terms, the duties (*dharma*) such as *varna dharma*, *ashrama dharma*, *rajya dharma*, *grihya dharma* and so on. The Brahmins wrote a number of *dharma shastras* which may be described as important sociological treatises. For example marriages were also classified according to the varna scheme as *anuloma* i.e. in the natural order of castes, and *pratiloma*, i.e., against the natural order of castes. Under the *anuloma* form, a brahmin male could marry not only a brahmin woman, but a kshatriya, a vaishya or a shudra woman; a kshatriya apart from marrying a kshatriya woman, could also consider a vaishya or a shudra and a vaishya, apart from a vaishya woman, could also marry a shudra. *Anuloma* marriages though never preferred, were recognised and the offsprings treated as legitimate. But a *pratiloma* marriage, that is the marriage of a male from a lower caste to a female of a higher caste, was prohibited and condemned. But both *anuloma* and *pratiloma* were practised and sometimes new castes or mixed castes emerged leading to confusion in social hierarchy. Both of these forms of marriage also led to caste mobility.

Jati Model

In an honest and frank appraisal, M.N. Srinivas says that the varna model has produced a wrong and distorted image of caste. The varna model was an ideal form of Indian Social Stratification . It was more an ideal or desired form of social stratification rather than an actual one. In precise terms, it was a loose and broad categorization of Indian or Hindu society. Ideally speaking it had a definite hierarchy where the Brahmins occupied the top rung and the shudra the lowest in the ladder with untouchables having been placed outside it's pale. Some mobility was also allowed. But the later one i.e. *Jati* model has always been an ethnographic and empirical reality. When exactly the *Jati* model emerged is still a matter of debate among the social historians. But one thing is almost clear i.e. by Gupta period it had crystalized and people were living alongwith it.

With the emergence of the *Jati* model the system had become closed. Thus *jati* represented the watertight compartmentalization of society with it's definite rules. The morphology of the Hindu Caste (*Jati*) system can be described in terms of three key characteristics (Bougle, 1908) all of which are religiously underpinned by the religious values of purity (Dumont, 1970). In *Social Science Encyclopaedia*, J.P. Parry summarises the situation by saying that (1) there is a hierarchy of castes which is theoretically based on their relative degree of purity. As the purest of all, the Brahmins rank highest, and are in principle both distinct from and superior to the caste which actually wields politico-economic power, (2) since the pure can maintain their purity only if there are impure castes, to remove the pollution they inevitably incur by their involvement in the natural world, there is a division of labour between castes resulting their interdependence, (3) pollution is contagious, and a caste must therefore restrict it's contact with inferiors in order to maintain it's status. Thus, separation takes many forms, a rule of endogamy precluding marital alliances with inferiors, restrictions on commensality, the outcasting of those who transgress the rules lest they pollute the rest of the group, and the phenomenon of untouchability debarring physical contact between 'clean' and 'polluted' groups. If we analyse these three major features we get the following characteristics of the caste (*jati*) system:

(1) ***The Innate Nature :*** The membership of Jati is determined by birth. A man dies in the same caste in which he is born and it is his caste that determines his social status. The caste status is simply ascribed status.

(2) ***Endogamy :*** A strict endogamy is one of the most important features of *jati*. Every *jati* or sub-jati permits marriage within the group. The system has been so rigid that traditionally inter-caste marriages were prohibited. Even today endogamy is quite rigidly followed.

(3) ***Hierarchy :*** Because of fixed hierarchy what we see is a hierarchical social structure. A village or cluster of villages or a region maintains a definite hierarchy in which each jati's place is well defined. But the jati hierarchy unlike the varna hierarchy is local or regional in nature. It means that the place of a particular *jati* may be varying a bit from region to region while varna hierarchy is fixed throughout India. Thus in *Jati* hierarchy the place of Brahmins is predominant and the untouchable jatis are placed at the bottom. However, the jatis placed at the intermediate levels may be showing minor variations in the hierarchy.

(4) ***Commensality :*** Sharing or acceptance of food and water is governed by detailed rules. Severe restrictions are found in eating and social intercourse. Food has been divided into *Pucca* food (fried) and *Kuccha* food (boiled) and well defined rules are followed in the matters of who accepts from whom.

(5) ***Occupational Restrictions :*** Occupation of each caste is predetermined by birth and every caste is supposed to treat it's occupation as a religious duty.

(6) ***Disabilities and Privileges :*** The Brahmins and other higher castes (*dwija*, twice born) enjoy a number of privileges in religious and secular matters while the untouchables suffer from a number of social disabilities.

(7) ***Caste Councils :*** The existence of caste panchayats having authority to compel obedience from it's members is also an important feature of caste system. The violation of all sorts of taboos is dealt with by these caste councils. Using it's socio-political authority it can outcaste or excommunicate any of it's members.

Merits and Demerits of Caste System

Social scientists, over the years, have been discussing the positive and negative aspects or merits and demerits of the caste system. Following are some of the points discussed most frequently:

Merits :

(1) Social and psychological security

(2) Efficiency in occupations and security of occupational secrets

(3) Selection of spouse or life partner

(4) Controlled behaviour

(5) System of division of labour.

Demerits :

(1) Hinders economic development because of lack of occupational mobility.

(2) Exploitation and oppression of lower castes

(3) Religious conversions have taken place mainly because of highly exploitative, rigid, harsh and oppressive nature of caste system

(4) Untouchability

(5) Harmful to national unity

(6) Detrimental to the very essence of democracy

(7) Such hierarchies hamper social communication between different segments of society.

Ritual Aspect or Binary Opposition Between Pure/ Impure (Pollution)

1. The opposition between pure and impure has been regarded by Louis Dumont as the fundamental principle underlying the Hindu Caste System.
2. This principle is implicit in the three predominant features of the caste system which were systematically spelt out by Bougle and later endorsed by Dumont. According to Bougle the caste system comprises a series of hereditary groups (the socially relevant *jatis*) characterized by (*i*) 'hierarchy' or gradations according to ritual status; (*ii*) 'mutual repulsion', implying rules governing contact, ensuring their separation; and (*iii*) division of labour and consequent inter-dependence.
3. Dumont shows that the opposition between the pure and the impure is implicit in all the three attributes: in hierarchy because the pure and impure must be kept separate; and in the division of labour because pure and impure occupations have to be segregated.
4. Following from this, the caste system is viewed as a 'whole' which is founded on the necessary and hierarchical co-existence of the opposites (the pure and the impure). This represents a view point of caste according to which both the pure and the impure have their *rightful place* in the system and each has it's privileges and co-exists with the other.
5. One way of assigning rank to castes in terms of their relative purity and impurity is to study their attributes and accordingly order them in relation to one another.

The attributes of purity include features such as wearing sacred thread, veneration of cow, vegetarianism, teetotalism and prohibiting widow remarriage. Pollution is associated with human emissions, death, disrespect of cow and consumption of meat and alcohol, to mention the principal elements.

6. The attributes of purity and pollution discussed above may be used to identify the two broad extrems in the caste hierarchy — the Brahmins and the untouchables. But the precise determination of the highest and the lowest among Brahmins and untouchables respectively is conditioned by local interpretations of the pollution concept. Thus, while scavenging and beef eating would make a caste group untouchable almost anywhere, it may still be able to establish it's precedence over some other group through fine distinctions of behaviour. The fact that the empirical referants of the pollution concept are subject to local interpretations highlight the point that caste hierarchy when viewed as a specific phenomenon, is confined to a given local area. Hence caste (*jati*) hierarchy shows regional variations.

7. The tendency which results in the hierarchical arrangements of castes in a given locality is often replicated within a caste and leads to the grading of segments both in the same local community and over a wider territorial area.

8. The operation of local interpretations of pollution explains various regional differences in the evaluation and ranking of castes. However, even within a given locality, the multiplicity of attributional criteria and the necessity of evaluating them in relation to one another render it difficult to grade all the castes in a fixed hierarchical order.

9. Dumont attempts to show how these attributes may be used to establish a series of divisions, each more precise than the other, between superior and inferior castes. For example, the vegetarian castes may be placed above the non-vegetarian ones : among the vegetarians those who prohibit widow remarriage would be superior to

those who permit it. Similarly among the non-vegetarians further dichotomies may be established between beef eaters and non-beef eaters; and among the later still further gradations may be made between those who eat only mutton or birds and who eat pig (pork) raised by lower castes and fed by garbage. Dumont argues that such dichotomies, which establish distinctions of relative purity and impurity, reaffirm the importance of the hierarchical principle.

10. At the same time it is difficult to explain that any particular village hierarchy solely depends on the basis of attributional criteria. A vegetarian caste, in some cases, may actually rank below a non-vegetarian caste. It is also not clear how the various attributes of pollution combine together to form an unambiguous hierarchy of values. For example, are the attributes of diet more important than those of occupation? Among certain occupations, such as butchering goats, cutting hair and tapping toddy, which would be lowest?

11. Such difficulties led Mckim Marriott to propose an interactional theory of caste ranking based on intercaste relationships as manifested in the '*ritualized giving and receiving of food, and the giving and receiving of ritual services.*' He considers food transfers more decisive in establishing rank than the receiving of ritual services, but the two are connected since the services are paid for partly in food.

12. The circulation of food is one significant index of rank because a caste which receives more of the purer kinds of food than it gives to other caste groups may be regarded as the recipient of relatively more ritual honour in relation to the others. Following the same principle, a caste which receives more ritual services from other castes than it gives to them ranks higher; It is lower if it gives more ritual services than it receives or renders these to lower castes.

❑

19

Scheduled Castes and Other Backward Classes

The term 'SCHEDULED CASTE' has been in vogue for about half a century. The term appeared for the first time in the *Government of India Act* 1935. In April 1936, the British Government issued the *Government of India (Scheduled Castes) Order, 1936*, specifying certain castes and tribes as scheduled castes in the then provinces of Assam, Bengal, Bihar, Bombay, Central Provinces, Madras, Orissa, Punjab and United Provinces. Prior to that these castes were generally known as 'depressed classes'. The depressed classes were systematically categorised in the 1931 census. The list of 'scheduled castes' issued in 1936 was in continuation of earlier list of 'depressed classes'. The list drawn in 1950 was revised version of that list. After proclamation of the constitution these lists were notified by the President in accordance with the provision of Article 341 of the constitution. Meanwhile the term 'Harijan' continued in vogue for non-official purposes. The activists among the scheduled castes don't like the term and prefer the term *dalit* for themselves which, incidentally, means 'Depressed'.

Population and Distribution

The scheduled caste population constitutes 16.73% of the total population of India. This population may be divided into about one thousand castes with a number of names being synonymous. Some of these scheduled castes number several million members each. Some of the large scheduled castes are the Chamar (constituting about one fourth of the total population of the scheduled castes), Bhangi, Adi-Dravida, Pasi, Madiga, Dusadh, Mali, Parayan, Koli/Kori, Mahar, Adi-Karnataka, Namasudra, etc. Each has its own list of scheduled castes.

Following is the tabular description showing the position of the prominent states:

S. No.	State	No. of Scheduled Castes
1.	Karnataka	95
2.	Orissa	88
3.	Rajasthan	76
4.	Tamil Nadu	74
5.	Madhya Pradesh	60
6.	Maharashtra	60
7.	Uttar Pradesh	60
8.	West Bengal	60
9.	Andhra Pradesh	60

If one goes through the demography of the scheduled caste population, one comes across some important and interesting facts. For example, almost half of the total number of scheduled caste population inhabit five states of the Hindi speaking belt namely Uttar Pradesh (23.5 million), Bihar (10 million), Madhya Pradesh (7.3 million), Rajasthan (5.8 million) and Haryana (2.5 million). Among the southern states they are concentrated mainly in Tamil Nadu (8.8 million) and Andhra Pradesh (7.9 million), and in the East in West Bengal (12 million). Interestingly the highest ratio of the scheduled caste population in the total population is in Punjab (31%), closely followed by Himachal Pradesh (25%), West Bengal (24%), Uttar Pradesh (21%) and Haryana (19%). The bulk of the scheduled caste population (84%) live in rural areas as agricultural workers, share croppers and marginal farmers. The rate of literacy among them has been reported at 67%.

Decomposition of Scheduled Castes/Dalits: Internal Differentiation

Discussion on the dalits, in particular the atrocities and violence on their person and corporate entity, has generally tended to give the impression as though the entire dalit community is of the same type and reflects the similar characteristics. This is certainly not true. The dalit is a grouping that comprises of a basket of communities that were pursuing a large number of occupations in the Indian society. While it is indeed true that they all shared certain types of debilities, they were quite different in terms of their ritual sufferings. They are not a homogenous group. There is rank ordering even among them on the basis of ritual status. The example of the scavengers, vividly portrayed by Bhagwan Das in his book, Main Bhangi Hoon (2017), dramatically shows that this particular community was treated as the untouchable even among the dalits. Nor is the example of ill treatment of the Bhangis by the dalits themselves the only one of its type. That there exists a ritual hierarchy even among the Dalits is demonstrated by P Muthaiah's (2009) study of the dalit hierarchies in Andhra Pradesh. His study shows that the Malas and the Madigas had two different ritual hierarchies among the dalits in Andhra Pradesh. The Madigas and Malas, who constitute roughly 14 and 12 per cent of states' SC population, are two major castes within the larger grouping of the dalits in the state. The notions of purity and pollution have continued to determine hierarchies even among the dalits in this state. Not only that, it has continued to play a similar role in determining the life chances of these dalit groups in the secular sphere of sharing reservation benefits under affirmative action. The Madigas have been deprived of their due share in the reserved sphere of education, employment and politics as the Malas have been cornering reservation benefits disproportionate to their population. These new inequalities among the dalit castes have strengthened dalit hierarchies in Andhra Pradesh-Telangana. The AP case study is only a more dramatized example of internal differentiation among the dalits. It is present in almost every other state in varying degrees.Same is the case of Chamar caste in Uttar Pradesh where they dominate in terms of their share in reservation benefits.

There is second type of differentiation that has emerged among the dalits as a result of their endeavours in education, employment -particularly through the reservation route in government bureaucracies-and other fields such as literary pursuits. Those who have received education and joined the government positions have, following in the footsteps of upper castes, improved their life styles. In doing so, a large number of them have left their native places and settled down in urban areas, where ritual distance is somewhat insignificant if not altogether absent. This change of occupation, employment, place of residence and acquisition of new life style has, in turn, produced a social distance between them and their brethren still living in the rural areas and pursuing their traditional callings. The Dalit Panthers have described the former as the 'Dalit Brahmins', who are not much concerned with the unfortunate fate of those left behind. Others have called this development as the emergence of 'creamy layer' among them. In states like AP and Tamil Nadu this internal differentiation has caused fissures in the solidarity of the dalit mobilization against repression.

Identity assertion of single SC communities is quite often dependent on their numerical strength. The SCs constitute a large group in which the population of the majority of the constituent large number of communities is quite small. This has led to domination of their organizations by just a few dominant ones. There are classic rivalries between/among some of the leading SC communities in states like UP (Chamar vs. Pasi), Andhra Pradesh (Mala vs. Madiga) and Maharashtra (Mahars vs. non-Mahars). These rivalries have quite predictably undermined the overall dalit solidarity.

From Untouchables to the Dalits: The Process of Identity Formation: The scheduled castes had to pass through various stages of identity formation. In an incisive narration of the journey HS Verma(ibid) says that two sets of opinions exist among the scholars on the issue of dalit identity formation and assertion. One of these argues that the driving force behind the lower caste consciousness is to get recognition within the ambit of 'great tradition'. To achieve this end, they say that the dalits have selected and applied three consequential processes: construction of a counter culture, parallel to the 'great tradition'; creation of a space by invoking pity and sympathy for themselves within the psychic parameters of 'great tradition'; resistance to the ongoing oppression and exploitation. The second set of scholars (i.e., Kancha Illaiah, Kalpana Kannabiran, Anupama Rao) argues that the identity formation among the dalits is to show that they have their own history, traditions, and practices which are diametrically opposite to those of the Hindu religion and that the dalits are pursuing aggressively recognition and respect at par with others as a separate group, not as a part of Hinduism or for that matter other religions. Some segments of Dalits (i.e., Sikhs) have indeed formed their own theological traditions and practices. This process has in fact been termed as a process of 'Dalitisation' by Kancha Illaiah. Increasingly, empirical evidence is indicating that the majority of Dalits are veering round to accept the second viewpoint. The process while unfolding itself displays different forms in different theatres such as Maharashtra (first Republican Party, later Dalit Panthers), Bihar (nexus with the Naxalites and extremist groups), Tamil Nadu (offering tacit support to some extremist elements - selectively but clandestinely- and in main – openly participating in political field by establishing their single caste parties after disillusionment with the practitioners of Dravidian nationalism on the Dalit question), and Punjab (establishment of several sects, Deras, and an alternate view of Sikhism). Interestingly enough, resistance and struggle have generally been more visible among the Dalits of the Hindu order than the non-Hindu religions.

Anupama Rao (2009) argues that caste is a specific form of embodiment, universally salient as the process of inequality. This explains why caste has grown rather than diminished in significance as democracy has taken roots in India, producing a form of politics that forefronts collective rights and group emancipation rather than individual autonomy. A radical view of caste is to view it as a historical form of violence and inequality. Several earlier researchers like Eleanor Zeallot, Eugene F Irshchick and Gail Omvedt have written on Dalit identity formation. But these studies were period analyses and much water has flown down the rivers Krishna, Kaveri, Ganga and Yamuna since then. Dalit identity formation process has continued to unfold itself in myriad forms right to this day in different parts of the country. The most up-to-date, authentic and authoritative analysis of the history of transformation of the untouchables to Dalits is provided by Anupama Rao (ibid). According to her, this process is a history beset with reversals, failures, and contradictions produced by caste subalterns' engagement with the colonial, nationalist, and upper caste power. She traces the paradoxical manner in which an identity predicated on a future outside or beyond caste was conceived with humiliation and suffering as its enabling grounds. It is a narrative of how a new political collectivity was constituted by resignifying the Dalit's negative identity within caste structure into a positive political value.

Socio-Economic Problems and Disabilities

Since the very creation of the scheduled castes is the product of highly discriminatory and sometimes inhuman nature of the functioning of the caste system, one cannot understand the problems being faced by the scheduled castes and suggest the remedial measures required without having a sound understanding of the caste system. The idea of ritual purity/pollution manifested through untouchability is the corner stone of the highly discriminating nature of the caste system. An entire segment of population was assigned 'unclean' occupations like scavenging, flaying, tanning, etc. and converted into untouchables. To be untouchable did not mean only that his physical touch was to be shunned or avoided due to ritual reasons; it was to enter a fatal and futile universe totally impervious to hope. One problem led to the other and one social disability created another. For example is a section of the society is barred from entering a sacred place like temple and in the traditional set up if the formal education is imparted within the temple premises this section of society shall definitely be deprived of education. If a section of the society is forbidden to own land by force of custom, it will be without any economic backbone. Moreover in an agrarian society where all powers emanate from the ownership of land, landlessness forms a vicious cycle of deprivation. If a section of society is prohibited from touching/using gold, it cannot ward off an economic crisis by mortgaging or disposing off a gold ornament; it will be clearly vulnerable to all sorts of exploitation. To top it all, because of reasons of ritual pollution it may not be getting the services of washerman, barber, priests etc.

Among the main social-economic disabilities the bulk of the scheduled caste population has been suffering from (i) lack of freedom to choose occupation (ii) landlessness (iii) forced labour (iv) lack of access to education (v) segregated housing and (vi) lack of freedom to exercise political rights may be enumerated. Obviously, the mother of all these is the enforced notion of ritual purity-ritual pollution, the resultant obnoxious practice of untouchability and the perpetuation of all these by a highly discriminatory social system. The main socio-economic problems afflicting the bulk of the scheduled caste populations are:

(i) chronic indebtedness and bonded labour
(ii) landlessness/land alienation
(iii) lack of education
(iv) lack of productive assets
(v) forced labour and prostitution
(vi) lack of 'minimum wages'
(vii) child labour, etc.

Because of the traditional landlessness, chronic indebtedness has been a concomitant problem with the scheduled castes. Those who got some land after independence as a result of Zamindari abolition and the ensuing land reforms have to part with the land as a result of land alienation. Whether landless or marginal farmer the lot of an average scheduled caste person in the rural areas has been pitiable because his existence is characterized by all sorts of deprivations and exploitation. Education takes a back seat in such a scenario. Obviously, when children play important role in family economy, sending them to school means depriving oneself of their contribution. In such a situation opening schools and providing free education may not bear any fruits because of lack of takes of such amenities. Wherever feudal tendencies persist and the agricultural workers are not organised (as in the case throughout the country) forced labour (*begaar*) or very low wages has been a normal phenomenon. Because of a number of factors the Jajmani system even in rural areas has been crumbling during the last four decades. It has made important bearing on the inter-caste relations and caste equations in rural India.

The adoption of laws meant to protect the rights of the scheduled castes, the realization of socio-economic measures in their interests and the atmosphere of support to the just and lawful demands of the scheduled castes that was created as a result of the work done by some government bodies, democratic and left organizations and the progressive press have led to further activisation of both socio-economic and political life of the scheduled castes.

Constitutional Safeguards

When our founding fathers sat down to frame the Constitution for free India they took care to see that the protection and safeguards for the Scheduled Castes especially, or by way of the general rights of citizens was totally ensured with the object of promotion of their educational and economic interests and of removing their social disabilities. The important articles in the constitution which are intended to protect and promote the interests of the scheduled castes are as follows:

1. Article 15(4) says that nothing in this article or in clause (2) of Article 29 shall prevent the state from making any special provision for the advancement of any socially and educationally backward classes of citizens or for the scheduled castes and scheduled tribes.
2. Article 16(4) states that nothing in this Article shall prevent the state from making any provision for the reservation of appointment or posts in favour of any backward class of citizens, which, in the opinion of the state, is not adequately represented in the services under the state.
3. Abolition of untouchability and forbidding of its practice in any form is the basis of Article 17 of the Constitution. (It is being dealt with separately in this chapter because of its implications of far reaching importance).
4. Article 25b deals with throwing open, by law, of Hindu religious institutions of public character to all classes and sections of Hindus.
5. Article 15(2) deals with removal of any disability, liability, restriction or condition with regard to access to shops, public restaurants, hotels and places of public entertainment or use of wells, tanks bathing ghats, roads and places of public resort maintained wholly or partially out of state funds or dedicated to the use of general public.
6. Forbidding or any denial of admission to educational institutions maintained by the state or receiving grant out of state funds-Article 29(2).
7. Article 46 states that the state shall promote with special care the educational and economic interests of the weaker sections of the people and in particular, of the scheduled castes and scheduled tribes, and shall protect them from social injustice and all forms of exploitation.
8. Under Article 330 and 332 seats are reserved in Parliament and state legislative assemblies for the

scheduled castes except in the tribal areas of Assam, Nagaland, Meghalaya, Arunachal Pradesh and Mizoram.

9. Under Article 338, a special officer (designated as Commissioner for Scheduled Castes and Scheduled Tribes) is to be appointed to investigate all matters, relating to safeguards provided under the constitution and report to the President upon the working of those safeguards. With 65th amendment of the Constitution Article 338 stands amended and from 1992 the special officer's post has been substituted by the National Commission for Scheduled Castes and Scheduled Tribes, and now there is an exclusive Scheduled Castes Commission.

10. Article 341 empowers the President to declare a caste, race or tribe as Scheduled Caste.

Legislation against Untouchability and Protection of Civil Rights

For enlarging the scope and making the penal provisions more stringent the Untouchability (offences) Act, 1955, had been comprehensively amended by the Untouchability (offences) Amendment and Miscellaneous Provision Act, 1976, which came into force from 19 November, 1976. With this amendment, the Principal Act has been renamed as Protection of Civil Rights Act, 1955. The act provides for penalties for preventing any person on the grounds of untouchability, from enjoying the-rights accruing on account of abolition of untouchability. Enhanced penalties/punishments have been provided for subsequent offences.

Under the provision of Section 8 of the Representation of Peoples Act, 1951, a person who is convicted of an offence under the act is disqualified from contesting elections to Parliament and State Legislature for a period of six years commencing from the date of such conviction.

The PCR Act, 1955, is administered by the State Government. Under the provision of Section 15A (4) of the act, the Government also places every years, before each House of Parliament, an annual report on the working of the provisions of Section 15A of the act.

Measures to Check Atrocities against Scheduled Castes

With a view to effectively deal with crime against Scheduled Castes and Scheduled Tribes and to tone-up administrative machinery to tackle this vital issue, comprehensive guidelines containing precautionary, preventive, punitive and rehabilitative measures exist which States/UTs have to follow. Still these communities continue to be vulnerable and atrocities are committed against them in one form or the other. In order that Scheduled Castes and Scheduled Tribes are fully protected from atrocities, Government enacted the Scheduled Castes and the Scheduled Tribes (Prevention of Atrocities) Act, 1989. The act came into force from 30th January, 1990. It specified the offences which are considered as atrocities' and provides for different punishments for commission of the same. The act also envisages preventive measures and states have to evolve schemes, among other things, for economic and social rehabilitation of such victims.

Other Backward Classes

The Constitution of India recognizes three categories of backward segments of Indian society i.e., Scheduled Castes, Scheduled Tribes and Other Backward Classes. The third segment, that is, 'the other backward classes' carried lot of ambiguity. But it was generally assumed that this category was meant to include the whole of middle bands of caste and communities situated above the Scheduled Castes and Scheduled Tribes excluding only prominently well-advantaged groups at the top. In simpler and popular terms, the *agde* (forwards) are the *dwija* castes like the Brahmins and the Kshtriyas but the Kayasthas (north India), Vaids (Bengal) and Nayars (Kerala) have also joined this division on the strength of their economic, political and bureaucratic power. The *Pichhade* (backwards) are lower castes, other than untouchables, who do not exercise control over sources of power—political, social and economic. The Scheduled castes and Scheduled tribes are clearly listed in the constitution. The non-dwija, non-scheduled castes not listed in the constitutional order are the OBCs. They comprise a little over 3,700 castes in all. In the absence of Census enumeration of OBCs, we have estimates only. The Mandal Commission estimated it at around 52% while the National Sample Survey Organization (NSSO) put it around 41% but various organizations and NGOs claim their population somewhere around 65% of the total Indian population.

The framers of the constitution, instead of using the term 'Castes', applied the term 'Classes' for this segment of backward population. There may be several reasons for this. First, they followed the old historical process (whereby the term 'depressed classes' was used even for the untouchable castes, now scheduled castes). Secondly, the word 'Caste' sounded obscurantist and outdated and the torchbearers of modern India wanted to banish this word from new and modern India. And thirdly, the usage might have created problems *vis-a-vis* the placement of the non-Hindu counterparts of the other backward castes in the list. This is certainly true in the case of Muslim community which, despite embracing the egalitarian ideology of Islam, has also developed caste like stratification under the social impact of the Hindu society.

The non-dwija intermediate castes or lower castes other than scheduled castes have also been victim of caste system. Most of these have been small peasants or artisans. They also come under the category of disadvantaged groups suffering in poverty. For the peasant segment of OBCs agriculture is the chief means of economy. But they have little land except for castes like Yadavas and Kurmis in parts of Uttar Pradesh and Bihar and such other castes in different parts of the country. Quite a substantial number of OBCs in different parts of the country have no land at all. The second category of OBCs are mainly artisans and their plight is really miserable. Because of growing industrialization, their traditional skills and crafts are in ruined state. The socio-economic condition of weavers, potters, carpenters, fishermen/boatmen, blacksmiths, vegetable vendors, butchers and a host of other castes in village India is there for all to see. Educational deprivation has worsened the situation further. The organized Industrial Sector enjoys subsidized credit, infra-structural support and other advantages at the cost of the tax-payer, the handicrafts and artisans hardly get all these benefits. The net result of this state of affairs is that they are always trapped in the vicious cycle of poverty and deprivation. As a number of surveys and studies in different parts of the country indicate that the OBCs have little access to employment and education, enjoy low rates of literacy and are trapped in indebtedness. The high incidence of indebtedness is attributed to illiteracy, poverty, social customs etc.

In order to help the OBCs come up in socioeconomic development, the first Backward Classes Commission was set up by a Presidential Order under Article 340 of the Constitution of India on January 29th, 1953 under the chairmanship of Kakasaheb Kalelkar. It submitted it's report on March 30th, 1955. After sorting out the facts the commission formulated the following criteria for identifying socially and educationally backward classes:

(i) Low social position in the traditional caste hierarchy of Hindu society.

(ii) Lack of general educational advancement among the major sections of a caste or community.

(iii) Inadequate or no representation in Government services.

(iv) Inadequate representation in the field of trade, commerce and industry.

The commission could not present an unanimous report. The majority of members including the chairman were opposed to the view of linking caste with backwardness. They were also opposed to the reservation of posts on the basis of caste. While rejecting the main recommendations of this commission the central government ultimately took a decision that neither all India list of backward classes should be drawn up nor any reservation made in the central government service for any group of backward classes other than scheduled castes and scheduled tribes. However, the central government informed the state governments that they were free to draw their respective lists of backward classes on the basis of criteria worked out by them and take whatever further action they deemed necessary in the matter. Consequently, a number of state governments set up their own commissions or committees for defining criteria for backwardness and recommending measures for its removal. So far eighteen states and union territories have set up commissions and have notified lists of *Other Backward Classes* for the grant of various educational, employment and other benefits. These are Andhra Pradesh, Bihar, Gujarat, Jammu & Kashmir, Karnataka, Kerala, Maharashtra, Punjab, Uttar Pradesh, Tamil Nadu, Assam, Delhi, Haryana, Himachal Pradesh Meghalaya, Orissa, Pondicherry and Rajasthan. The Last to fall in line was West Bengal.

The new commission, the Second Backward Classes Commission is popularly called the Mandal Commission. It's chairman B.P. Mandal was appointed by a Presidential order under Article 340 of the Indian Constitution on 20th December, 1978. It was required:

(i) to determine the criteria for defining the socially and educationally backward classes;

(ii) to recommend steps to be taken for the advancement of the socially and educationally backward classes of citizens so identified;

(iii) to examine the desirability or otherwise of making provision for the reservation of appointments or posts in favour of such backward classes of citizens which are not adequately represented in Public Services and posts in connection with the affairs of the Union or of any State; and

(iv) to present to the President a report by setting out the facts as found by them and making such recommendations as they think proper.

The commission was required to submit it's report by 31st December, 1980. In view of the enormity of its task and paucity of time at it's disposal, the commission worked with speed. To begin with, it conducted a countrywide socio-educational survey, covering 405 districts, with the help of the Bureau of Economics and Statistics of various states. The data gathered from the Survey were computerized and thirty-one primary tables were generated from this data in respect of each State and Union Territory. Then, on the basis of these tables, 11 indicators or criteria for social and educational backwardness were derived under three heads- Social, Educational and Economic. These are as follows:

A. Social

(i) Castes/classes considered as socially backward by others.

(ii) Castes/classes which mainly depend on manual labour for their livelihood.

(iii) Castes/classes where at least 25% females and 10% males above the state average get married at an age below 17 years in rural areas and at least 10% females and 5% males do so in urban areas.

(iv) Castes/classes where participation of females in work is at least 25% above the state average.

B. Educational

(v) Castes/classes where the number of children in age group of 5-15 years who never attended school is at least 25% above the state average.

(vi) Castes/classes where the rate of student drop-out in the age group of 5-15 years is at least 25% above the state average.

(vii) Castes/classes amongst whom the proportion of matriculates is at least 25% below the state average.

C. Economic

(viii) Castes/classes where the average value of family assets is atleast 25% below the state average.

(ix) Castes/classes where the number of families living in *Kuccha* houses is atleast 25% above the state average.

(x) Castes/classes where the source of drinking water is beyond half a kilometer for more than 50% of the households.

(xi) Castes/classes where the number of households having taken consumption loan is atleast 25% above the state average.

Weightage was given to the indicators in each group for evaluation. The social indicators were given 3 points each, educational indicators, 2 points each and economic indicators one point each. This came to a total score of 22 points. All these 11 indicators were then applied to each one of the castes covered by the survey in each state. The castes obtaining a minimum of 11 points on this scale were listed as socially and educationally backward. Thus, the Commission identified 3,743 castes as backward. After this, the commission computed the strength of the OBCs which was little over 52% of the total population of the country.

A Research Planning Team of sociologists-anthropologists was also constituted to help the commission in the identification of the deserving backward castes. This team, consisting of some top sociologists and anthropologists of the country, in order to gauge social-educational backwardness of the castes in the present times, suggested a number of ways and means and used existing studies/literature. It also emphasized upon the importance of trends of upward mobility of a number of traditionally backward castes before reaching any firm conclusions. The team further suggested that while designing empirical studies extent of prevalence of the following variables may be taken into account.

(a) Socio-ritual services extended by other ethnic groups

(b) 'Low' status of occupations of the category concerned.

(c) 'Low' self-evaluation compared to other ethnic groups in the region (Gram Panchayat/Block/Taluqa).

(d) Literacy rates in relation to other neighbouring groups in Gram Panchayat/Block/Taluqa.

(e) Occupation requiring investment of child labour (upto 15 years).

(f) Economic levels of castes and communities.

(g) Representation in public or private sector services or in profession.

Besides the research planning team an expert panel was also constituted consisting of sociologists, political scientists and geographers. When the Mandal Commission submitted it's report containing a number of recommendations of far reaching importance, some of these social scientists disowned the findings and recommendations on the ground that the criteria, modus operandi and variables suggested by them were not employed by the commission while finalizing the findings and recommendations.

Undertaking this massive exercise, the Commission came out with a number of recommendations, of which some were found most important for upliftment of the socioeconomic conditions of the OBCs:

(i) The OBCs are not properly represented in public services and hence they should be accommodated there through reservations.

(ii) There is a legal obligation to keep the reservations under Article 15(4) and 16(4) of the constitution, below 50%, so the reservation should be 27%.

(iii) Special educational facilities designed a upgrading the cultural environment of the OBC students should be created in a phased manner in selected areas containing high concentrations of OBCs.

(iv) Special emphasis should be placed on vocational training of the students belonging to the OBCs, separate coaching facilities should be provided in technical and professional institutions for them to enable them to catch up with the students from open quota.

(v) Special programmes for upgrading the skills of village artisans should be prepared and subsidised loans from financial institutions granted to them for *setting* up small-scale industries.

(vi) To promote the participation of OBCs in the industrial and business life of the country, all state governments should create a separate network of financial and technical institutions.

(vii) Under the existing scheme of production relations, Backward Classes comprising mainly small land holders, tenants, agricultural labour, village artisans etc., are heavily dependent on the rich peasantry for their sustenance. In view of this, OBCs continue to remain in mental and material bondage of the dominant castes and classes. Unless these production relations are radically altered through structural changes and progressive land reforms implemented rigorously all over the country, OBCs will never become truly independent. In view of this, highest priority should be given to radical land reforms by all the states.

Through the Memorandum of Action, vide it's circular issues on 13th August, 1990, the Govt. of India accepted the recommendations of the Mandal Commission. This was followed by violent and sustained movement by different sections of Indian society against the acceptance of Mandal Commission Report by the government of India. Writs were filed in different courts and after prolonged hearings the Supreme Court of India decided in favour of the recommendations and held these constitutionally valid excluding the so called 'creamy layer' of the socially and educationally Backward Classes (SEBC). In pursuance of the Supreme Court verdict, an expert committee under the chairmanship of Justice R.N. Prasad, Former Judge, Patna High Court was set up for specifying the criteria for identification of Socially Advanced Persons among the Socially and Educationally Backward Classes. This expert committee submitted it's report on 10th March, 1993. The Government of India accepted the criteria formulated by this expert committee and announced a reservation of 27% of the vacancies in Civil Posts and Services in the Government of India for SEBCs subject to the exclusion of the socially advanced persons/sections known as the 'Creamy Layer'. Thus, reservation was applied to all vacancies for which recruitment commenced from September 8, 1993.

Creamy Layer

The rule of exclusion of 'Creamy Layer' is applicable to son(s) and daughter(s) of

- Persons holding constitutional positions;
- parents either of whom is a Class-I Officer;
- parents both of whom are class II officers;
- parents either or both of whom is or are in the rank of colonel and above in the Army or hold equivalent positions - in the Navy, Air Force and the Para Military Forces;
- Families owning irrigated land which is equal to or more than 85% of the ceiling in term of irrigated area as laid down by the State Land Ceiling Laws;
- Persons having gross annual income of Rs. 1 Lakh or above or possessing wealth above the exemption limit as prescribed in the Wealth Tax Act for a period of three consecutive years.

These criteria have been revised from time to time.

Income from salaries or agricultural land shall not be clubbed. The benefit of reservation is extended, in the first phase, to the castes and communities which are common to the lists of the Mandal Commission Report as well as the State Government's lists.

OBCs among Non-Hindu Communities

Since the caste system with all its concomitants have been replicated by Muslims, Sikhs, Christians and Buddhists their backward sections have also been included in the list of *OBCs* in Mandal Commission. After giving a good deal of thought to the obvious problems of categorization, the commission has evolved the following and ready criteria for identifying non-Hindu OBCs:

(i) All untouchables converted to any non-Hindu religion; and

(ii) Such occupational communities which are known by the name of their traditional hereditary occupation and whose Hindu counterparts have been included in the list of Hindu *OBCs*.

(Examples: *Dhobi, Teli, Dheemar, Nai, Gujar, Kumhar, Lohar, Darzi, Badhai,* etc.)

Muslim OBCs as Ethnographic Categories: A Brief Overview

It is now historically established that most of the Muslims in India did not come from Arabia or other regions from where the message of Islam came. The earliest phase of Islam in India was represented by Muslim traders and nomadic Sufi saints who were instrumental in attracting the oppressed and exploited lowest strata of Hindu society into the fold of Islam. Making a very interesting and significant observation on the transformation of a lower Hindu castes into a lower Muslim castes. Eijaz Ali (1997) reveals that ,"Most of the religious conversion among the Hindus occurred in 'Harijan' castes and not from such backward castes as Yadav, Kurmi or Koeri. The converted castes/ biradaris changed their names from Julaha to Momin, Khatik to Kunjra, Pasi to Dhuniya, Chamar to Qasai and so on. But the names of occupations and structure of settlements still provide enough evidence of this phenomenon. Julaha are found in both (Hindu and Muslim) communities, Kunjra are still known as Khatik in some regions. Qasab or Qasai (butchers) have come from the Chamar caste. The fact of the matter is that it is the Chamars who had a great expertise in skinning and butchering. Those who embraced Islam discovered that the dead animal was forbidden and then they started butchering live animals except pig. They were already expert in other related nuances. Even today, at several places, the settlements of Chamars and Qasai are adjacent to each other" (Translated from Hindi).

When we look at the occupationally specialized backward castes of both Hindus and Muslims we can identify three categories. This has also been substantiated by Ghaus Ansari (1960) and others:

(i) Castes which are now entirely Muslim.

(ii) Castes which have larger Muslim than Hindu sections.

(iii) Castes which have larger Hindu than Muslim sections.

In the first category come those occupational castes which are now entirely Muslim, their corresponding Hindu castes either do not exist, or if they exist, they have altogether different names. Some such castes are Atishbaz (firework maker), Bhand (jester), Bhishti (water carrier), Gaddi (grazier), Mirasi (musician and singers), Qasab (butcher), Momin Julaha (Muslim weaver), etc.

In the second category, which have larger Muslim than Hindu share, come castes such as Darzi (tailor) Dhuniya (cotton carder), Kunjra or Kabariya (green grocers), Manihar (bangle/ bracelet maker), Saiqalgar (metal sharpner) and Rangrez (dyer and cloth printer).

The third category may contain those castes which have a larger Hindu than Muslim share. In this category of clean occupational castes come Kumhar (potter), Nai or Hajjam (barber), Teli (oil presser), Dhobi (washerman), etc. The Muslim Bhangi/Mehtar/Lal Begia (sweepers and scavengers/sanitary workers) constitute perhaps, the only untouchable section of the Muslim population.

A significant aspect of the occupational castes among the Muslims is the disappearance of certain caste groups due to social or techno-economic change. The Rangrez (dyer and cloth printer), Bhatiyara (innkeeper) and Saiqalgar (metal sharpner) have almost disappeared as social units.

The Peoples of India Project conducted by the Anthropological Survey of India, gives brief but rich and reliable ethnographic accounts of all the castes and communities of India including the Muslim OBCs.

A notable fact about the Muslim OBCs, especially the relatively larger caste groups, is that though some members may have moved out of the traditional occupations, most still follow their forefather's. This lack of occupational mobility has been detrimental, yet it has another dimension which is equally important. Like their counterparts in the Hindu population they have been hardworking from the beginning. Many of the enterprising members of different caste groups made the best of their professions and attained prosperity. The Ansari and Qureshi of Uttar Pradesh and Rajasthan are the obvious examples. Some other artisan groups among them who upgraded their technology and adopted new marketing strategies and showed competitive entrepreneurial skills also prospered such as the artisans/entrepreneurs of Meerut, Moradabad, Aligarh and Ferozabad from western Uttar Pradesh and Bhadohi and Varanasi in eastern Uttar Pradesh. Yet, at the same time we find a vast multitude of masses living in impoverished conditions in rural as well as the urban areas of the country. These 'technological communities' of India and their Hindu counterparts deserve a better deal from the society and the government.

❑

20

Impact of Buddhism, Jainism, Islam and Christianity on Indian Society

India occupies a unique place in the world community. It is the home of the followers of all the major religious ideologies of the world viz; Hinduism, Buddhism, Jainism, Christianity, Judaism, Islam and Zorostrianism. All of these influenced Indian Society in varying degrees. This narration shall, however, be confined to the impact of Jainism, Buddhism, Islam and Christianity and especially of Islam which had a profound impact in various spheres of life of Indian Society.

Jainism and Buddhism :

It is popularly believed that both Jainism and Buddhism are, fundamentally, offshoots from ancient Hinduism. In terms of historical antiquity Jainism is a little older than Buddhism because Mahavira, the founder of Jainism, was an older contemporary of Budha. Mahavira's period is popularly believed to be between 599-527 BC and Budha's is 560-480 BC.

The ethical idealism of Jainism occupies the central place in any description of it's impact on Indian Society. It has contributed significantly towards the strengthening of ethical life and moral virtues. Jainism stand for austerity - both external and internal - to shut the influx of evil. In the scheme of external austerity come such things as begging, fasting and lack of fetishism while humility, service to humanity, acquisition of knowledge, meditation, penances and other values come under the later. Instead of esoteric and complex ideas Jainism has laid down a simple ethical code for the people. Among the essence of Jainism the observance of the principles viz. *Satya*(truth), *asteya* (non-stealing), *brahmacharya* (non-adultery), and *aparigraha* (non-possession) stand prominent. In the Jain terminology the observance of these morals are virtues known as *anuvarta. Ahimsa* (non-violence, peace) occupies the pivotal position in Jainism. It preaches kindness to not only human society but other forms of life too. This gave rise to strict and puritan vegetarianism. Both the lay persons or believers (*Shravakta*) and the ascetic (*Yati*) are supposed to be bound by certain vows. These are cultivation of right state of mind, regular practice of meditation, observance of fasts on the eighth and fourteenth day of moon's waxing and waning period and confession of faults and the consequent penance. Intoxication of any kind is strictly prohibited in Jainism.

In the field of public service, construction of *dharmashalas* (rest houses, inns), is widely acknowledged. In the field of fine arts their rock cut architecture, temple architecture and painting stand out as significant contributions. Because of several factors such as the orthodoxy of Jainism, it's affinity to Brahmanism, it's non-missionery spirit, and virtual absence of hostility with other rival faiths Jainism still flourishes in Indian Society despite the fact that like other religious ideologies it has also imbibed a number of distortions.

Gautam Budha was a younger contemporary to Mahavira. His earlier name was Sidhartha and he had a spiritual and humanistic outlook since his childhood. The religious movement espoused by him - Buddhism - gave the greatest jolt to the orthodox Brahmanism. Buddhism exercised profound influence in shaping the various aspects of Indian Society. It's impact in socio-cultural, religious and political spheres cannot be negated. Buddhism developed a popular religion, without any complicated, elaborate and unintelligible rituals requiring necessarily a priestly class. This was one of the reasons for its mass appeal. The ethical code of Buddhism is also relatively simple based on charity, purity, self sacrifice, truthfulness and control over passions. It laid great emphasis on love, equality and non-injury (non-violence). It is true that the Upanishads, too, had highlighted these virtues before the rise of Buddhism but credit goes to Buddhism for raising public morality to those heights never witnessed before. It became an article of faith for the followers of Buddhism. But more importantly Buddhism laid emphasis on the value that man is the architect of his own destiny, not any God or gods. There is a great element of individuality in Buddhism and it is devoid of any elaborate idea of God.

Although, Buddhism could never dislodge Brahmanism from it's high pedestal it certainly jolted it and inspired institutional changes in Indian Society. Rejecting the caste system and it's concommitant evils, violent rituals based on animal sacrifices, pilgrimae, fasting and conservation, it preached total equality. In the Budhist religious system gods and godesses, fatalism, previous birth and movement of planets are not believed to be responsible for man's present plight. It exhorts people to seek answers from this world. Thus '*this worldliness*' rather '*that worldliness*' should be the basis of man's quest for seeking answers of the unknown. Compassion, equality between all human beings including gender equality, protection of all life forms and welfare of all tried to bind the entire society into one. Promotion of social equality and social justice helped Buddhism cross the frontiers of Indian sub-continent and become a world religion. The impact of Budhist thought may be seen also in our foreign policy (*Panchsheel* and non-alignment), national integration, mutual cooperation, peace efforts, Mahatma Gandhi's philosophy of non-violence, upliftment of weaker sections and welfare of scheduled castes and depressed classes(*dalits*) and tribal population. Since Buddhism identified ignorance as the root cause of sufferings, it laid great emphasis on acquisition of knowledge. Promotion of democracy and democratic values is yet another contribution of Buddhism to Indian society. Budhist *sanghs* and *maths* promoted democratic conduct and in the course of time it's impact was felt in many Hindu *maths* and religious institutions.

In the field of education Buddhism tried to make education practical, action oriented and geared towards social welfare. Most of the ancient India's universities such as Nalanda, Taxila, Vikrampur, Vikramshila, Sompuri, and others are products of Buddhism. A free quest for the acquisition of knowledge in Buddhism produced such eminent scholars as Dignang, Ashvadhosh, Nagarjun, Vasumitra, Charak, Matrachet, Dharmtrat and similar ones of highest order. The flag of independent India carries the picture of Ashoka's wheel and the national emblem has been adopted from Buddhism. Buddhism also popularised the Indian vernaculars and thus promoted respect for different languages and dialects. Undoubtedly, Buddhism has exercised a great humanizing and philanthropic influence on Indian Society.

Islam :

The advent of Islam in India may be traced back to seventh century AD immediately after it's emergence in Arabia as a major religion. The word *Islam* has been derived from a root word which means "surrendering oneself to God". Thus, the true Muslim is supposed to submit to God's will and obey his Command and live at peace with his fellow men. The emergence of Islam revolutionised the Arab world and influenced all religions and territories where it could enter. Writing on the socio-historical role of Islam, Harbans Mukhiya (1969) rightly comments that when Muhammed preached the doctrine of one god in polytheistic Arabia - there is no God except

God - he was suggesting a great social change. For the concept of one God meant the concept of social equality. If there is only one God and He has created all, then everybody is equal before him as children are before the father and therefore, everyone is equal to every other. Thus, the concept of a Muslim brotherhood (*the millat*) also sprang up from this basic premise. Also Islam did not sanction any exclusive governing class or even an exclusive priestly class.

The impact of Islam was felt on Indian society mainly because of it's humanistic concepts. These include fraternity of human beings, justice as the governing principle of social ethics, charity towards the 'have nots', rejection of priesthood, simplicity of dogma, monotheism, emphasis on the beneficient (*Rahman*) and the merciful (*Raheem*) attributes of God, with implications for mercy and beneficence towards the creatures of God in fulfilment of the 'obligation towards humanity' (*haq-ul-ibad*). In his all-time classic *Influence of Islam on Indian Culture*, Dr. Tara Chand, an eminent historian-philosopher has emphasised also upon the message of *sulhe-kul* (peace for all and complete peace) of the Muslim *Sufi Silsilah* (mystic orders). "The Muslim Sufi Saints became popular heroes as the charismatic focus of human charity, fraternization of different communities, upholders of the rights of man and dissenters against the tyranny of the Muslim Sultan and the Muslim feudal aristocracy; their *Khanqahs* (monasteries) provided refuge to the oppressed and wretched, the miserable, the down-trodden and the disinherited, irrespective of caste and creed" (Rasheeduddin Khan, 1987). In this way they symbolized the true essence of Islam as defenders of the opressed and the under-privileged. However, many orthodox interpreters of Islam, tend to exclude or marginalise the *sufism* and *sufis* from the Islamic fold. Ironically, it was *sufism* and the *sufi saints* who were instrumental in the perpetuation of the 'humanistic Islam'; the 'imperial Islam' remained confined within the ruling dynasties. "The sufi tradition of Islam was not only responsible for the perpetuation of the Islamic religious beliefs and metaphysics but also played a significant role in the spread of Islam in India. It's emphasis on ascetic personal ethic, ephemerality of material phenomenon (*fana*), and on mystical self abnegation, though being of foreign origin, was also in many ways concomitant with the Hindu tradition and made a deep impact on a large section of the Hindus. Non-ritualism and abstract monotheism as preached by the Sufi saints and philosophers was not only appealing to the Hindu masses but also tended to be in harmony with the forces of introversion and retreatism which had overtaken the Hindu tradition after its loss of political power" (Yogendra Singh, 1988). Many Muslim scholars and rulers made overt efforts to reconcile some aspects of the Hindu tradition with Islam. Akbar attempted it through introduction of a new synthetic cult called Divine Faith (*Din-e-Ilahi*) which was a mixture of Islam, Jainism, Hinduism and Zoroastrianism. Dara Shikoh pleaded for a synthesis of Upanishadic monotheism with that of Islam and emphasized similarities between the two traditions. Among the literary figures Amir Khusro did a great deal to interpret the endogenous tradition of Hinduism to the Muslim world. In the sixteenth and seventeenth centuries AD, many Muslim poets and writers even choose to write in Hindi. Moreoever, millions of people of deprived castes were attracted to Islam and embraced it in quest for better social conditions retaining many of their local or little traditions, thus contributing to the composite culture of India.

The impact of Islam is clearly visible in our constitution accepting equality against the traditional hierarchical order of the Hindu society. Further, the enactment of Hindu Marriage Act allowing dissolution of marriage and giving more say to women and Hindu Sucession Act allowing share of women in the parental property were inspired by, among other factors, Islam's social ideology.

Islam deeply influenced the Hindu ceremonies, social habbits, thoughts and ideals, language and literature, sciences and arts. In the field of medical science the

Muslims introduced in India the Greek method of treatment which the Arab had learnt from the Greeks and conserved it. This is known in this country as the *Unani* system of medicine. B.S. Upadhyaya, an eminent indologist in his well known work *Feeders of Indian Culture* (1973) has described in detail the contribution of Islam and Muslims in the reconstruction of Indian Society. The field of music is a unique example. It is well know that music is one of the most hated things in the orthodox version of Islam but many of the best known exponents of *Shastriya Sangeet* have been and still are Muslims. Ghazal, Lawani, Thumari, Qawwali, Dhun, Chatrang were the creations of the Muslims which the Hindus accepted with gratitude. Muslim musicians invented numerous instruments of which some were Sarangi, Dilruba, Taus, Sitar, Rubab, Surbin, Sursingar, Tabla and Algoza. Dance was another aspect of fine arts which was jointly cultivated by the Hindus and Muslims. Its' *Kathak* style, cultivated in and brought from the Muslim countries, is the Muslim contribution which has held ground in Northern India for centuries. Music has been one rallying point where distinction between the communities has never been tolerated. In the field of architecture a whole change comes over in the field of Indian architecture when new measures and forms are given to it by the Muslim newcomers. Domes and turrets, arches and minarets adorn the buildings of numerous cities of India. "Muslims built in their newly choosen home, India, as they had built nowhere. There are no forts in the entire Muslim world outside India grander than those of Delhi and Agra, no towers more magnificient than the Qutub Minar, no gates more splendid than the Buland Darwaza of Sikri, no mosques as pretty as the Pearl and the Jama Masjid, none indeed as delicate, as subtle, as fascinating as the mausleum of Taj. There is no country in the world which can boast of greater or even equal number of Muslim monuments than those built in India either in variety or in surpassing beauty" (B.S. Upadhyaya, ibid). The Rajas of Rajputana errected their palaces, even their mausoleums in the Muslim style and donned the Mughal dress and affected the Mughal manners in their respective courts. The *Chughtai* style of painting risen from the Chinese background, has enriched the painting scene in India.

In the sphere of dress pattern and jewellary, *Nath* (nose ring) has become a veritable symbol of Hindu marriage. The ceremonial *sehra* and *maur* decks the Hindu bride grooms. Urdu language is a beautiful example of composite culture of India. It is one of the greatest abiding contributions of Islam to India. Urdu is a language of India created and developed by both Hindus and the Muslims together and it stands as a common cultural heritage of India. Citing the abiding influence of Urdu language, BS Updhayaya(ibid) expresses the view that there are words which, despite the best efforts of the purists, could not be ousted from the common vocabulary of Northern, Central and Western India. The list is endless but some of the examples are *bandook* (rifle), *top* (gun), *kaghaz* (paper), *sarai* (inn), *chaprasi* (peon), *bahi* (account book), *ghaban* (embezzlement), *barud* (gun powder), *sipahi* (soldier), *dehat* (village), *Zamindar* (landlord), *Naukar* (servant), *munim* (clerk), *Jild* (book binding), *lifafa* (envelope), *kurta* (upper loose garment), *pajama* (lower garment), *istree* (press), and thousands of such words which have been used in Hindi exclusively with or without an equivalent. Can there be a more important word than the Gandhian *Charkha, inquilab zindabad* and everyday *roti* or *chapati* ? It is high time that we again recognise our composite culture and rededicate ourselves to it's maintenance in the face of assault on these values both by the Hindu and Muslim reactionaries and fundamentalists.

Christianity :

Christianity is the religion found by Jesus Christ, but it has its roots in Judaic tradition. Christ was a historical figure born about 2,000 years ago. The church has played a key role in Christianity. It has determined the Christian world view. It is the popular view that Christianity has a long background in India. "Though, it can neither be proved nor disproved that Thomas evangelized India (*The Christian Mission Today*, 1960), according to traditions Thomas, one of the aspostles of Christ, landed on the coast of Kerala in

52 AD and set up seven churches in different areas." Then he travelled to Madras where he was martyred at Mylapore in 72 AD. But the spread of Christianity in India, in the true sense of the terms, came with the advent of the Europeans from the early 16th century onwards. Among the earliest missionaries were Portugese followed by the Dutch, the French and the British alongwith other European and American missionaries. Initially, the missionaries worked in the tribal areas and among the untouchable populations but later on spread their activities in urban areas too.

"In India Christianity has been one of the important factors of modernization and economic development through the social values it has legitimised" (Victor D'Souza, 1994). The essence of Christianity is universal brotherhood, egalitarian outlook, and service of the under privileged. Consistent with its' social philosophy. Christianity attacked the evils of the caste system in India and contributed immensely to loosening up the system through its preaching oriented towards the formation of an egalitarian society based on self respect and social justice. Undoubtedly, Christianityhas contributed to the '*opening up*' of Indian society and has provided a healing touch to the under priveleged especially the victims of the oppressive caste system. Christianity has been one of the earliest agencies of social welfare for the weaker sections and through the vast network of social services has been able to provide educational and medical facilities to the relatively isolated regions of India untouched by government support in these areas. The best evidence in favour of this statement is the high rates of literacy in areas where Christianity and it's social services network has been relatively strong.

❑

SECTION SEVEN

DIMENSIONS OF SOCIAL CHANGE IN INDIA

Introductory Note

India is on the move; contemporary Indian society is changing. This change is taking place both in it's structure and functioning. The amount and scope of change are stupendous and unprecedented. And what makes the change in contemporary Indian society specially significant and noteworthy is the fact that it is planned, sponsored, directed and controlled by the State.

The study of contemporary Indian Soceity, as indeed of all developing societies, is most fruitfully carried out in terms of social change. A concern with the structural features of Indian society e.g. the village community, caste the family itself will lead us to the study of social change, for these institutions are not showing unmistakable signs of new kinds of change. "Urban India, too, is becoming increasingly important as a source of change and as an expression of India's total poverty. A purely academic sociology or social anthropology, which does not come to grips with the present social conditions and with on-going social change in India, is bound to die out because of it's own sterility" (T.N. Madan, 1973).

India has always been described as a 'traditional' society in which "(i) the status of a person is determined by birth is fixed, that is, individuals do not strive for social mobility, (ii) individual's behaviour is governed by custom and ways of behaviour of people vary only slightly from generation to generation, (iii) social organization is based on hierarchy, (iv) individual identifies himself with primary groups and kinship relations predominate in interaction, (v) people are conservative, (vi) economy is simple and economic productivity above subsistence is relatively low, and (vi) mythical thought predominates in society". Does this description portray the totality of the present Indian society? It is in this light that we must appreciate the distinction proposed by M.N. Srinivas between the 'field view' and the 'book view' of Indian society. There were book views of every major institution: of caste, of joint family and of village community. Srinivas attacked these views as being out of date, out of touch with reality, and mistaken. He argued for their replacement by accounts based on fieldwork "that would reveal the dynamic tensions in their actual operation. This was largely a reaction against the Brahminical bias for the 'though out' as against the 'lived in' order" Andre Beiteille, (1992). Social institutions and values are changing in India. This will affect every one especially the Hindus whose way of life is "very largely dependent upon a triad of social institutions viz., Caste, Joint Family and Village Community, which are changing in important respects" (Srinivas, 1992). Going back again to 'book view-field view'dichotomy, let us refer to Andre Beiteille again when he pinpoints the new realities as observed through field view. He explains that differentiated institutional structures of various kinds have emerged. These structures are: (1) the growth of money economy as opposed to inherited status, (ii) a new caste-free occupational structure, (iii) a new kind of educational system, and (iv) the development of differentiated political structures. On the whole the numerous 'societies' in India and 'Indian society' is in the throes of a major social transformation; the entire India is in the midst of a social ferment. In this section some concepts and approaches have been dealt with through which some aspects of social change are sought to be analysed and understood.

❑

21 Sanskritization and Westernization

Contrary to the 'book view', the Indian caste system has never been absolutely rigid and static. This observation has led progressively to various attempts to explain, in systematic terms, the manner in which change or more precisely mobility occurs within it. The process of hypogamy may be the earliest attempt in this direction. Broadly speaking, four approaches could be delineated in the study of social mobility in India. These are: (i) "individual" or "family" mobility approach, (ii) "corporate" or "group" mobility approach, (iii) comparative approach, and (iv) reference group approach. M.N. Srinivas is the main protagonist of the corporate mobility approach in India.

As a sequel to multifarious rural studies some concepts have been developed which are significant theoretical contributions from Indian sociologists-social anthropologists. These may also be used as analytical techniques to study social change in India. Although, some stray attempts had been made to develop theoretical postulations and methodological exercises during the pre-independence period, the first systematic attempt to define, analyse and understand the process of social change in Indian society was made by M.N. Srinivas in his significant and pathbreaking study, *Religion and Society among the Coorgs of South India* (1952).

The term **Sanskritization** used by Srinivas in his study on Coorgs was primarily meant to describe the process of cultural mobility in the traditional rural India. Srinivas holds the view that Hindu caste system has never been so rigid that individuals or castes cannot alter or raise their status. He defines Sanskritization as the "process by which a low caste or tribe or other group takes over the customs, rituals beliefs, ideology and life style of a higher caste and in particular 'twice born' (*dwija*) caste". For instance, a low caste or tribe or any other group may give up non-vegetarianism, consumption of liquor, animal sacrifice, etc. and imitate the Brahmin's life style in matters of food, dress and rituals. By following such a process, within a generation or two, they may claim a higher position in the local caste hierarchy Originally, Srinivas used the term 'Brahminization' to denote this process. However, when he was confronted with other models for emulation he gave up the term 'Brahminization' in preference to the term 'Sanskritization'. Moreover, Sanskritization is much broader a concept than 'Brahminization' because not only it encompasses non-Brahmin models like Kshatriya model, Jat model, Vaishya model and models of other 'twice born' castes but also denotes a wide spectrum of values and life styles.

On the basis of a number of field studies we have, in our possession, a list of changes adopted by an aspiring lower caste as part of this cultural emulation. The talk of cultural imitation should be in concrete terms so that one could visualize the scenario as it exists. Sanskritization may result in the erosion of cultural autonomy of the women folk which includes erosion in the freedom to choose life partner and prevalence of a rigid sexual morality, changes in family structure include a movement towards the orthodox Hindu joint family and the concomitant strong authority of father, monogamy, a stronger caste organization with increased tendency of outcasting/ostracism. Also, a rigid commensality prevails alongwith changed food habits outlawing beef and pork eating and consumption of liquor, more emphasis is placed on the acquisition of higher education, adoption of dowry practices instead of the token bride price. In the realm of religion and religious practices, it frequently results in the donning of sacred thread, giving up sacrifice of pigs at the time of wedding and increased emphasis on pilgrimage etc.

Srinivas has further explained that political and economic factors have also affected the process of Sanskritization. With the establishment of British rule in India the lower castes got more opportunities to sanskritize themselves and subsequently raise their social status because the new rulers and a new political order were not socially involved in the dynamics of caste hierarchy.

Sometimes a lower caste aspiring to climb upward in caste hierarchy through the process of Sanskritization may have to face hostility from the castes of middle strata. Their hostile attitude may be explained in terms of clash of interests. It is a familiar problem with people of lower castes in many parts of rural India to face hostility and ridicule from the higher castes even when they try to start using shoes or wear neat and clean clothes; the lower castes are not supposed to look like them, not to speak of adopting their names, rituals, customs and practices.

Moreover, in some cases even Sanskritization may not lead to elevation in caste status and they may continue to suffer the traditional social disabilities.

Expanding means of transport and communication have facilitated and hastened the process of Sanskritization because of new avenues and opportunities of culture contact. Democratic value system also provides more freedom to choose and hence more avenues for Sanskritization but at the same time it gives boost to conservative tendencies. Ironoically, despite their lowly social status, many lower castes are found more liberal, permissive and progressive. Their liberal and positive attitude especially towards the position of woman, sexual conduct, freedom to choose life partners etc. are worth emulating but they tend to become conservative and adopt retrograde measures in order to become 'sanskritized'. Conceding its highly complex and sometimes confusing nature Srinivas himself admits that "Sanskritization is an extremely complex and heterogeneous concept. It is even possible that it would be more profitable to treat it as a bundle of concepts than a single concept. The important thing to remember is that it is only a name for a widespread cultural process."

Sanskritization refers to a cultural process but it is essential to realize that it is usually concomitant of the acquisition of political or economic power by a caste. Both are parts of the processes of social mobility. An interesting contradiction is seen here: "lower" castes which have become prosperous or powerful or educated like to assert their claim to a higher place in the herarchy by resorting to Sanskritization. On the other hand they struggle fiercely to retain their "backward" status for taking advantage of educational concessions and government job. Modern India is full of contradictions.

Pinpointing the limitations of Sanskritization, S.C. Dube made the comment that the sanskritization hypothesis has served it's limited purpose well, but when we seek to adopt it as a major tool for the analysis of the complex cultural scene in India, it is found wanting in many respects. In broad outlines, the "Sanskritic Model" appears to be attractive, but careful analysis shows that it is extremely deceptive. Sanskritic sources provide not one model but many models, some of them involving even fundamentally opposed ideals. What we call Hindu philosophy is not just one school of thought, it is a compendium of many systems of thought, recognizing and advocating many divergent images of society and many different schemes of values. The margin of choice is wide indeed, and the selection of specific items out of the wide spectrum provided by Sanskritic sources is conditioned by regional contexts and historical antecedents of particular groups and communities. It will be seen, thus, that a generalized all India Sanskritic Model will be too vague to be useful as an analytical tool; it will be necessary to have a series of such models to suit to different regional conditions and historical antecedents. Without wishing to enter into a semantic controversy, it may be mentioned that not all groups and communities draw their "models" from Sanskritic sources. Apart from Muslims, Christians and Parsis, even within the fold of Hinduism there are significant groups whose religious classics are not in Sanskrit but in other languages. The followers of Buddha, Kabit, Ravidas, Dadu or Jyothiba Phule - to take only some examples off hand-draw their inspiration from the writings of these mentors. These writings are not in Sanskrit; often they are in a language that can be understood by the masses. Only a part of what they have said can be attributed to Sanskritic sources; there is a great deal, in what they have said, that stands for conscious rejection of some of the central ideas implicit in the Sanskritic Model. Will it not be more useful to speak of 'Classical Models' rather than of a Sanskritic Model? But Srinivas's explanation of Sanskritization does not lay total emphasis on the semantic aspect either.

Talking of new agents of Sanskritization, Srinivas (1992) talks of the festivals of the village deities and the calenderical festivals being increasingly sanskritized. *Harikathas*, *Yagna*, *Jagran* etc. are being celebrated with much more ostentation in Indian towns and cities. Religious figures, whether in ochre robes or not, promising salvation or more concrete things to the people, continue to appear on the Indian scene. In fact, they enjoy audience which they could not have dreamt of before the newspapers, the microphone and the radio/ television became popular. Everyone of them can be regarded as a sanskritizing agent. Indian films frequently make use of religious themes taken from the epics and *puranas*. The availability of low priced books has enabled people to become acquainted with Hindu religious literature in a way not possible before.

Sanskritization as a process of social mobility may be observed empirically even among the non-Hindu communities especially those with well defined social hierarchy such as Muslims and Sikhs and in lesser degrees among other communities too. Cultural emulation for the sake of status elevation has been the prime motive force among the non-Hindu communities too. Talking of the cohesive role fo sanskritization especially in the case of a group external to Hinduism such as a tribe, sanskritization resulted in drawing it into the Hindu fold, which necessarily involved its becoming a caste having regular relations with other local castes. When we talk of tribal absorption into the Hindu fold, the examples of Meena from Rajasthan, Santhal and Munda from Bihar and West Bengal, Jounsari and Tharu from Uttar Pradesh and similar others immediately come to mind.

When we talk of cultural imitation of the higher castes/dominant castes by an aspiring lower caste we must not forget that in several cases the motive force is not always cultural imitation per se but an expression of challenge and revolt against socio-economic deprivation and frustration like in the case of a lower caste insisting to carry its bride in a palanquin or the bridegroom riding a horse. And here comes the most significant question — why do the sanskritizing lower castes imitate or emulate the life style and cultural elements of their traditional 'exploiters' and 'oppressors'? Why does a human group imitate a group hated by it? One of the plausible explanations as given by Harold Gould (1988) tells us that the "prime motive force behind Sanskritization is the factor of repressed hostility which manifests itself not in the form of rejecting the caste system but in the form of it's victims trying to seize control of it and thereby expiate their frustrations on the same battelefield where they acquired them. Only then, can there be a sense of satisfaction in something achieved that is tangible, concrete, and relevant to past experience."

Because of erosion in the importance of the ritual component of our lifestyle, especially in towns and cities, some observers make the comment that the process of Sanskritization seems to have been halted as ritual hierarchy lost its' relevance in determining social status. Such observations are nothing but sweeping generalization otherwise why do the vast majority of our so called 'modern' and 'forward looking' population still take into consideration the factor of *Jati* in the selection of spouse? While it is true that power and wealth are the main components of secular status, any status achieved by such means alone still seeks to be legitimized by acceptance into a higher born social group or by the burying of one's true community or birth origins. Thus, these new principles of status operate contingently together with the caste principle of social stratification and only rarely do they operate autonomously.

Before concluding this discussion, let us quote Harold Gould's (ibid) observation again when he says that "Srinivas's concept rests ultimately on the notion that the caste system, like all status hierarchies, causes the low to invidiously compare themselves with the high and to try in every way they can to soften, modify, reduce, and even eliminate altogether the basis for these status differences. This is not unique to the Indian Castes System. What is unique is the manner in which this process must work itself out in India, given the empirical nature of the status system that prevails there. It is this with which sanskritization comes to grips". The changes that creep into the Indian Society through the adoption of the process of sanskritization have implications of far reaching importance which help the students of Indian Society understand the nature of social change in the contemporary Indian Society.

Westernization

Westernization seems to be much simple concept when compared with its twin concept of Sanskritization. It refers to all cultural changes and institutional innovations in India as this country came into political and cultural contact with the western national specially

Britain. More precisely, it is "changes brought about in Indian society and culture as a result of over 150 years of British rule, the term subsuming changes occurring at different levels..... technology, institutions, ideology and values". He prefers to call this process Westernization and not modernization. There should be a line of demarcatin. On a wider plane Westernization includes a scientific approach, emphasis on materialism rather on spiritualism, individualism, liberal approach towards various problems of the society, humanism, equality, egalitarianism and rationalism. Establishment of scientific, technological and educational institutions, rise of nationalism, new political culture and leadership in the country are all by-products of Westernization.

The impact of Westernization on Indian society may clearly be observed in a number of spheres. It has influenced caste system and the lessening rigidity may be assigned, to a great extent, to the impact of Westernization; it has promoted the disintegration of joint family and it has induced a number of social reform movements. In the economic and political sphere it has disintegrated cottage industries, promoted variety in cultivation, introduced new measures in land management; it has promoted democratic values and ideals, national conciousness, social justice and uniform administrative system in the whole length and breadth of the country. To be more precise, emphasis on humanitarianism and rationalism is a part of Westernization which led to a series of institutional and social reforms in India.

Srinivas expresses the view that increase in Westernization does not retard the process of Sanskritization; both go on simultaneously. Interestingly, in some cases, increase in Westernization accelerates the process of Sanskritization. For instance, the expanding means of communication like postal facilities, railways, newspapers and periodicals, etc. which are the result of the western technology have given fillip to pilgrimages, religious propaganda, and caste and communal congregations. Moreover, a significant by-product of

Westernization is that under its impact many higher castes (who are more exposed to Westernization through English education) give up their traditional life style.

It is observed that usually the westernized ones live minimally in the universe of caste and maximally within the universe of class; they may practice non-traditional occupations, ignore rules of ritual pollution, dietry restrictions and many outside the caste/region/religion; they may give up the practice of maintaining *gotra* or caste names, adopt non-vegetarianism, give up the practice of eating in the kitchen or *chauka* and may give up sacred thread. In other words, the westernized ones tend to adopt western models and lifestyle giving up the traditional ones. The lower castes aspiring to attain higher status in the caste hierarchy try to fill this vaccum by adopting the sanskritic models given up by the higher castes under the impact of Westernization. This is yet another instance of Westernization and Sanskritization going together.

We, as the lower castes spend a lot of energy on Sanskritization while several higher castes turn to Westernization as a means of maintaining the social distance between themselves and the lower castes which is no longer possible within the old order in the face of the later's current ability to Sanskritize themselves. Supplementing this line of argument further, Harold Gould (ibid) comments that if one is already Sanskritized, as the Brahmins and the Rajputs are, then one cannot go any higher up in the traditional stratification system. If one cannot maintain things as they are through the application of political and economic power, then one can only go down or accept the notion of equality which, in effect, means accepting the nullity of the caste system itself and hierarchial relationship in general. This is patently impossible for the higher castes, with their deeply embedded conception of their inherent superiority, and so they must ironically move outside the caste system which spawned them in order to preserve their pretensions to paramount status in Indian Society. Meanwhile, the lower castes keep chasing the mirage of equality with the higher castes. But, by the time they reach their destination, however, they discover that the Brahman has himself vacated the spot and moved on to the higher hill of Westernization where he still gazes contemptuously down upon them from on elevated perch, (ibid). Perhaps, that is why in a number of cases, the well off and aspiring sections of the lower castes in towns and cities may be going straight to Westernization. But for the majority of the lowercaste population the idiom of westernization may be too complex, incomprehensible and difficult to understand and adopt. Thus, we find an important dynamic interplay between the process of Sanskritization and Westernization.

However, the term Westernization itself is not free from controversy and complications. Some scholars have advocated the term 'de-sanskritization' for Westernization with the British impact on India. This is not a correct assessment when viewed in totality. The post-independence period has witnessed a lot of Russian and American influence on Indian society. The Russian and American versions of modernization in our economic measures of far reaching importance have also influenced the Indian society to a large extent. The continuing five year plans, emphasis on public sector and nationalizaiton or socialization in our economic planning are the instances of distinct socialist impact through our strong ties with socialists states. Of late some Chinese impact is also discernible in our health care measures especially in rural areas. To some other scholars the term Westernization sounds value loaded because of its colonial connotation. Hence they advocate the term 'Modernizaiton'.

Secularization

The process of Secularization is intimately related with Westernization. In a way it is a part of Westernization while some people consider it to be a by-product of Westernization.

Secularization got impetus during British rule in India. Industrial Revolution and the consequent expansion in the means of transport and communication, spread of education, especially English education increased development of towns and cities and growing use of various tools of modern science and technology radically affected the thinking and mental horizon of the people. For the first time Indian people specially of towns and cities were exposed to newer ideas and ideologies. Social interaction between the otherwise isolated groups and communities increased tremendously. The ideas of rationalism and humanitarianism gave new dimensions to the thought process of the people. All these factors strengthened the process of secularization. Many myths were exploded and stereotypes about other peoples changed and moved closer to realities.

The most important consequence of secularization witnessed in Indian society was that for the first time Indian people started adopting non-religious approach for analysing and understanding many social-economic and political problems. Now it was possible for a large segment of society especially of urban areas to view many 'worldly' problems in their independent form completely isolated from the trappings of religion. Most significantly the process of secularization gave insight to the people of intellectual class to analyse the issues of morality and moral values on purely rational and humanistic ground completely independent of religion. Previously, it was the established view that ethics and morality could not be seen independent of religion because of the view that it is only the established and normative religions which provide the society with guidelines in ethics and morality and religion is the only fountainhead of these virtues.

The rise of nationalism and national movement for freedom gave further impetus to secularization. People of diverse cultural backgrounds even having conflicting religious ideologies stood together under the banner of freedom movement. The constitution of independent India gave it the ideal form of a republic; the essence and spirit of our Constitution have the moving force of Secularization behind various provisions reconciling diverse socio-religious interests. Though, the opposing force of religious fanaticism and revivalism have also been active, yet the process of secularization continues to attain deeper roots. What more evidence of it is required than our secular Constitution continuing even after the partition of our country and formation of a theocratic state in our immediate neighbourhood.

Secularization is a wider process than Sanskritization. While Sanskritization is mainly concerned with the Hindus, Secularization covers all sections of the society. Secularization has more appeal for urban, educated class and Sanskritization attracts mainly lower castes. Secularization is the gift of modern age, a by-product of Westernization; Sanskritization is related with traditions and conservatism.

Modernization

Modernization has been a dominant theme after the second world war (specially in nineteen fifties and sixties) and a central concept in the 'sociology of development', referring to the "interactive process of economic growth and social change. Modernization studies typically deal with the effects of economic development on 'traditional' social structures and values". The process of modernization is related to the industrialization, urbanization, high standard of living, development of civilizatoin and broadness of view point. Defining modernization Eisenstadt (1966) says that "from a historical viewpoint modernization is the process of change towards those types of social, economic and political systems which were developed in Western Europe and North America from the 17th to 19th century, and after that spread over to south America, Asia and Africa during the 19th and 20th centuries." In the context of contemporary times, the concept of modernization is the response of western social science to the many challenges faced by the Third World in the decades immediately following the Second World War. Therefore, some scholars considered modernization to be the child of Westernization. In a brilliant analysis of the ethical aspect of modernization, S.C. Dube (1988) says that "an attractive feature of the concept was that it showed an apparent concern for the cultural sensitivities of both the elites and the masses of the Third World. The term *modernization* was much less value loaded than it's predecessor-westernization. Most countries in the Third World were proud of their cultural heritage and deeply attached to it. While desiring western standards of plenty they had no desire to abandon their own life styles and values. The concept of modernization recognised the strength of roots; it did not pose any overt threat to the cultural identity of the people aspiring for rapid change. To the elite of the Third World the ideal of westernization was difficult to swallow; they accepted modernization readily because it did not appear to offend their cultural dignity". According to Lerner (1958) three features constitute the core of modernized personality - empathy, mobility, and high participation. Empathy is the capacity to see things as others see them. All societies possess this capacity in some measure, but to sharpen and strengthen, it can make a qualitative change in human interaction. Such a change is desired in modernized societies. The second attribute, mobility does not refer only to geographical mobility- it is used in a more comprehensive sense. The imperatives of change demand, a capacity to assume, as occasions demand new statuses and learn to play associated roles. Unlike the traditional society, which had ascribed statuses and roles, the modernized society has an open status system. The third attribute - high participation - refers to the increased role of individuals in realizing social goals and objectives in more active ways; high participation requires the capacity in individuals to visualise new goals or altered objectives and modify their roles accordingly. In traditonal societies social objectives are not open to question. The core of modernization is, of course, rationality.

One of the most significant features of modernization is that modernized societies operate through institutional structures that are capable of continuously absorbing the changes that are inherent in the process of modernization. Let us see, very briefly, as to how the contemporary Indian society is striving to adopt modernization for economic growth and social change. On the agricultural and industrial fronts the country's performance is not as poor as some of it's critics make it out. Our record in these fields is better than that of many Third World countries. But the development has been lopsided and full of regional imbalances. The distributive aspects of economic growth and the diffusion of the benefits of modernization appear to have receive little serious thought. The growth of elitism is alarming and it should be curbed. Rampant corruption and nepotism are the product of the prevailing state of moral decay. All possible political and administrative steps should be taken to arrest this trend. The cohesive bonds of society should be strengthened.

A modern society is a rational and scientific society, surrounded by the forces of fundamentalism in the neighbouring countries we have, in recent times, shown signs of succumbing to these pressures. The rising tide of religious revivalism, obscurantism and fundamentalism in the wake of Babri Masjid-Ram Janambhomi dispute is dangerous. The happenings of the fateful day of Dec. 06, 1992 is alarming; it threatens to tear our social fabric apart. The minorities, too, should shed their tendency of clinging to obscurantism and strengthen the democratic, progressive and secular forces to save the country. More conditions should be created to ensure increased participation of all sorts of minorities in the nation building process. During the Ayodhya controversy enough damage has been done to rationalism and scientific temper. We are left with no other option but to contribute to strengthen rationalism and scientific temper through all the available institutional networks. Our failure to achieve this objective shall be fatal setback in modernization.

As very rightly observed by S.C. Dube (1974) "there is no standard model of modernization and no fixed path for it's attainment. Developing societies can adopt a model of their choice and can chalk out their own path for it's realization." We have chosen democracy and secularism as the basis of the aspired for modernized

Indian society. Adoption of modern science and technology shall go a long way in the achievement of India's cultural and technological modernization.

❑

22 Dominant Caste

In the agrarian Indian society, an understanding of land owning dominant castes in rural India is necessary to have some idea about the process of social change in India. Despite it rapid industrialization ownership of land is still the main source of wealth, status and political power. In a path breaking research paper titled '*Dominant Caste in Rampura*', published in 1959 in *American Anthropologist*, Srinivas put forward the concept of Dominant Caste. It gave some new insight about the process of social change in India. Since then many sociologists and social anthropologists have been applying themselves on the various aspects of dominance in rural India.

Srinivas asserts that to be a dominant caste, a caste must have the following characteristics:

1. It must own a sizeable amount of cultivable land.
2. It must be of considerable numerical strength.

3. It must enjoy a high place in the local caste hierarchy.

The ownership of land has traditionally been vested in a few castes only. With these land owning castes have been aligned a number of artisan castes and landless labour. Even after four decades of land reforms, about one third of scheduled caste population is still landless and the remaining population has small land holdings. Moreover, the 'Green Revolution' has further enhanced the price and importance of cultivable land with the result that many trading castes are focussing their attention on the ownership of land; they are investing more and more money to procure land.

Despite all these factors mere ownership of land, numerical strength and high place in ritual hierarchy are no more the only determining factors in conferring the status of *dominant caste* on any particular caste. Western education, jobs in administration and political clout and contacts are the new and additional factors of dominance. Therefore some castes which were earlier dominant no more enjoy dominance. Moreover, introduction of adult franchise and democratic decentralisation (*Panchayati Raj*) have provided leverage to many middle level and lower

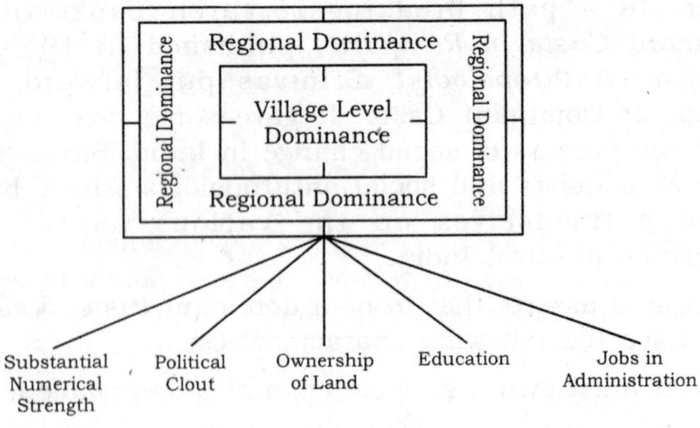

castes. The status of Scheduled Castes and Scheduled Tribes has improved due to reservation in State and Central legislative bodies. Spread of education among these erstwhile depressed groups has futher altered the yardstick of dominance.

Due to immense expansion in transport and communication village level dominance is no longer enough to make a caste dominant caste. Instead regional dominance seems to be a better criterion of dominance. This situation may further be explained. A particular caste may be numerically, economically and politically dominant in a particular village. However, if it is surrounded from all sides by other castes with antagonistic interests the village level dominance of that particular caste does not carry much weight. Hence, dominance spread over a vast contagious tract of land is more important.

Significantly, the model of Sanskritization for lower castes is not always the Brahmin. Instead in most of the areas the dominant caste serves as the model for Sanskritization. For instance, if a Kshatriya caste is dominant in a particular region the model for Sanskritization will be Kshatriya; likewise Vaishya, Brahmina and so on. This dominance is so all pervading that in regions where non-Brahmins are dominant castes even Brahmins are looked down upon and often treated with contempt. For instance in certain areas of eastern Uttar Pradesh the dominant *Thakur* landlords make the Brahmins cook food except their *Kulguru* (family priest). Likewise in many villages of Punjab the jat landlords consider Brahmins as their servants.

The dominant caste usually keeps a distance from others in the village and the whole region of dominance. It considers itself as the protector and watchdog of culture. It sets certain norms of behaviour the violation of which is dealt with severely. The whole value system of a particular region carries the stamp of dominant caste.

The Dominant Caste plays important role in the settlement of disputes through the traditional village and caste council. The influential members of the dominant caste settle disputes not only between members of different castes, they are also frequently approached by members of the same caste for the settlement of their intra-caste disputes and problems.

S.C. Dube and Peter Gardner raised serious objections to the very concept of dominant caste. Pinpointing an empirical aspect of the situation, Dube comments that it will be meaningful to speak of 'a dominant caste' only when power is diffused in the group and is exercised in the interest of the whole group or atleast a sizeable part of it. When there are pronounced inequalities of wealth, prestige and power between different individuals in a so called dominant caste, and where dominant individuals exploit the weaker elements in their own caste as well as the non-dominant castes it will perhaps be inappropriate to think of it as dominant caste. Unity and concerted action in terms of caste interest, therefore, must be assumed before we locate dominance in a caste on the basis of criteria specified by Srinivas. The fact that a number of dominant individuals occupying most of the power positions belong to a particular caste is, by itself, not enough to characterize the caste as dominant. Further, intra-caste unity and articulation in terms of power are essential for it's emergence as a dominant caste. Where these conditions exist a caste can become dominant. In their absence, however, the community power structure can be better understood in reference to *dominant individuals, dominant faction* and their complex alignment.

In his rejoinder, Srinivas says that "although Dube concedes the existence of 'dominant individuals' and 'dominant faction' he is hesitant to go the whole hog and concede the existence of 'dominant caste'. Here Srinivas's basic contention is that both 'dominat individuals' and 'dominant faction' owe their dominance to the fact they are a part of the dominant caste. It may be observed here that most, if not all, of the leaders of the 'dominant faction' hail from the dominant caste except in areas where there are two rival castes each striving to establish its dominance." The dominance of the dominant caste is not a local or village level phenomenon. As mentioned earlier in this discussion the village level dominance of caste does not carry much weight. The dominance shall be complete only when it is spread over a substantial region. If this is the case then even a family or two in a village, belonging to a dominant caste, shall count locally because of the network of ties binding them to their dominant relatives and fellow members of the caste. In such situations others in the village will always be aware of this nexus or network and hence the affairs in the village get conducted accordingly.

Taling of the possible diversity of interests and still putting up a united front on the part of the dominant castes, Ghanshyam Shah (1985) points out the formation of caste associations - an important innovation introduced by the 'dominant group' of a dominant caste to maintain harmony among the various economic strata within the caste structure. It there by maintains it's hegemony as well as protects it's own 'class interests'. The history of caste associations go back to the late 19th century, although their number has increased after independence. The Sardar Kurmi Kshatriya Sabha of Uttar Pradesh and Bihar, the Nadar Mahajana Sangam in Tamilnadu, the Gujarat Kshatriya Sabha in Gujarat are some of the examples of powerful caste association. "These caste associations projected economic interests of the dominant group as the caste-interest. In order to win over the support of the poorer strata of the castes concerned, the associations generally adopt two strategies. Firstly, in the beginning the leaders of the associations invoke the caste ideology based on the concept of purity and pollution. Caste members are exhorted to maintain or improve their caste status. Legends are created glorifying their past. A sense of 'weness' among the caste members is promoted around rhetoric such as 'economic backwardness', 'economic development', etc of the caste members. Secondly, in order to bind together the caste members, the caste associations occasionally pass resolutions ventilating grievances of the exploited strata of the caste against the government."

When one views caste, both theoretically and empirically, one finds that Srinivas never claimed that the concept of dominant caste provided the *total* explanation for the phenomenon of power in rural India. Moreover, the unity of a caste, particularly that of a dominant caste, is not something static and constant, but dynamic and contextual. It emerges especially in relation of opposition to the other castes. With the increasing emphasis on the popular participation in the implementation of welfare schemes and schemes of economic development through democratic institutions, the role of dominant castes has assumed crictical importance because of their ability and capacity to control and manipulate these institutions. In this fierce competition to control economic and political resources not all the members of the dominant castes may be receiving 'power' directly but they as a collective whole are definitely exercising the powers. Thus, the political process and economic development at the micro and mecro levels definitely carry the stamp of the respective dominant castes.

❑

23 Social Change in India: Some Dimensions

Contemporary Indian Society is changing. This change is taking place both in its structure and functioning. Social institutions and values are changing in India. This will affect every one especially the Hindus whose way of life is *very largely dependent upon a tria of social institution* viz., *Caste, Joint Family and Village Community, which are changing in important respects* (M.N. Srinivas, 1992).

India has always been described as a traditional society in which (i) the status of a person is determined by birth and is fixed, that is individuals do not strive for social mobility, (ii) individual's behaviour is governed by customs and ways of behaviour of people vary only slightly from generation to generation, (iii) social organisation is based on hierarchy, (iv) individual identifies himself with primary groups and kinship relations predominate in interaction, (v) people are conservative, (vi) economy is simple and economic productivity above subsistence is relatively low and

(vii) mythical thought predominates in society. Does this description portray the totality of the present Indian society?

II

Recent studies of caste has shown that caste is not evaporating or dying away but is undergoing adaptive process. Membership of caste is still determined by birth and caste still remains strongly endogamous but the religious basis of caste has shown lot of dilution. Caste is, no longer, in a position to impose strong restrictions on the individual freedom, especially freedom to choose one's occupation. We stand at the threshold of a caste free occupational structure. As far back as 1950, F.G. Bailey, an eminent British anthropologist, who has contributed significantly on Indian society, observed in his study of a relatively backward state like Orissa, ..."*not every person works at his traditional occupation. The distillers do not touch liquor. The kond potters do not know how to make pots. The fishermen do not fish. The warriors are cultivators.*" Around the same Katheline Gough, another keen observeer of Indian society noted a similar trend in Tamil Nadu "*The caste/community is no longer homogeneous in occupation and wealth, for caste is today a limiting rather than a determining factor in the choice of occupation. Exactly half of Kumbarpettai's adult Brahmins are now employed in town as government servants, school teachers or restaurant workers. Of the remainder, some own upto thirty acres of land, other as little as three. One runs a grocery store and one a vegetarian restaurant. Among the non-Brahmins, Marathas, Kallans, Koravas and Kuttadis have abandoned their traditional work. Village studies of other parts of the country bear out this trend.*"

The preceding narration prepares the ground for the study of a more pronounced caste free occupational structure in urban Indian. Under the impact of industrialization, urbanization, secularization/ modernization the caste system has shown an amazing flexibility and adaptability. What better evidence one could use in support of this contention than the vaste range of occupational mobility that includes a movement from ritually pure to ritually impure/polluted occupations in the case of several higher castes. The mushrooming growth of beauty parlours, manicure/pedicure centres, massage parlours, hair styling centres being run by mainly higher caste people bear testimony to this fact. Involvement with hide and skin, the leather and leather products has always been considered ritually impure/ taboo for higher castes because of obvious ritual reasons. Now tanneries, footwear trade and even retailing of these has been taken over by people of a number of higher castes. Even rules of commensality are no longer strictly observed.

The socio-economic, political and ritual axis of the caste system viz... *Jajmani system* in rural India is crumbling. The new market forces, new political process and technological modernization have seriously affected inter-caste relations. However, the ritual components of the *Jajmani system* still remains operational to a large extent. The emergence of new dominant castes and state support to the traditionally deprived castes have severeally and seriously affected the Jajmani system.

The new political process based on adult franchise has brought into operation the factors of caste hitherto unknown. Rajni Kothari in his path breaking studies on Caste and Politics has explored new areas of enquiry. In his ruthlessly frank analysis he has compared politics in India with enterprise. He says that Indian politicians are enterpreneurs and like any intelligent entrepreneur, a politician is sure about his resources. He knows that the bulk of the Indian masses live by and live along their respective castes, therefore, he always goes for the mobilization of his resources. If castes are used like any other resources, the politics can never be the same again. In this interactional process the politics as well as the caste have undergone changes: both have been alterted. Caste has been politicised and this is nothing but 'politicization of caste'. The democratic process - the democratic decentralization and adult franchise - have aroused new hopes among many traditionally deprived castes who have now realized that political mobilization promises to give them fruits. Ironically the same castes — the traditionally privileged ones — who have been singing about the virtues of democracy and democratic process may now be cursing the same.

Rajni Kothari has specified three typical stages in the relationship between caste and politics in a region.

Stage I: This involves politicization of a powerful elite caste, usually one which responded earliest to the opportunity for western education. In Maharashtra and Tamil Nadu, this was the Brahmins : In Bihar, it was Kayasthas. With some political success on the part of the entrenched caste, the members of other high castes in the area would respond with resentment, feelings of relative deprivation and possibly antagonism. These castes then challenge the entrenched caste as what Kothari calls an *ascendant caste*. In three examples given in Kothari's work, the *ascendant caste* is one of respectable cultivators who had been slower than the entrenched caste in accepting western education. In Rajasthan, the Rajputs were the entrenched and the Jat cultivators the ascendant caste. In Tamil Nadu, the Brahmins were the entrenched and the Shudra non-Brahmins were ascendant; and in Maharashtra the Brahmins are the entrenched and the Marathas were the ascendant.

Stage 2: Factionalism and fragmentation take place within the competing castes and multicaste and multifactional alignments develop. Lower castes are often brought in to support high caste leaders and to strengthen a faction.

Stage 3: Caste identity tends to languish with the progress in education, urbanization and the development of an orientation towards individual achievement and modern status symbols. Individuals participate in networks which include persons of several *loyalities has been overlaid by a more sophisticated system of social and political participation with cross-cutting allegiances. Institutions are distinctly different.* The present political realities suggest that the Indian society is not fixed in either Stage 2 or Stage 3. It is something beyond State 2 with the traditionally deprived moving towards domination of society at several levels.

III

In the changed socio-political scenario some sociologists and anthropologists have also talked about the new functions of caste in terms of expressive and instrumental functions. The former refer to the sense of social and emotional solidarity that caste can bring about among it's members. The behaviour of individuals tends to be caste centric because caste provides them not only a sense of identity but also acts as a protective force. The later functions, on the other hand, are more pragmatic and concern the achievement of personal or group goals in political or economic fields. Because of positive discrimination towards the backward segments of our population and the direct intervention of state in the process of social change, a number of higher castes are feeling threatened. Therefore, many of them feel justified in using caste channels and their nepotic networks for achieving educational, economic or political goals.

IV

The emergence of new dominant castes is yet another factor of critical importance in the structural aspect of caste system in India. M.N. Srinivas in his path breaking work *Dominant Caste in Rampura* (1953) first talked about the emerging dominant castes. He enumerated numerical strength, ownership of cultivable land of good quality and a high place in the local *jati/ritual* hierarchy as the main factors of dominance. The follow up studies added English education (or westernization?), jobs in local administration and political contacts or clouds as some other factors of dominance.

The term *dominance* is used to refer to the exercise of authority in society by groups who achieved politico-economic superiority, and claimed legitimacy for their commands in terms of superior ritual status or through alliances with those who controlled status distribution. By contrast, the term *power* is used to refer to the exertion of secular authority by individuals appointed or elected to offices of the state, who claimed legitimacy, under law, to make and implement decisions binding on the population within their territorial jurisdiction.

If we analyse the regional patterns of dominance, we can identify two most important models among several ones. As Francine Frankel and MSA Rao (1989) put it, *notions of an underlying cultural unity should not obscure the substantial regional variations which existed in patterns of social stratification. Outside the Aryan heartland, there was often a disjunction between the configuration of actual local or jati hierarchies, and the abstract general Varna categories of Brahmin, Kshatriya, Vaishya and Shudra used across regions to order proliferous subcastes.* The closest approximation to the stratified social system of the Varna order survived in the Ganga valley of it's origin. Within this area viz., Uttar Pradesh and Bihar, the *dwija* (twiceborn/higher) castes are fully articulated and represented by area wide subcastes of *Brahmin, Kshatriya* and *Vaishya* ranks. The *Varna* divide between the twice born castes and the *Shudras* in the Hindi heartland areas has historically demarcated a rigid social hierarchy, one in which lower castes were deprived of education, denied social dignity and were confined to manual work of cultivation or to other low status artisan and service occupations. Untouchables, by definition, performed ritually polluting tasks and in addition, worked in the fields, commonly under conditions of begar or bonded labour. In south India, the Varna structure by itself could not legitimize the secular stratification of wealth and power. The *Brahmins* constituted no more than about three to four percent of the population. While they remained at the apex of the ritual hierarchy, they were unevenly distributed, and controlled extnesive land only in some localities. The *Kshatriyas,* if present at all, were settled in extremely low concentration. Vaishyas of indigenous origin were outnumbered by immigrant *Marwaris, Jains* and other mercantile castes. In most of the south India, land controlling groups came from origins which marked them as *Shudra* by brahmincal criteria.

Thus, we find that from 1940's onwards, when the new dominant castes emerged, these were mainly of Shudras origin in the south and the jats at middle rungs in the local hierarchies like *Yadav*, *Kurmi*, *Gujjar* and *Jat* in the north. Since the untouchable castes in north India were, by and large, traditionaly landless, they could not take advantage of *Zamindari* abolition and ensuing and reforms. Therefore, the middle level non-polluting castes had all the ingredients of future dominant castes. The Green Revolution further strengthened their position. In a nut shell, one can say that socially, the Green Revolution has been basically a contribution of the middle caste peasantry, who have had traditionally a strong attachment to land and agriculture as a mode of life and livelihood. The *Jats*, *Kurmis*, *Yadav* in the north, the *Kunbis*, *Patels* and *Patidars* in maharashtra, the *Khammas*, *Reddis* and *Rajus* in Andhra Pradesh, the *Vanniyars* and *Nadars* in Tamil Nadu, the *Vokaligga* and *Lingayats* in Karnataka etc., have been the leaders of Green Revolution and most of them emerged as dominant castes in their respective regions.

V

A number of western social scientists and political thinkers have been making prophesies about India - the traditional Asian social order. I have chosen two of these made by two giants of their age, Karl Marx and Max Weber.

> Modern Industry, resulting from railway system, will dissolve the hereditary division of labour, upon which rest the Indian castes, those decisive impediments ot Indian progress and Indian Power.
>
> —Karl Marx in Articles on India

> If the stability of the caste order could not hinder property differentiation, it could at least block technological change and occupational mobility, which, from the point of view of caste, were objectionable and ritually dangerous. Today, the very fact that new skills and techniques actually lead to the formation of new castes or subcastes strongly handicaps innovation. It sustains tradition no matter

how often the all powerful development of imported capitalism overrides it.

— Max Weber in the *Religion of India*

The crux of Marx's, Weber's and other early scholars analyses of the caste system and other related aspects of India's traditional social order was their assumption that a real dichotomy existed between the type of society which sustained the caste system the type of society which accompanied the rise of modern industrial economies. They were quite incorrect in this perception. It was because of the inherently and amazingly flexible nature of caste that proved their prophecies wrong. For example, most jobs in modern industry are new in content and method, and since most are viewed as *ritually neutral*, persons of any caste, including untouchables and *Brahmins*, may fill them. Moreover, in the towns and cities violations of ritual norms were condoned by the castes. This was one area where most of the western social scientists erred in making correct forecasts.

Summarising the changes in the structure and functioning of caste, one may borrow Harold Gould's statement when he says that *in the rural areas, caste despite many modifications, is persisting in it's traditional form, as a system of hierarchically graded, locally integrated, occupationally and ritually specialized, endogenous social strata. In the contemporary, urban based order, caste is persisting the form of complex networks of interest gruops preserved through endogamy and legitimized by region. In both forms, caste remains an extremely viable social institution and thus appears to be an instance where simultaneously old uses have been retained and new ones found for a traditional Asian social structure.* Significantly, the changes are taking place within the same social order based on caste. More than forty years after indepndence, it is becoming apparent just how much society in modern India has undergone, and continues to undergo, profound change. Social groups, which, for centureis, were accustomed to command, within decades found their moral authority challenged and political power undermined. Indian society is in ferment. If the Indian state can not keep the tensions, coming out of a traditionally unequal social order, within manageable limits, we are in for serious trouble. Status distribution and fruits of development have to follow just path.

❑

SECTION EIGHT

ASPECTS OF INDIA'S VILLAGES and SOCIAL ORGANIZATION OF AGRICULTURE

24 Rural Society in India

India may be described as a nation of villages. It has around six lac villages and around 68% of Indian population lives in villages. All of these villages are not similar. These may be classified into different types such as (i) Nucleated Villages, commonest all over India, a tight cluster of houses surrounded by the fields (ii) Linear Settlements, where houses are strung out, each surrounded by its own compound. There is little to physically demarcate where one village ends and another begins (iii) Scattering of homesteads or clusters of two or three houses where physical demarcation is not clear. Beside these and other types size of population and density of population may also represent important types.

Further, India's villages portray an overwhelming diversity of form, style, custom and ritual. Each is a product of a long evolution, an overlapping of separate peoples and cultures over a period of thousands of years. Contemporary village India is a mirror of it's past.

The main components of rural social structure in India have been and still are, despite social change, family and kinship, caste, class and village. Several sociologists while describing village India talks about caste, Joint family and village community as forming a trinity. However, on a wider plane, we look at such social institutions rooted in recorded history as described above are longest enduring. The all pervading nature of these social institutions may be observed in all spheres of life — social, cultural, economic and political. We get their reflection in social norms, and values, statuses and roles, and rights and obligations. Within India's rural social structure family, usually joint family, functions as unit of economic, socio-cultural, political and religious domains.

When we examine the essential nature of India's villages the issue of 'village autonomy' immediately comes to the fore. This has been a controversial issue. Among the earliest scholars Henry Maine (1881), Charle's Metcalfe (1833) and Badon Powell (1896) laid emphasis on the notion of village autonomy in an exaggerated manner. The Indian village was portrayed as a 'closed' and 'isolated' system. Charles Metcalfe (*ibid*) went a step further and described the Indian villages as 'little republics', almost independent within themselves, monolithic, atomistic, non-changing and self sufficient. The later researches done by the historians, sociologists and social anthropologists have demolished this myth. The Indian village was never self sufficient. It always maintained links with the larger society and centres of India civilization. Migration and movement for work and trade, village exogamy, administrative linkages, inter-regional markets, inter village economic ties, caste network, pilgrimage, fairs and festivals and other activities always served as bridges with the neighbouring villages and the larger society. During later years new forces of modernization further expanded the inter village and rural-urban interaction. This has been described by Oscar Lewis (1955) as 'Rural Cosmopolitanism'. But despite the increasing external linkages village remains, by and large, a fundamental social unit and people living in a village have a sense of common identity and loyalty.

Traditional Characteristic Feature of Villages and Changes Coming into them

1. **Isolation and self sufficiency:** Historically speaking, till 19th Century Indian villages were more isolated and self contained. There was minimal contact with the outside world. There used to be fixed division of labour (because of fixed status and roles as per caste system). Villages consisted of peasants, agricultural labour and artisans. Human labour was the main resource in the absence of mechanization and use of machines.

   Due to rapid development of transport and communication since the 20th century, villages began undergoing rapid changes in all respects. With increasing use of machines division of labour has undergone changes. With increased economic and political empowerment of disadvantaged groups and castes *Jajmani* system has virtually crumbled.

2. **Conservation:** Our villages have always been characterised by strongly traditional and conservative attitude. Changes may also be seen in their attitudes towards women, youth and social institutions.

3. **Caste Mobility:** Through the process of sanskritization, economic and political empowerment caste system does not remain static. A virtually occupation free caste system has developed where caste and occupation are now almost delinked.

4. **Joint Family:** Once the hallmark of agrarian society in India, it is now crumbling as a social institution because of rising aspirational level, individualism and assertiveness of educated women.

5. **Marriage:** Decision making in choosing a spouse is becoming more democratic. Education, economic pursuit and status, beauty and appearance are now more important than merely social/caste status through caste endogamy is still very strong.

6. **Living Standard:** Now there is better availability of food, dress and jewellary, more *pucca* houses, toilets

and sanitation. With the opening of primary health centres and hospitals the health status has improved and infant mortality rate has declined appreciably. Small family norm is also picking up.

7. **Economic System:** Preciously private moneylenders were the only source of credit. Now their dependence on *sahukar* (moneylenders) has decreased with the increased availability of institutional finance — cooperative credit societies, self help groups, rural banks and commercial banks. Plastic money (credit and debit cards) has also entered into villages of most of the states. There is also improved agricultural technology.
8. **Political System:** The traditional village/caste panchayats have declined and under Panchayat Raj, statutory panchayats looking after development work are making rapid inroads. Thus, the democratic decentralization coupled with reservation for scheduled castes, scheduled tribes and women have facilitated the emergence of a new leadership with new ideas. The power structure is changing.

Indian Village as a Social System

System implies an orderly arrangement, inter-relationship of parts in which every part has a fixed place and definite role. These parts do not exist in isolation but are bound by a constant interaction. When this understanding of system is applied to Social System we get an insight into the working of social system. Arrangement of social interactions based on shared norms and values provides the basis of social system. In practical sense, individuals constitute it and each individual has a place and function to perform. Talcott Parsons gives a clear understanding of social system by telling that "plurality of social actors engaged in more or less stable interaction according to shared cultural norms and meaning" is a precondition. Here the interaction is 'patterned interaction'. He further tells us that social system is a comprehensive arrangement. It takes under its orbit all the diverse sub-systems such as economic, political, religious and others. Moreover, social system, in itself neither exists in isolation nor totally independent. It is also bound by environment. Thus, geographical factors have also a crucial role to play in the maintenance of social system. Breaking this conceptual understanding into parts, we may have the following points:

- Plurality of individual actors which means there should be a number of interacting individuals
- Every social system must have certain aims and objectives. It can never be aimless.
- There must be some order and pattern among various functional constituents or units.
- The unity between the constituents of the social system is based on functional relationship.
- Adjustment between the constituents or units.

Perhaps, the most important aspect of social system is maintenance. The maintenance of social system is based on socialization and social control. The former refers to the process through which the children or younger generation learns or adopts the norms, values, and behavioural pattern of the family and the larger group while the later implies the power of enforcement because without social control, social system cannot survive for long.

Now, if we look at the Indian village we find all the important feature of social system in it. There is constant interaction between the individuals and there is no anonymity because of small population and high density of population. Indian villages are caste based with a deep rooted caste system. There is functional relationship and mutual interdependence between different castes as per *Jajmani* norms and obligations. Though, the *Jajmani* system, the socio-economic-political basis of the caste system, has weakened a lot, crumbling or has crumbles in many villages but the caste based interaction is still there. With the enforcement of *Panchayat Raj,* democratic decentralization has been adopted where individuals and castes as units may be competing with each other but adjustment is also sought and achieved to minimise frictions and conflicts. Joint family, and wherever it has disintegrated, nuclear family and caste through caste panchayat supported by statutory panchayat serve as agency of socialization and social control for the maintenance of social system. Since all the important features of social system are found in Indian Village, it can safely be concluded that it represents social system.

Village Study in India and Its Significance:

Study of small scale, isolated primitive tribal communities have been the dominant field for social cultural anthropologists upto 1930s or so. Credit goes to Robert Redfield and his students from Chicago (Later prominent anthropologists) for making a significant departure from the past. Redfield initiated the study of civilization and with this the anthropologists turned their attention towards peasant society and villages and urban centres or cities. Redfield provided a model for village study through his own work — a systematic study of a village in Mexico by the name of Topoztalan. It was followed by anthropologists all over the world.

In village study, a village is chosen as a unit of investigation. It is an ethnographic account of a village written on the basis of data collected, largely, through participant observation. In this way anthropologists utilized their experience and expertise achieved over a century of study of tribal societies through this method.

By the turn of 20th Century in India, being the first among social scientists, some economist had begun village studies. But obviously, their work and orientation were different. In 1930s William Wiser, though not a trained anthropologist, did two remarkable and pioneering works. His *Hindu Jajmani System,* study of village of Karimpur in north India came in 1930 followed by *Behind the Mud Walls* in 1936. These were pioneering work of anthropological tradition as these were based on intensive field work. By 1950s a sudden explosion of interest in village studies was witnessed.

In post-independence period rural reconstruction and development occupied a high priority. The American anthropologists were also attracted to village studies and with them anthropologically oriented village studies gained momentum. Morris Opler, Oscar Lewis, Mickim Mariot, David Mandelbaum, Bernard Cohn, Allan Beals alongwith British anthropologists such as F.G. Bailey, A.C. Meyer, Scarlett Epstein etc. did excellent village studies. They used high levels of scientific method. Now entered India anthropologists in a big way. In late 1950s M.N. Srinivas published *Indias' Villages*, *S.C. Dube* did *Indian Village*, D.N. Majumdar published *Rural Profiles* in two volumes, *Village India*, an edited volume by Mickim Marriot, and some others heralded a new beginning. S.C. Dubes *Indian Village*, a study of Shamirpet village near Hyderabad is considered a classic in village studies. It provided a complete picture of village life. D.N. Majumdars' *Caste and Communication in an Indian Village* (1958) showed how the introduction of new means of transport and communication impacted caste mobility. *Life in a North Indian Village* by Oscar Lewis and *Caste and the Economic Frontier* by F.G. Bailey was a path breaking work on the interface of caste and economic pursuit while K.S. Mathurs' *Caste and Ritual in Malwa Village* looked into the dynamics of caste and religious rituals.

The Significance of village studies may be understood at two levels — theoretical and practical or applied. In depth ethnography of village resulted in the emergence of concepts such as Sanskritization and Dominant Caste developed by M.N. Srinivas on the basis of his study of religion and society of Rampur village. Great and Little Tradition were developed by Robert Redfield on the basis of his study in Mexican villages while the Concepts of Universalisation and Parochialization have been given by Mickim Marriot to understand the cultural process of Indian Civilization.

On the practical/applied level village studies helped the planners involved in rural reconstruction and development. Village studies provided, for the first time, first hand knowledge of villages in an objective manner. It not only helped in planning - at micro and macro level both - but also helped other disciplines in social science to think of village objectively. It also negated the colonial outlook of villages and in the post independence period negated the stereotype and image of villages developed by urban people. It helped the government to locate the channels of social change and barriers to change. It also helped to understand the role of communication in the development of new economic pursuit and breakdown of caste prejudices and practices besides understanding the emerging new power structure and leadership. Thus, one can see that the village studies are not merely an academic pursuits of anthropologists and sociologists but may go a long way in its contribution to the nation building process.

RURAL COSMOPOLITANISM:

The propounder of this concept is Oscar Lewis and this is the outcome of his comparative study of a North Indian Village, Ranikhera near Delhi and Tepoztalan, a village in Morelos, Mexico (earlier in 1930 the same village was studied by Robert Redfield thus initiating 'Village Studies' in anthropology).

In 1953-54 Robert Redfield, Mickim Marriot and Milton Singer organized a seminar on Indian Village Studies at the University of Chicago, to which they invited eight outstanding social anthropologists to discuss their respective field studies in eight different regions of India. The two central questions that were addressed to were:

(1) To what extent is the Indian Village an isolated and self sufficient "little community"?

(2) What can be learned from village studies about Indian Civilization as a whole?

In the paper submitted by Oscar Lewis to this seminar, he beings out contrasts between these two villages of India and Mexico. He found the Mexican villages 'Inward looking', it's people marrying within the village. The inter-village networks of relationships are constituted of trade and not of other cultural bonds such as pilgrimage to shrines, etc. Moreover, the Mexican villages are "relatively self contained nuclear groupings or pockets of a small number of villages centrally located within municipos."

In contrast each Indian village was linked to other villages in it's region and to towns and cities by complex networks of social relations based on caste, kinship and marriage, trade and occupation, religious pilgrimage, and administrative and political organization. In the words of Lewis himself, "a villagc in India is part of multiple intervillage networks and where a single village is related by affinal and lineage ties with over four hundred other villages, thereby making for a kind of Rural Cosmopolitanism." Thus we find that the concept of Rural Cosmopolitanism is largely based on the villager's social relations beyond the village and it further extends his cultural horizons.

TRADITIONAL CULTURE

The concept of Traditional Culture is commonly associated with a very important work of George Foster, Traditional Change (1962). This work is a product of his long experience in Latin American countries (Mexico, Columbia, Peru and Brazil) where some socio-cultural factors affected the functioning of public health centres. Thus, largely, this concept deals with cultural barriers to change because the peasant/rural societies because of their traditional cultures are often resistant to change — socio-economic and technological.

The stereotyped portrayal of Traditional Cultures is often in terms of non-rationality, inactivity, fatalism and 'other worldliness' (non-secular attitude). One of the most characteristic features of traditional culture is the anonymous character of it's original producers and contributors. Apart from direct oral transmission and practical demonstration the folk/peasant communities may also develop some other means to transmit their traditional knowledge from one generation to the other such as linguistic formula put into rhyme which may contain facts about climate, weather conditions, agriculture, animal farming, religious and moral instructions as well as a whole range of experiences forming what is popularly known as 'wise sayings'. Many of these formulae belong to the category of proverbs. These may be common in current speech.

Institutionalized social gatherings are very important media for the preservation of traditional culture. Such gatherings may be meetings at home, ritual occasions, fair and festivals etc. Glorification and sanctification of the past is, perhaps, the most important part of the traditional culture. "Out fathers and grand fathers have always done this, thus we shall do" - is a statement often heard from peasants from the traditional cultures.

Thus, we find that traditional rural communities have a traditional culture with it's own values and rationale. Their "cultural ethnocentrism" often makes them stubborn and resistant to change. Therefore, the planners must know and understand this before introducing a new idea or technology into such traditional societies. Even otherwise all the traditions are not bad and a happy convergence of tradition and modernity is not impossible.

AGRARIAN SOCIAL STRUCTURE & SOCIAL ORGANIZATION OF AGRICULTURE

The study of agrarian social structure has been a matter of serious study in rural sociology and social anthropology. If we go by the dictionary meaning, 'agrarian' pertains to land or it's tenure or to a general distribution of lands and organizing or furthering agricultural interests. Agrarianism refers to a set of values which holds that agriculture is the most natural and desirable vocation and the farm the ideal place to live.

Thus, an agrarian society may be accepted as "any form of society, especially traditional societies, primarily based on agricultural production and associated crafts rather than industrial production" (*Collin's Dictionary of Sociology*, 1991). If we wish to elaborate further, we may say that an agrarian society "focuses it's mode of production primarily on agriculture and the cultivation of large fields. This distinguishes it from the 'Hunter-Gatherer Society' which produces none of its own food, and the 'Horticultural Society' which produces food in small gardens rather than fields" (*The Blackwell Dictionary of Sociology*, 1995).

Besides others, A.R. Desai and Andre Beitelle have contributed significantly to the understanding of agrarian social structure in India. Beitelle while defining the agrarian social structure is clearly of the view that only peasantry does not constitute it. It means something more than the study of peasant societies and cultures. Thus, all those playing a role in agrarian society from various parts of it. He further says that the study of agrarian social structure revolves round mainly two aspects (i) technological arrangements, and (ii) social arrangements. While the former refers to the ecological conditions and agricultural technology, the later refers to land ownership and control, power structure, land tenure and related social dimensions.

The understanding of agrarian social structure and the Social Organization of Agriculture, described as 'Social Framework of Agriculture' by Andre Beitelle (1974), as not possible without having a sound understanding, of 'Peasantry' or 'Peasant Society' and its various implications and dimensions in the Indian setting.

Talking about the Social Framework of Agriculture Andre Beitelle (*ibid*) says that the economic activities and economic change cannot be adequately understood in isolation from the social framework within it takes place. This is particularly true of the under-developed (and developing) countries of Asia where economic organization has a lower degree of autonomy than in the industrial societies of the West. Thus, in such Asian societies the economic organization is found to be more closely intermeshed with a variety of social institutions whose functions are partly economic and partly non-economic. He further emphasises upon the relevance of the social framework to economic activities by elaborating that the economic activities involve the mutual interaction of individuals whose rights and obligations are socially defined. The same broad set of activities, as in agriculture, can be socially organized.

Peasant Society

A peasant society is a small scale social organization in which peasants predominate. Anthropologists have defined and explained peasant societies in different ways. A.L. Kroeber was the first anthropologist who tried to provide a formal definition of peasant societies. He described peasant societies as a 'part society' indicating it's dependence in technological, economic, political, administrative religious and moral spheres on a larger society. George Foster taking clue from Kroeber described peasant society as a 'half society'. He implied that a larger society, such as a nation may consist of two parts - the first part consisting of cultivating class living in villages and the second part consists of upper classes living in urban centres. That part of a larger society which is composed of cultivating classes is peasant society or half-society. Robert Redfield followed Kroeber and he also defined peasant society as a 'part society'.

Until 1960s, the peasantry was largely ignored in sociology as having no significant role to pay in history. This was despite the fact that peasants have existed for most of recorded history and in many parts of the world. From the 1960s, the publication of key works, such as Eric Wolf (1966) and Barington Moore (1967), began to change this perception, introducing to sociology perspectives developed in anthropology and political economy. "The role of peasantry in the Vietnam war, and the growth of peasant political activity in Latin America and Asia raised questions about the assured passivity of the peasantry. Within Marxist work, partly under the influence of Maoism and events in China around the 1949 Revolution and subsequently, there emerged the question of whether the peasantry in the Third World represented the revolutionary force of socialism. There is now a major area of interdisciplinary peasant studies. Till date the debate continues over whether a distinctive category of peasantry can be identified both conceptually and empirically. Shanin presents one of the strongest and most influential defences of the concept. Drawing his inferences from various peasant studies in this century, he argues that there are six inter-related characteristics of the peasantry (Shanin, 1982; Shanin (*ed.*) 1988, *introduction*)

(a) The family farm is the major economic unit around which production, labour and consumption are organized.
(b) Land husbandry is the main activity combined with minimal specialization and family training for tasks.

(c) There is a particular 'peasant way of life' based on the local village community which covers most areas of social life and culture and which distinguished it from urban life and from those of other social groups.

(d) Peasants are politically, economically and socially subordinated to non-peasant greaps against whom they have devised various methods of resistance, rebellion or revolt.

(e) A specific social dynamics involving a cyclical change over generations which irons out inequalities over times via land division and the rise and fall of the availability of family labour through the domestic cycle.

(f) Especially in the contemporary world, a common pattern of structural change, drawing peasants into market relationships, often through the influence of outside bodies such as agribusiness, and incorporation into national politics. There precise outcome of these common changes is not predetermined."

Robert Redfield in his landmark work '*Peasant Society and Culture*' (1956) placing Peasant Society between folk and urban communities has described the following three as the most important features of a peasant culture.

(a) Highly reverent attitude towards land,

(b) Acceptance of agriculture as the noblest, best and the ideal job, and

(c) A pronounced, industrious attitude of the people demonstrating a firm belief in the dignity of labour.

Among the other important features of Peasant Society are:

(i) family is the primary unit of multilateral social organization.

(ii) the main source of livelihood is land and agriculture which fulfill almost all the requirements of life,

(iii) they maintain a distinctive, traditional culture in terms of day to day life and its' schedule, and

(iv) usually, they are dominated by outsiders.

For the peasant societies, agriculture is not an enterprise but a way of life which cannot be given up in favour of any other activity promising more money or profit. If agriculture becomes an enterprise instead of a way of life, a peasant becomes a farmer like the rich farmers of Punjab, Haryana, Maharashtra or Karnataka. Thus, peasants are subsistence cultivator of agricultural land. They may be owner-occupiers or tenants, participants or non-participants in the market. Some writers (for example Chayamov and Eric Wolf) have attempted to isolate a distinctive peasant economy, others (for example, Redfield) stress the notion of a peasant culture.

As the above description indicates, all definitions of the peasantry agree on emphasising the importance of the opposition or contrast between the peasant stratum and the urban elite. The peasantry and the urban centre are two opposing poles of a single socio-economic system, and this is reflected not only in their economic inter-dependence but also in the complex relationship which exists between peasant and urban culture. This may be seen in the concepts of Great/Little Tradition and folk-urban continuum. Among the anthropologists, Eric Wolf (1969) in his '*Peasants*' defines the peasants as those whose surplus production is transferred to a dominant ruling group, which employs this surplus both to maintain itself and to redistribute it to other non-agricultural sectors of the population.

Peasants can be most clearly distinguished in Agrarian Societies. Significantly, cultivators are not the only segment of population constituting a peasant community. People, who are not analytically defined as peasants but still a part of the peasant community are also parts of it. They may be traders, labourers without land and artisans who may have close social and economic links with the peasants. Further, people who are analytically defined as 'peasants' will often engage in some of these activities for part of their time. Thus, while, definitions of the peasantry sometimes rest on the functioning of the household, it is essential to see how this is firmly integrated into a wider social, political and economic network. David Lehmann (1985) stated that "it seems best to discard the term 'peasants' as a comprehensive descriptor of rural populations of any sort and to use it instead as an adjective describing features of rural production systems without pretensions to exhaustive definition."

Characteristics:

Anthropologists and sociologists like Kroeber, Foster, Redfield, Wolf, Norback, Thorner, Shanin, Andre Beitelle and many more who have written about peasant societies have agreed on the following features as characteristics of peasant societies:

(i) A peasant society has long history commensurate with that of city and state.

(ii) A peasant society has a social system based on face to face relationships. It includes village communities. The inhabitants of each village communities. The inhabitants of each village are known to one another through shared experience in work, ritual and leisure activities. This close association entails a social system based on face-to-face relationships. The inhabitants of each village may also have personal ties with individuals outside their village community.

(iii) A peasant society views agriculture as a means of livelihood not as a business for profit. It is not so much that peasant's lack an interest in selling a portion of their crops but rather that such sales are not an end in themselves. These sales can best be understood as transactions that help maintain a given style of life and permit the acquisition of basic necessities. Consequently, peasants are primarily concerned with subsistence production and generally consume a major portion of the food and other articles they produce.

(iv) A peasant society is based on antiquated technology and low agricultural productivity. Its technology in many parts of the world has changed little since Neolithic times. The productivity of peasant agriculture is low. The peasant economy reveals reliance on agriculture, simple technology, an emphasis on subsistence production, a limited range of items produced, and a direct dependence on the environment.

(v) A peasant society directs its economic behaviour at a pattern of immediate consumption and at meeting the material demands of ceremonialism. First, a peasant society is characterized by lack of deferred gratification i.e. the tendency to spend rather than to save, to spend now rather than tomorrow. Second, every peasant society directs its effort at meeting the material demands of religious observances and social position in terms of festive foods, fireworks, incense, traditional payments and obligations, taxes, shares and other dues and rents.

(vi) A peasant society always maintains communication with the urban centres. It produces some exchangeable surplus food which goes to support towns and cities which in turn provide certain types of manufactured or processed goods and services. These exchanges are frequently organized and carried on through a system of market places usually in the towns or cities. Many of its institutions are local manifestations of national institutions such as the use of a national currency in economic exchange and national educational system. Further, the religious, intellectual and moral life of the urban centres influence the life at the village level and link the peasant community to the wider society.

(vii) A peasant society is resistant or very slow to change. Peasants have survived for thousands of years through a series of techniques designed to make them less tempting targets. It is difficult to convince peasants that they can now discard

> these defences with impunity. Peasants make the economists sigh, the politicians sweat, and the strategists swear all over the world-Moscow and Washington, Peking and Delhi.

Power Structure and Class Stratification:

The usual and universalistic way of describing social structure has been through institutions based on birth such as Family, Kinship and Caste. Another way of describing it is through class. Thus, the agrarian class structure may be used to understand the power structure and class stratification in Indian rural social structure. However, both caste and class are necessary to describe the agrarian social structure in India. It also explains the power structure in rural India. In this way when we talk of agrarian class stratification we get a better view of rural India which was, traditionally, viewed through caste stratification only. K.L. Sharma (1980) putting the whole issue in proper perspective makes the incisive comment by saying that "caste incorporates the elements of class and class has a cultural (caste) style, hence the two systems cannot be easily seperated even analytically."

Broadly speaking, the modern agrarian class structure in India evolved during the British colonial rule. It was the outcome of the land revenue system evolved and enforced by the British rule. There were three classes:

(i) land owners
(ii) tenants
(iii) agricultural labourers

Daniel Thorner (1973) in his classical work describes these three classes as:

(i) proprietors
(ii) working peasants
(iii) labourers

In vernacular language he uses the terms *maalik*, *kisan*, and *mazdur* for these three classes respectively. The landowners or proprietors traditionally belonged to the upper caste groups. They were tax gatherers and non-cultivating owners of land. Thorner (*ibid*) understands that the category of proprietors of *maalik* refers to families whose agricultural income is derived primarily (although not necessarily solely) from property rights in the soil. That is to say that whatever other sources of family income may exist, such as from a profession or business, the main, agricultural income is derived from a share of the produce of lands belonging to the family. Typically, this share will be realized in the form of rent. Usually, the rent will be taken in money, but it may be in kind of the tenants are on crop sharing basis. Instead of renting out his lands, however, a proprietor may hire labourers to cultivate them for him. He may manage these hired labourers himself or he may hire someone else as manager. He may actually go into the fields and perform some of the work alongside of his hired labourers. The main determinant should be his mode of income —if his agricultural income from that part of his holdings which he cultivates with his own lands is less than the amount he receives from renting out the rest of his lands, or having them tilled by hired labourers. Within this group or class of proprietors, it is possible to separate out two subgroups. One consists of large absentee land lords who typically have holdings in more than one village. The second consists of smaller proprietors who reside personally in the village in which they own land, and usually exercise some degree of management and control over its cultivation. Most of the members of this class come from the higher castes.

The second class (referred to as *Kisan*) of working peasants have also a recognised property interest in the land (Thorner, *ibid*). They may be small owners, or tenants with varying degrees of security. By and large (but not in every state) their legal and customary rights will be somewhat inferior to those of the *malik* (proprietors) in the same village. The chief distinguishing feature, however, is the amount of land held. In the case of the working peasant the size of the holding is such that it supports only a single family and then only if one or more members of the family actually perform the field labour. In fact, the produce from the land owned by the *Kisan* may not even provide the entire income required by his family, but at least it provides a larger share than whatever funds he may receive from other agricultural sources, such as doing labour on other people's lands. *Kisan* as defined here are those villagers who live primarily by their own toil on their own lands. They do not employ labour, except briefly in the ploughing or harvest season, nor do they commonly receive rent. They come from the middle level cultivating or artisan castes, most of them being OBCs or backward castes as per the current terminology.

The third agrarian class referred to as labourers or *mazdur* comprise those villagers who gain their livelihood primarily from working on the people's land. Families in this class may indeed have tenancy rights in the soil, or even property rights, but the holdings are so small that the income from cultivating them or from renting them out comes to less than the earnings from fieldwork. Wages may be received in money or in kind. If the latter, they may be fixed or in the form of a crop share. In practice the lower ranks of croppers and tenants-at-will are almost indistinguishable from mazdur, they will tentatively be included in this category. Most of the members of this class come from the traditionally landless, deprived, lonely untouchable castes or scheduled castes and backward castes as per the current terminology.

As Thorner (*ibid*) rightly points out, the maintenance of this hierarchical structure of interests in the land had required that quite a substantial proportion of the produce be reserved for persons who perform no agricultural labour. What was left to the actual cultivator, after the claims of the various superior right holders were satisfied, might still be subject to collection as unpaid debt by the moneylender. Thus, the power structure in the agrarian class is largely based on exploitation and deprivation. In his landmark work D.N. Dhanangre (1983) says that although Thorner's categories and sub-categories are nearer the realities of the Indian agrarian social structure there is still a need to read just or regroup these categories into such a broader and more comprehensive model and redesignate them commonly used concepts and criteria in the study of peasant societies. Such a model can be drawn from the works of Lenin and Mao, especially those relating to the analysis of agrarian classes in the Russian and Chinese societies respectively:

(i) Landlords
(ii) Rich Peasants
(iii) Middle Peasants
(iv) Poor Peasants
(v) Landless labourers

Dhanangre (*ibid*) further opines that the social composition of these agrarian classes in terms of specific status groups like castes, religious or ethnic groups, etc. is far too complex in different regions of India to reduce into any simplistic formulae. However, for a loose and broad classification this may hold ground. For example, landlords and rich land owners (including non-cultivating urban money lenders/owners) belonged to the upper castes such as Brahmin, Thakur, or Banias in northern India. In Andhra Pradesh the Kammas, Reddis and Raos, in Mysore the Okkaligas and Lingayats, the Patidars in the Gujarat region while the Kunbi Marathas and Deshmukhs in Maharashtra could be cited as more examples of the locally dominant landowing castes. The middle and poor peasantry, mostly debt-ridden, came primarily from the traditional castes of cultivators, artisans and soon. The landless labourers belonged mostly to untouchable castes, the scheduled castes.

The past-independence period witnessed significant changes in the agrarian class structure in India. The impact of land reforms and rural development programmes facilitated the emergence of new forces of change. Infact, the challenge to the feudal class structure emerged with the rise of the nationalist movement. Analysing these changes Yogendra Singh says that the agrarian class structure everywhere in India had a feudal character. The challenge to the feudal class structure came with the nationalist movement when not only was a radical agrarian ideology accepted but the nationalist leadership also actively undertook the cause of the exploited peasantry and led *Kisan* (peasant) movements in various parts of the country. Following independence, therefore, land reforms were introduced in most states and a beginning was made for transformation in the agrarian class structure. Most sociological studies of the agrarian structure refer to these processes of social change. Moreover, the significant trends mentioned in such studies are:

(i) that there is a wide gap between land reform ideology projected during the freedom struggle or even thereafter and the actual measures introduced for land reforms consequently, socialist transformation in the class structure of the villages has not take place;

(ii) this lag could partly be explained by the class character of the Indian political and administrative elite who are resistant to the needed radical reforms;

(iii) the existing land reforms have initiated a process by which the security of tenure and economic prosperity of the rich peasantry has increased, but the condition of the small peasants, both in respect of economic level and tenurial stability, has deteriorated;

(iv) the feudalistic and customary type of tenancy has declined and it has been replaced by a capitalistic form of lease labour or wage labour agrarian system;

(v) a new class of rich middle stratum of peasantry system has come into being, and not all of these are from among the ex-zamindars;

(vi) the class inequalities between the top and the bottom levels of the classes have increased rather than decreased.

(vii) the benefits of land reforms have so far not gone so much to the agricultural workers or even to ex-zamindars as to the emergent middle peasantry;

(viii) as a result of these contradictions in the agrarian class structure the tensions in the rural social system have increased and are bound to increase further; and finally,

(ix) the sociological process, that is dominant in the current class transformations in the villages, is the 'embourgeoisiment' of some and 'proletarianization' of many social strata.

P.C. Joshi (1971) in his celebrated work has made very incisive comments on the trends in the agrarian class structure. Some of these are summarized as under:

(a) it led to the decline of feudal and customary types of tenancies. It was replaced by a more exploitative and insecure lease arrangement;

(b) it gave rise to a new commercial based rich peasant class who were part owners and part tenants. They had resource and enterprise to carry out commercial agriculture;

(c) it led to the decline of feudal landlord class and another class of commercial farmers emerged for whom agriculture was a business. They used the non-customary type of tenancy.

Thus, the rural India witnessed and still witnessing the process of social mobility and transformation. Depeasantization of small and marginal peasant is also a by product of the transformation of village India.

Jajmani System:

It has been the socio-economic basis of the Hindu Caste system and an integral part of the agrarian social structure in India. It is said that the term *jajmani system* has been introduced in the vocabulary of Indian sociology and social anthropology by William Wiser through his pioneering work, *The Hindu Jajmani System* (1936). He carried out this study in a village called Karimpur in Uttar Pradesh. In this seminal contribution Wiser described in detail how different castes interact with one another in the production and exchange of goods and services. Though there are regional variations of this term in different parts of the country the term *Jajmani system* has become a standardized term in sociological literature.

Under the *jajmani system* each caste group within a village is expected to give certain standardised services to the families of other castes. In general terms it stands for the exchange of goods and services between the landowing higher castes and landless services castes. These castes have always been occupationally specialized following certain traditional occupations and thus are known also as artisan castes. Those artisan castes such as black smiths, gold smiths, weavers, oilseed pressers, leather workers, barbers, washerman, musicians and a wide range of occupationally specialized groups alongwith the traditionally landless untouchable castes providing agricultural labour constitute the 'service castes' and known as either *Kamin*, *prajan* and other terms in different parts of the country. The landed higher castes are broadly known as *jajman* (patrons). These service relations which are governed by a hereditary tenure, are called the *jajman* - *prajan* relations.

The jajmani system is essentially an agriculture based system of production and distribution of goods and services. Through jajmani relations these occupational castes get linked with the landowning dominant castes. The land owning castes maintain a paternalistic attitude of superiority towards their occupational or service castes.

Oscar Lewis (1956) rightly points out that under this system, each caste group within a village is expected to give certain standardised services to the families of other castes. Pauline Koleanda (1963) looks at it as a system of distribution whereby the higher caste land owing families called *Jajmans* are provided services and products by various lower castes. The system, thus, explains the occupational division of labour in an Indian agricultural village with distribution of services and products under a network of role relationship and payments. Tradition approves of such an arrangement, and mutual trust and inter-dependence in the Indian agrarian system based on Caste. Talking about the social dynamics of the jajmani system S.C. Dube (1953) says that it is not easy for an agriculturist to remove a family attached to his household and secure the services of another. No one else would be willing to act as a substitute for fear of being penelized by the caste panchayat. David Mandelbaum (1972), a keen observer of village India emphasises upon the internal functioning of the jajmani system and says that the jajmani relations essentially operate at family level. A Rajput landowing family has its jajmani ties with one family each from brahmin, barber, carpenter, etc., and family of service caste offers its services to specific families of jajmans. However, jajmani rules are enforced by caste panchayats.

The jajmani relations are durable and are of hereditary nature. The jajmani rights however may be regarded as a form of property passing from father to son. These relations are in a way informed and governed largely by the local traditions. On the whole, the jajmani system carries strong elements of dominance, exploitation and conflict. There is wide difference in exercise of power between landowning dominant patrons and poor artisans and landless laborers who serve them. Another very important feature of the jajmani system is that though, the jajmani relations operate at village level, they are often not confined to a single village only, because not all the villages have all occupational castes and therefore the services of 'occupations'. Castes from other villages are frequently borrowed. Moreover, for certain occupational castes, such as goldsmiths, blacksmiths an carpenters, a single village may not be adequate to provide sufficient job round the year. Such castes, therefore, cater to the needs of a number of villages in a given region. Summarising, one can say that the jajmani system is an age old social institution which refers to the inter-caste and inter-family social, economic, political and ritual ties prevalent in Indian village. It is one of the most important constituents of social organization of agriculture in India.

Decline of Jajmani System:

Gradual modernization of Indian economy coincides with the decline of the jajmani system. But it's rapid decline was witnessed in the post-independence period. In loose and broad terms the decline of jajmani system can be discussed under the following heads:

(a) Role of the State

(b) Introduction of technological innovations and industrialization

(c) Political mobilization of the dalits and the backward classes

Traditionally, the jajmani system, based village economy, was primarily a subsistence economy oriented to meet the consumption needs of the local population only. Due to the localized self-sufficiency and immobility of labour and capital, commercialization and the capitalist transformation of agriculture did not take place. After independence deliberate and planned attempts were made to link the village economy to the regional and national markets. In order to facilitate it, the government made huge investments towards the expansion of transport and communication networks. The state's policies contributed to rapid monetization of economy in village India. Increasing productivity in agriculture was very high on government's economic agenda to feed the huge population.

The process of planned development initiate immediately after independence brought about capitalistic transformation in agriculture sector. Moreover, the State took initiative in providing various inputs like credit facilities, technical know how, fertilizers, irrigation, high yielding varieties of seeds etc. Now came a sea change in the mindset of landowning classes and the entry of market forces encouraged them to generate surplus for the market rather than sustaining the age old jajmani system. It gave rise to contractual relationship between the landowning classes and agricultural labourers and artisans. The traditional informal ties started giving way to formal relationship as per formal contractual obligations.

Technological innovations and industrialization also created a situation where there was hardly and need for functional interdependence. With the machine made goods flooding the market and reaching even remote rural areas the rural artisan castes were literally made to compete with the machines. Let us take a look at a few ordinary technological innovations. With the growing availability and the consequent increased use of safety razor the practice of self-shaving became popular minimizing the role of village barber. With the advent of stainless steel utensils the importance of village potter declines. And with the availability of hand pumps in the village the dependence of higher castes on the Kahars (drawers and carriers of water to the households) declines. All this rendered the majority of artisan castes jobless. Many of them opted for the market or started providing their services against cash payment in a formal economic transaction. This, coincides with the rapidly increasing migration of the service castes to the emerging urban centers and industrial townships. Those who stayed behind became wage labourers working on the lands of the landed elite. Village economy was now being increasingly integrated with the urban and national economy.

Before independence, the nationalist movement took a principled and rather quasi-ideological stand on social equality. The weaker sections - dalits, tribal and backward classes were promised an equality based and injustice - exploitation free new order. For that matter Backward Classes Movement had already made its' impact on southern and western parts of India. With the promulgation of the constitution the State became committed to their upliftment and empowerment. One of the profound changes in contemporary Indian society has been the emergence of a new sense of identity among the dalits and the other backward classes. The democratic assertion of the backward segments of Indian population and their political mobilization in different parts of the country was a serious blow to the exploitative jajmani system based on the monopolistic rights of the landed higher castes controlling the means of production in the traditional agrarian economy. With the new found confidence and democratic assertion by the backward classes the jajmani system has suffered a serious set back. Yet it, also seems to be true that whatever the weaker sections gained, the new economic policy and globalization threatens to take away from them.

Peasant Movements

Peasant Movements and agrarian struggles continue to be one of the central themes of the 'old' movement study tradition of sociology and social anthropology in India. Systematic interests in peasant movements can be traced back to the 1960s largely because it was a period when the 'agrarian question' and unequal distribution of land in the 'Third World' were prominent political issues. Peasants came to represent a possible alternative revolutionary subject (Alavi, 1965). However, Erick Stokes (1978) finds that peasant rebellions look strangely absent in Indian society. This situation is attributed to the peculiar Indian social structure, i.e. the caste system and the village structure. However, the 'passive' and 'docile' character of Indian peasants has been challenged by Kathleen Gough (1974), A.R. Desai (1979), D.N. Dhanagare (1983), RanjitGuha (1983) and others. They argue that historians have overlooked a number of peasant rebellions before and during the British rule. Furthermore, according to Andre Beteille (1974), the areas with a larger number of agrarian revolts are predominantly rice-producing regions. These regions not only have a large proportion of agricultural labourers but land is also unequally divided among the cultivators.

Peasant movements in India are generally classified in terms of pre-British/pre-Colonial, British/Colonial, and post- independence periods. In terms of classification, A.R. Desai (1986) classifies colonial India into Ryotwari areas under British territory, Zamindari areas under princely authority, and tribal regions. Kathleen Gough (1974) classifies peasant revolts on the basis of their goals, ideology and methods of organization. The five types suggested by her are:

1. restorative rebellions to drive out the British and restore earlier rulers and social relations;
2. religious movements for the liberation of a region or an ethnic group under a new form of government;
3. social banditry;
4. terrorist vengeance with the idea of meting out collective justice; and
5. mass insurrection for the redress of particular grievances.

Talking of issues, Ghanshyam Shah (1990) says that there was a tendency among the British officers and historians to depict some of the revolts as communal riots, or mere banditry. The Moplah rebellion of the nineteenth century and the early 1920s in Malabar was interpreted primarily as Hindu-Muslim communal clashes, rather than as conflict of economic interests between tenants and landlords, merely because the two groups happened to belong to different religious communities. It was the revolt of Muslim peasantry against the non-Muslim landed gentry. Dhanagre (1983), Panikkar (1979), and Namboodripad (1943) argued that the uprisings were mainly related to agrarian conflicts between tenants and landlords. Moreover, some of the leaders of the Moplah rebellion were Hindus. Shah further argues that in most of the cases the peasants revolted against exploitation and oppression when their economic condition deteriorated. These changes may be classified under the three heads:

1. deterioration of their economic condition due to price rice, famine, etc;
2. structural changes, which cause an increase in the exploitation of peasants, consequently deteriorating their condition; and
3. rising aspirations of peasants to improve their condition.

Famine was almost a regular feature of rural India in the eighteenth and nineteenth centuries, and it continued to be so in isolated pockets to some extent even after independence, though it is now called 'draught' and not famine. Begaar, vethorvethi (forced labour) was widely prevalent in the last century as well as today. During the peasant movement in Oudh (1919-22), the peasants took a pledge that they would not work as labourers without payment. Eviction of tenants as cultivators by moneylenders, landlords or government officers was one of the causes for widespread resistance and revolts in the nineteenth century.

It is generally believed that the Bhoodan Movement, launched by Vinoba Bhave in the early 1950s, was largely to counter the leftist movements, also focused the issue on the distribution of land. "Changes in the mode of production in agriculture have disturbed the traditional agrarian relationships which also led to peasant unrest. Under the British rule, land became a marketable commodity and commercialized agriculture developed during the late nineteenth century" (Shah, ibid). Barrington Moore argues that 'where a large scale commercial agriculture has resulted in proletarianization of peasantry, and consequently in snapping of the old traditional bonds of caste, etc. the possibilities of insurrection are much greater'. The demand for higher wages has been a central issue in the struggles of agricultural labourers in the nineteenth as well as the twentieth century.

Kisan Sabha

Kisan Sabha, the leading leftist organization, played very important role in organising the peasants and has been in the forefront of peasant struggles in the country. Born on April 11, 1936 and carrying a membership of more than 10 millions, it was instrumental in pushing the peasant's agenda to the centre. The first meeting of the Kisan Sabha was held along the 49th convention of the Indian National Congress. It was presided over by the legendry peasant leader Shahjanand Saraswati. On this occasion it released a 'peasant's manifesto'. Reviewing the plight of the peasantry in India it said that the peasants were leading a life of slavery and back breaking poverty. The Zamindars, Taluqadars, Malguzars, Inamdars and other land owners were exploiting the peasants. The main reason for this condition was the prevailing land revenue system and the system of debts and credit developed by the British imperialist. With the passage of time the peasants were attaining more and more economic and political consciousness. This declaration presented the following four basic demands of peasants:

(i) The prevailing condition of land ownership with all its forms should be abolished.

(ii) All the old debts and interest should be cancelled and the administration should formulate new schemes of credits for the fulfilment of immediate needs of the peasants.

(iii) All the cultivable barren land should be distributed among the landless and those peasants having less than 5 acres of land.

(iv) A new land tax system should be promulgated in place of prevailing land revenue system. The new system should be applied on those peasant families enjoying the net income of more than 5 thousand rupees and having family members up to five.

Among the other major demands, exemption of uneconomic landholdings from tax, security of tenure, declaration of all types of feudal and traditional extortions as unlawful, stay on repayment of loans for five years formed the nucleus of the charter of demands. Though in the initial stages the Kisan Sabha supported the Congress government before Independence, the peasant movements in Bihar, Bengal, Punjab and Andhra Pradesh created a major rift between the rightist and leftist elements in the Congress party and most of the leftists sided with the Kisan Sabha and carried the peasant struggles through the Kisan Sabha and Communist Parties. Rest is now part of the history.

Telangana Movement

The attainment of independence was marked by two mass uprisings of peasants who had become quite politicised by this time largely because of the involvement of the leftist leaders. The Tebhaga Movement (1946-47) was a struggle of share croppers in Bengal for a two third share of the produce (instead of the customary half) had the support of the Kisan Sabha and the Communist Party of India. The Telangana Movement (1946-51) was largely against the feudal conditions in the princely state of Hyderabad and it was launched by the Communist Party under its leadership. It was an organized movement against the feudal conditions and ruthless exploitation by the muscle men of the feudal lords, police and the Razakars (volunteers) of the Nizam of Hyderabad.

The Telangana region comprised almost half the area of the erstwhile Hyderabad State. The Telangana revolt began in the middle of 1946 and lasted for over five years till it was called off in October 1951. In order to understand the Telangana Movement we should have a clear idea of the prevailing agrarian social structure in Hyderabad State. There were two main types of land tenure:Khalsa or Diwani tenure was on the lines of Raiyatwari - the peasant proprietary system. The land holders, in this type of land tenure were not called 'owners', per se but were treated as pattadars (registered occupants). D.N. Dhanagre (2002) analysing the intricacies of this type of land tenure says that the actual occupants within each patta were shikmidars, who had full rights of occupancy but were not registered. As the pressure on land grew, the shikmidars, previously the cultivators of lands, began to lease out lands to sub-tenants (asami shikmis) for actual cultivation. They were tenants at will having neither legal rights in land nor any protection against eviction. The second main type of land tenure was called jagirs: one,sarf-e-khaas was obviously the most important of them being assigned to the Nizam himself as 'crown lands'. Scattered in several parts of the state, the sarf-e-khaas covered a total area of 8,109 square miles (1,961 villages), and fetched revenues totaling about 20 million rupees which met the Nizam's houshold, retinue and other expenses and partly met the cost of his army. Nowhere in Hyderabad was feudal exploitation of the peasantry more intense than in Telangana district.

The movement began rather modestly in 1946, under the leadership of the Communists, in the Nalgonda district and then spread to the Warangal and Bidar districts. Makhdum Mohiuddin,a prominent communist leader and revolutionary Urdu poet was one of the leading lights of the peasant movement. As Hamza Alvi (1968) points out, the initial aims of the Telangana movement reflected the broad demands of the whole of the peasantry against illegal and excessive exactions of the Deshmukhs and the Nawabs. One of the most powerful slogans of the movement was for writing off all peasant debts. The repression let loose by the feudal lords and their governments was met by armed resistance by the peasantry. The movement then entered a new revolutionary stage. "Local communists participated in the movement vigorously, although it did not receive the official sanction of the communist leadership until later. By the time of the Second Congress of the CPI in March, 1948, the Telangana Movement had already entered its revolutionary phase and was one of the factors which influenced the leftward swing in the Communist Party line at the Congress" (Alvi, ibid). By 1947, the Telengana Movement had a guerrilla army of about 5,000. The peasants killed or drove out the landlords and the local bureaucrats and seized and redistributed the land. They established governments of peasants. Peasant rule was established in an area of 15,000 square miles. The government of the armed peasantry continued until 1950 and was crushed by the so called Police Action and Indian army.

The movement had been crushed but continues to inspire the exploited peasantry even today.

Naxalbari Movement

When we look at the peasant movements in the post-independence period we should not miss the fact that certain issues which had dominated in colonial times lost their significance in independent India, when land reforms, Zamindari abolition, declining importance of land revenue, and a public-credit system began to alter rural conditions. The period after 1947 was characterized by two major social movements: The Naxalbari Movement and the 'New farmer's Movements'.

Some idea about the political background and the prevailing political situation is essential to understand the Naxalbari Movement, now popularly known as the Naxalite Movement. On 2 March, 1967, a non-Congress, United Front government was sworn in West Bengal. The government was dominated by the CPI(M), C.P.I, and other leftist groups and a breakaway group from the Congress, the Bangla Congress. The United Front government was pledged to bring about the long overdue land reforms in favour of the poor and landless peasants and release from the burden of chronic indebtedness to the sahukars and moneylenders. After assuming power, the CPI(M) found itself in a difficult situation. The bureaucracy, the judiciary and vested interests were found to be hurdles in any smooth and quick implementation of this agenda.

Meanwhile the euphoria generated by the left front government especially among the downtrodden peasantry was fast giving way to disillusionment. At Siliguri, Charu Majumdar and Kanu Sanyal, two very popular leaders representing the 'ultra-left' within the CPI(M) were quietly explaining to their followers that the measures for land redistribution announced by the revenue ministers Hare Krishna Konar of CPI(M) would not only fail to satisfy the landless but also prove to be detrimental to the interests of the future peasant movements. "They reiterated the need for moving beyond economism towards the task of politicising the peasants" (Sumanta Banerjee, 2002).

Thus, it is clear that the peasant uprising shows the existing schism within the CPI(M). The 'extremist radical groups' were either expelled or they disassociated themselves from the party.

The succeeding Congress government resorted to the brutal suppression of the movement and consequently led to the unusual phenomenon of mass emigrations from the Communist party to other parties especially the Congress Party. Thousands of bright and educated young boys and girls were arrested and tortured to death. The still committed leadership and cadre formed a breakaway CPI(ML) party which remained underground for some time and is now functioning as a revolutionary democratic party in several states and also fight elections.

The consequences of the Naxalbari uprising are of far reaching importance. It left a "far reaching impact on the entire agrarian scene throughout India. It was like the premeditated throw of a pebble bringing forth a series of ripples in the water. It was also a watershed in the Indian communist movement. It helped to expose the political failure of the parliamentary leftists in power, and unrolled a process of rethinking among the communist ranks. While the immediate and spontaneous response to the Naxalbari uprising was eruption of militant peasant's struggles on limited economic demands, a more long range and predetermined sequal was the number of organized struggles" led by the communist revolutionaries in selected areas of the country with the ultimate political aim of seizure of power. It was this political aim at which the Naxalbari rebels directed their movement, which posed a challenge to the Leftists in office" (Sumanta Banerjee, ibid). Thus, the Telengana and Naxalbari movements continue to inspire the revolutionary zeal of the tribal and non-tribal peasantry and a section of the urban, educated class.

Changing Mode of Production in Indian Agriculture:

'Mode of Production' is a central concept in the Marxist analysis. It is understood as the way a society is organized to produce goods and services. Mode of production has two major aspects:

- Forces of production
- Relations of production

'Forces of production' or productive forces include manpower or human labour power. It also includes means of production that is, tools, productive machinery, other infrastructure, technical knowledge, materials, plants, animals and land. The 'relations of production' or social and technical relations of production include property, power and those controlling productive assets and relations between social classes. Allan G. Johnson in The Blackwell Dictionary of Sociology (1995) writes that "since production is a social activity, any mode of production must also include a set of social relationships- the relations of production through which the forces of production are used and decisions are made about what to do with the results. Karl Marx's own conception revolved around the key idea that people produce not only "linen and flax" but in so doing also produce definite social relations. The social relations of production are the basis of the Marxist analysis of society.

In the light of this understanding let us examine the changing mode of production in Indian agriculture.

An analysis of caste based system of production represented by Jajmani System needs to be understood. In the traditional caste system land ownership was vested in higher castes only. This system of production developed an elaborate system of exchange of goods and services. The landed higher castes were called Jajman (patron) and the service providers- the occupationally specialized lower castes such as carpenters, barbers, blacksmith ,oilseed pressers, landless untouchable castes and poor Muslims etc were called Prajan or Kamin or by some other names as per regional languages. The landless service castes were providing their services and in exchange got a share in the harvest. The Jajmani relations were permanent and hereditary in nature. In the post-independence period the Zamindari and Jagirdari system was abolished by the Indian State. With this Jajmani system also declined. Now a number of traditionally landless castes got some land. Further, with the advent of democracy and adult franchise untouchable and backward castes mobilised themselves politically and the entire gamut of relationship in the production system underwent change in most parts of the country. In many regions technological innovations such as safety razor and hand pumps freed such castes as barbers and kahars (carriers of water) from Jajmani obligation. Moreover, with the introduction of new tools and mechanized agriculture, manual labour did not remain the only input in agriculture. This altered the very nature of relationship between the land holders and agricultural labour.With the increasing avenues of transport and communication rural to urban migration increased many fold. Now those who remained in the village and were either landless or had small and unproductive land holding insisted and got wages in cash. It became cash based wage transaction and that is how mode of production in Indian agriculture changed.

Green Revolution and Social Change:

One of the most significant and laudable achievements of post- independence India is in the field of agriculture where a revolution was brought in. When India announced in 1984 that it would provide to the drought hit countries of Sub-Saharan Africa 1 lakh ton of wheat as its contribution to the alleviation of human suffering, the gesture evoked universal praise and admiration. This pronouncement was particularly significant since not long ago India itself was struggling with food shortages and was depicted as a country which could survive only with a begging bowl. All this transformation was possible because of forward looking policies of the government, its enterprising and hard working farmers, brilliant scientists, extension and development workers, inputs, agencies and by the country's sheer determination to transform itself from food deficit and importing country to a self sufficient nation.

While these achievements are significant, India has to go a long way to provide its people with the amounts of food, fats, sugar and other commodities comparable to what is consumed in the most developed countries. The Green Revolution has brought changes in the agrarian relations. It has been successful in realizing production in large land holdings but has increased the economic disparity among the rich farmers, the small and marginal farmers and agricultural labourers. One of the effects of the Green Revolution has been the swelling of the bulk of 'agrarian proletariat' in some parts of the country. The landless have been getting organized; the organization of the landed is also emerging as a counter to this. It has also resulted in large-scale migration of labour to the enclaves of prosperity. Large migrations of agricultural labour from Bihar-Jharkhand and eastern Uttar Pradesh to Punjab and Haryana is a case in point.

The emergence of new dominant castes is, to a great extent, linked with the advent of Green Revolution. This is more obvious in the case of a number of backward castes placed in the middle or lower rungs of the local caste hierarchy. Several studies by sociologists and social anthropologists have shown that it is the socially backward castes (OBCs) and not the traditionally landless scheduled castes that have really benefited more from land reforms. Since these backward peasant castes were excellent cultivators, when more land was added to their kitty they became very enterprising. Moreover, they were already numerically strong in their respective regions. The only criterion left to be achieved by them to become dominant castes was higher status in the local social hierarchy which they achieved by going for sanskritization. The Jats of Punjab, Haryana and western Uttar Pradesh; the Ahirs, Kurmis and Gujjars of Uttar Pradesh, Bihar and parts of Madhya Pradesh; the Marathas of Maharashtra; the Patels and Pattidars of Gujarat; the Reddys and Khammas of Andhra Pradesh; the Vokkaligas and Lingayats of Karnataka and several other peasant castes from other parts of India may be cited as examples of this phenomenon. These upward climbing castes took full advantage of Green Revolution and through a plethora of cash crops and commercial agriculture, accumulated wealth and property not only in villages but also in the adjoining urban centres. Thus, Green Revolution played an important role in the altered social structures of different regions of the country.

Another Interesting and significant fallout of Green Revolution is a shift of authority from the older generation to the younger generation. Since the Green Revolution involved a new technology, economic transactions, institutional finance for credit, a little knowledge of English language and new varieties of seeds and plants, the well-entrenched older generation found itself ill equipped to handle this situation. Thus, the younger generation got a better and stronger role in the decision making process.

Impact of Market Economy on India's Villages

When we look at India's villages we find that traditionally, rural economy was primarily a subsistence economy oriented to satisfy the consumption needs of the local population. The *jajmani* system served as the basis of the economic organization under which the local people belonging to different castes were involved in exchange of goods and services as per the local traditions. But it is also true that within this subsistence economy there was some role of the market. There used to be local, informal markets with varying periodicity but they served social-cultural functions more than a place of formal economic transactions. These periodically held markets provided avenues for inter-relationship between the clusters of villages. Significantly the economic exchange in such markets was predominantly either redistributive or reciprocal type. Thus, we can say that limited degree of cash economy and market exchange did exist in the pre-industrial urban centers in India from the medieval period onwards.

With the advent of the British rule and the consequent process of modernization the pace of change increased rapidly. The colonial vested interests of the British rule pushed a new kind of capitalistic economy in agriculture. Land become a commodity and property. A new kind of land revenue system was introduced promoting monetization. Simultaneously, the process of peasantization and depeasantization were witnessed especially in the case of tribal communities. The system of land revenue settlement introduced by the British rulers required the payment of revenue in cash. This became instrumental for a rapidly increasing tendency of raising more cash or commercial crops. In this way the village economy got linked to the urban and later to the national economy. This was the beginning of monetization and extension of market economy to Indian villages.

After independence modern means of transport and communication were introduced by the government as part of massive economic development programmes resulting into full fledged extension of market economy to village India. Now the commodities of daily use in urban markets such as soaps, tooth paste, hosiery etc. are also available in village and town's markets. On the other hand poultry items from a village in northern India has reached to the markets of metropolitan cities of far off regions. The emergence of a rich class of peasantry created enormous demand of luxury goods in villages. A.R. Desai in his pioneering contribution has identified four major trends of change in village India:

(a) Rapid transformation of agrarian society from subsistence economy to market economy

(b) Rapid transformation followed by the introduction of modern technology

(c) Abolition of intermediaries such as *Zamindars* and *biswedars*

(d) Emergence of associations and institutions having linkages with urban and national organizations.

With the introduction of market economy, there was a change in the nature of production and consumption. Now the prime motive behind agricultural production was to generate a surplus for the market thus facilitating the entry of more and more market forces. It also promoted a consumption oriented life style among the rural folks. The demand for urban, machine produced items increased rapidly. Consumption and possession of these items became status symbols. Thus, the rural transformation promoted by the market economy may be summarized as under:

(a) The new market economy created a new class of rich peasants, big traders, petty officials and political workers;

(b) It promoted a large number of new facilities especially related with credit. Now, even credit cards have entered into rural society

(c) It facilitated the entry of improved implements such as tractors, water pumps, threshers etc.

(d) Polarization of peasants into rich landowning class and extremely poor landless labourers increased manifold.

(e) Monetization has expanded the avenues of social mobility. It had a deep impact on such traditional social institutions as joint family. The differential capacities of various members of the joint family to generate income led to a tendency towards nuclear families.

(f) It led to occupational mobility and diversification

(g) An occupation free caste structure started emerging proving to be a big blow to the traditional jajmani system.

(h) Caste barriers to economic mobility are crumbling. New avenues of health care and education have entered into rural life.

(i) It indirectly promoted empowerment of women.

Among all these features the most glaring phenomenon of recent origin is the agrarian distress and the resultant suicides of the peasants even in regions of green revolution such as Punjab, Haryana, Karnataka, Andhra Pradesh, etc. A.K. Vasavi (1999), analyzing the phenomenon of suicides among the peasants has identified certain general trends and factors. He rightly points out that the promotion of commercial agriculture based on the utilization of hybrid seeds, chemical manueres and pesticides, in a predominantly semi-arid region has had several repercussions. As a whole, there is a lack of compatibility between the ecological specificity of the region and commercial agricultural practices Climatic changes, especially changes in the rainfall pattern compound the conditions of uncertainty and risk in agriculture subjecting agriculture to an ecological crisis.

Alongwith the ecological crisis the economic crisis worsen the situation further. Though commercial agriculture is promoted on the basis of utilization of external inputs, institutional credit facilities to purchase these inputs are available to a limited number of agriculturists (mostly large landowners). Most agriculturists incur heavy debts in order to engage in commercial agriculture. Small and marginal cultivators for whom institutional credit in not readily or easily available resort to non-institutional debts at high rates of interest in order to take to modern cultivation or to remain in cultivation. The local moneylenders and *sahukars* are the mostly easily available sources of credit who thrive on usury. In time of ecological crises such as an outbreak of pests or diseases, such peasants incur more debts.

The introduction of commercial agriculture in a predominantly dry agriculture belt has its' impact on the social fabric too. This type of agriculture no longer draws on the established principles of local or indigenous knowledge and caste and kin based ties. The agri-business agents and agencies alongwith the agriculture extension workers enter the scene at the cost of the traditional institutions of dissemination of knowledge. They are not always congenial to the interests of hopeless peasantry.

Sharp fluctuations in prices, a part of market economy, compound the problem. Increased cost of production without assured procurement or support prices from the government agencies push the cultivators into a corner. Cultivators also complain of the large scale dilution of pesticides and lack of guarantee of many commercial seed varieties. The loss of crops for two successive seasons has been devastating. Under such conditions of changing agricultural practices, minimal state and administrative support, increasing subordination to market forces, high risks in agriculture and declining community support, it is not hard to imagine the personal distress that cultivators experience. The subordination of cultivators to market and capital forces without any safety net to support them in terms of crop loss or radically fluctuating prices beyond their control accounts for the devastation and pauperization of small farmers. Just as the suicides are symptoms of passive distress in the region, the loss of staple food grains in the region must also be considered to be a serious issue. As Susan George (1985) says, the loss of staple grains in any specific region without a substantial alternative economic base indicates a threat to the food security and hence the fragility of the local communities. Thus, the phenomenon of suicides is directly related with the economic factors as part of market economy.

Impact of Globalization on Villages:

1. Though, forces of market economy had entered into Indian villages before the advent of Globalization, it has further increased after Globalization has set in.
2. Globalization has facilitated greater mobility and faster connectivity mainly because of faster means of transport and communication. Easy availability of cell phone and internet is transforming the villages.

3. This has contributed to rapid migration to nearby and distant places in search of better employment.
4. With increasing mechanization and improved variety of seeds fertilizers and pesticides, agricultural production has increased substantially.
5. Cropping pattern is changing rapidly and more and more peasants are taking up commercial crops though, it has also added hazards. In case of repeated crop failures, the farmers get trapped in distress and many of them commit suicide.
6. Globalization has created markets outside the states and even country but the big, rich farmers are the main beneficiries.
7. Increased use of plastic money.
8. Increased aspirational level for the educated youths.
9. The self-sustaining nature of villages is destroyed.

❑

SECTION NINE

RELIGION AND RELIGIOUS COMMUNITIES IN INDIA

25 Religions and Religious Minorities

India is widely known as 'a nation of 'pluralism/ multiculturalism'. People speaking hundreds of languages and dialects and followers of all the major religions of the world inhabit this land of amazing cultural pluralism. However, there appears to be substantial, differentials in the socio-economic and demographic profiles of major religious communities in India, mainly emerging from socio-cultural and historical reasons. The status of linguistic communities is also largely related with these factors.

The Constitution of India uses the term 'minority' but does not define it. In order to have some understanding of the term 'minority' one refers to the works and interpretations of social scientists and to judicial decisions. The term 'minority' is a compound of the Latin word 'minor' and the suffix 'ity' meaning inter alia "the smaller in number of the two aggregates that together constitute a whole." The Webster dictionary defines it as "a group characterised by a sense of separate identity and awareness of status apart from a usually larger group of which it forms or is held to form a part." The Oxford English Dictionary defines minority as "the condition or fact of being smaller, inferior, or subordinate or as a number which is less than half of the whole number." The meanings and definitions just referred to contain a common criterion, namely, the statistical criterion. "Apart from the statistical criterion mentioned above the term 'minority' may also be defined on the basis of certain characteristics which are commonly possessed by the members constituting it. In this sense, the term signifies such groups of people as are united by certain common features and feel they belong to one common unit. Such groups may be held together by ties of common descent, physical characteristics, traditions, customs, language or religious faith or a combination of these" (G.S. Sharma, 1973). In any case, therefore, there is a sense of akinness, a sense of community or unity prevalent in the group or groups that distinguishes them from the majority of the inhabitants of the area where such minorities function. It is this sense of akinness within the group couples with the consciousness of a difference with the majority which may serve as the basis of various political or other claims. There may also be cases when differential treatment alone is the pointer that may determine the minority status. Such differential treatment may be shown by another group or other groups of people towards this group or it may be self-imposed by the 'minority' group itself.

Sumanta Banerjee (1999) adding a very important dimension to the meaning and interpretation of minority says that "in the context of human rights today, the term 'minority' is no longer a numerical concept, but has come to signify a non-dominant and disadvantaged group in a state or society, be it ethnic, religious or linguistic. The Muslims for instance are a disadvantaged minority group in India." Thus, the place of a group of people in the power structure of the society and the state becomes very crucial in identifying it as a 'minority'.

Though, the Constitution of India does not define 'minority' yet it recognizes two types of minorities, based on religion and language. That is how and why we talk about religious and linguistic minorities. The Constitution uses the term 'minority/minorities' only in four articles, namely, Articles 29, 30, 350-A, and 350-B:

Article 29 (1) Any section of citizens residing in the territory of India or any part thereof having a distinct language, script or culture of its own have right to conserve the same.

(2) No citizen shall be denied admission into any educational institution maintained by the state or receiving aid out of state funds on grounds of religion, race, caste, language or any of them.

Article 30 (1) All minorities, whether based on religion or language, shall have the right to establish and administer educational institutions of their choice.

(2) The state shall not, in granting aid to educational institutions, discriminate against any educational institution on the ground that it is under the management of minority, whether based on religion or language.

Article 350 (A) It shall be the endevour of every state and of every local authority within the state to provide adequate facilities for instruction in the mother tongue at the primary state of education to children belonging to linguistic minority groups; and the President may issue such directions to any state as he considers necessary or proper for securing the provision of such facilities.

Article 350 (B) (1) There shall be a special officer for linguistic minorities to be appointed by the President.

(2) It shall be the duty of the special officer to investigate all matters

> relating to the safeguards provided for linguistic minorities under this Constitution and report to the President upon those matters at such interval as the President may direct, and the President shall cause all such reports to be laid before each House of Parliament, and send to the Governments of the State concerned.

Thus in the absence of any formal or definite definition we largely go by the judicial pronouncements given from time to time. But one thing is absolutely clear and that is the fact that all the internationally recognized normative principles are enshrined in the constitution of India. On practical 'plane the word 'minority' in India is most often used in the context of religious communities - Muslims, Christians, Sikhs, Parsees (Zoroastrians) and Jews. This category also includes Budhists and Jains which means that all the non-Hindu communities come under the category of minorities. Following are the profiles and important facts and figures about the social, economic and political status of the religious minorities:

Muslims

Muslims in India are the largest and the most important religious minority of the country. Though a minority in its' numerical strength, it is so big as to make it the second or third biggest Muslim population in the world, after Indonesia. They constitute about 14% of the total population of India and form an important segment in the social fabric of the coutnry. They are distributed all over the country and live in every region, state and union territory in varying numbers.

Muslims are in majority in Jammu and Kashmir and Lakshdweep and constitute a significant minority in several other states. They are:

— more than 20% of the total population of Assam, Kerala and West Bengal.

— 10-20% in Uttar Pradesh, Bihar-Jharkhand and Karnataka.

— 5-10% in Telangana-Andhra Pradesh, Madhya Pradesh, Haryana, Rajasthan and Gujarat.

— In terms of absolute number they are most numerous in Uttar Pradesh and Bihar.

— In the remaining states they constitute 1-5% of the total population.

— In states like Sikkim, Mizoram, Meghalya and Nagaland they are less than one percent.

— Significantly, states with higher percentage of Muslims do not account for larger Muslim population.

A significant fact about Muslim demography is their higher urban population. About 35% or more of Muslims live in urban areas and it has significant bearing on their economic profile and access to health care and educational facilities.

Economic Scene

All the available studies, surveys and reports reveal that Muslims are an educationally and economically backward community. A sizeable majority of Muslims live in abject poverty. The percentage of Muslim population below the poverty line stands at 43 - higher than the national average. In rural areas, they are mostly landless and lack access to employment opportunities and other wage employment avenues. The majority (53%) of Muslims are self employed and earn their livelihood through petty business, small scale enterprises and low paid jobs. In the rural areas their overwhelming majority is agricultural labourers and artisans while in the urban areas they earn income from artisan and industrial works. As compared to other religious communities the participation of women in their work force is much lower. They contribute to the family economy largely through jobs performed within the four walls of the house especially in the urban areas where they are involved in such works as *Bidi* making. *Chikan* work in and around Lucknow and similar other occupations.

It is unanimously accepted that, through the ages, Muslims have been excellent artisans involved in different types of handicrafts and this has proved to be their undoing. In the face of the challenges of mechanization and industrialization, emergence of new market forces and lack of access to institutional finance they have been reduced to mere wage labour and cease to be the owners of these units in most of the cases. The following table may give the reader some idea of this problem:

Substantial presence of Muslim in the following industries

Bangles, glassware etc.	Ferozabad (U.P.)
Woolen, Wood work	Saharanpur (U.P.)
Carpets	Bhadohi, Mirzapur (U.P.)
Brasspots	Moradabad (U.P.)
Lungis	Madras (T.N.)
Woolen shawls, carpets	Kashmir
Handloom	Madras, Bhiwandi (Maharashtra), Mau (U.P.)
Chikan embroidery	Lucknow (U.P.)
Locks	Aligarh (U.P.)
Shoes	Kanpur (U.P.)
Leather	Calcutta, Chennai
Scissors	Meerut (U.P.)
Silk	Ram Nagram (Karnataka)

Survey reports reveal that only in some of these industries they dominate while in others most of them are wage earners.

Education

As stated earlier, the Muslims are below the national average in literacy and education. Some attribute it to their economic backwardness, some are of the view that it is on account of their religion. There is a popular perception that Islam prohibits secular education and encourage only religious education and that's why there are so many *Madarsas* and very few schools and colleges maintained by them. If the religion is any hindrance to secular education then why even a theoretic country like Iran ruled by religious priests put so much emphasis on the teaching of science and technology or Indonesia with the largest Muslim population of the world invest so much on secular education? Moreover, only a small percentage of children go to madarsas.

The partition of the counrty in 1947 had an important bearing on the educational status of Muslims. The modern, educated middle and upper class Muslims left for Pakistan, specially from the north and western India and among those left behind were a large number of poor and illiterate masses. Apart from a small middle class community of Muslims, those left behind were artisans, small traders, coolies, rickshaw pullers, tangawallas and lumpen elements in urban areas and small peasants, landless labour and others in rural areas. With such backward economic status there was hardly any incentive for modern secular education. There are some other factors contributing to the educational backwardness. Firstly, most of the Muslims in urban areas are artisans and others like dyers, weavers and bangle makers. They consider it beyond their means to send their children to school and also a sheer waste of time as their children supplement the parental or family works. However, they can be sent to a *madarsa* either in the early morning or late evening. Moreover, Muslim's low economic status and the parental perception that their children will not get jobs anyway on account of prejudices (though this may not always be correct) also discourage them to send their children to schools or colleges. The lack of higher aspirations and opportunities for upward mobility are also discouraging factors. On account of low economic status of their parents, the rate of dropout is also high among them. Beyond the primary level, it exceeds 60 percent and therefore the percentage of graduates among them is hardly two percent though their population is more than 14 percent.

The much maligned and condemned *madarsas* have played an important role in Muslim education especially promoting literacy among the Muslims. Though Islamic theology, logic, philosophy and history have been the traditional areas of knowledge in madarsas education, modern and secular areas of knowledge are now being added to them. The existing *maktabs* and *madarsas* need to be revamped so as to provide scope for the introduction of modern education alongwith religious education. States like Karnataka, Kerala and Telangana-Andhra Pradesh and some madrasas from Uttar Pradesh and Bihar have already introduced the teaching of science, mathematics, geography and computer education in madarasa curriculum. The Union Government as well as a number of state governments are helping in the modernization of madarsa education. Part of the reason why *maktabs* and *Madarsas* flourish is becasue the state has not done enough to promote modern education in mofussil towns and the rural hinterlands. Hence, children of poor Muslim families flock to religious schools — *Madarsa* among the Muslims and HIndu *pathshalas* among the Hindus. Of late some political vested interests have launched a vicious campaign of mis-information against the *madarsas* by dubbing them as centres of anti-national activities. One may condemn the *madarsas* for their orthodox, conservative, dogmatic and outdated syllabi but the generalized accusation that they harbour ISI agents and terrorists is highly irresponsible. Education is both a challenge and a solution to most of the problems faced by the Indian Muslims.

Social Conditions

Indian Muslims are not a 'cultural community' in the sense that they do not have a common language or adhere to the same life style. They do not occupy a common geographical space. They are not regional communities either. "They are born, live and die in different parts of India and speak a multiplicity of languages. What is, however, common to them is their religion, which they share with fellow Muslims all over the world. Therefore, to identify religion as the sole basis of their identity is incorrect and illogical" (T.K. Oomen, 1998). But the irony is that the religion based socio-cultural specialities are magnified and utilized to mark out the religious minorities.

To many people, they are held responsible for the partition of India. But three important facts should not be ignored here. First, the allegation that the Muslims where responsible for partition may be applicable to Urban Muslims of North India, particularly of Uttar Pradesh. Second, a substantial section of the Muslims were vigorous participants in the anti-colonial, freedom movement. Third, at the time of partition only a small number of Muslims from the territory allocated to India migrated to Pakistan; the vast majority stayed back.

Indian Muslims, like Hindus and others, are steeped in the caste based social stratification contrary to the ideology of Islam. They, too, have higher and lower caste groups — *Ashraf* is referred to the higher castes such as Saiyyed and Shaikh and *Ailaf* referring to the lower castes mostly the occupationally specialized castes and artisan groups such as *julaha* (weaver) *Qasai* or *Chikwa* (butcher), Raeen (vegetable venders), *Manihar* (bangle setter), *Badhai* (carpenter), etc. At the same time there is a strong backward class movement among them marginalizing the *ashraf* castes.

Doctrinal variety, social hierarchy and economic stratification are quite pronounced characteristics of Muslims as well - though they are, perhaps, not as marked, open, obvious and proclaimed as in the case of Hindus. The *Shias*, the *Sunnis* and the *Wahabis*, or the *Khojas*, the *Bohras* and the *Aghakhanis* are just a few examples of a large number of differentiations based on religious as well as quasi-religious beliefs and ritual practices.

The status of women, polygamy, and family planning (birth control) and 'uniform civil code vs. personal law' have been issues steeped in subjective prejudices, preconceived notions and speculations. For having a correct understanding of their social status one must have an objective understanding of these issues in their proper perspectives. When we have a look at the status of women among the Muslims we must honestly acknowledge the fact that the status of women in India as a whole is lower than the western societies. If the status of Muslim women is sought to be determined only on the basis of one determinant i.e. easy divorce or tiple *talaq* (divorce) then what about the rampant dowry problem, maltreatment and bride burning among the Hindus? The case of several Muslim countries where women are more empowered and enjoy a higher social status point to the fact that religion has never been a barrier to social mobility among the Muslim women. The case of theocratic Iran, Egypt, Indonesia, Turkey, etc. may be cited in support of this argument. Look at the educational backwardness of Indian Muslim women. The traditional society always tried to keep her uneducated or gave her only elementary religious education so that she can perform certain religious duties, nothing more. However, this is more a social than religious or ideological problem. Our attitudes are determined as much by social factors as by religious or ideological one. At times societal aspects prevail overriding religious or ideological aspects. If educational level among them is comparatively lower the reason is socio-economic rather than religious. It is true that education and socio-economic status are closely related. But it is also conditioned by the value system prevalent in a given society. The fact remains that what Islam had given her, the male dominated society has taken away. But the situation is fast changing. The winds of modernization is sweeping the Muslims too. The Muslim girls are going for modern education, participating in all the spheres of life, have a better share than ever in the decision making process at the family level and quite a few of them have started refusing to be cowed down by the religious threats.

Powerful myths are promoted to achieve sectarian political ends in India. One glaring example is the prevailing communal propaganda about polygymy and population growth. A rational and objective examination of empirical data is essential to know the truth. Though the religion and the law allows a Muslim to have more than one wife but is it empirically true? As per the 2011 census data there are 951 females per 1000 males among the Indian Muslims, better than Hindus, Sikhs and Jains. Is polygamy possible on a substantial scale? Any demographer worth his salt would immediately rubbish it. When the Report of *National Committee on the Status of Women in India (1971-74)* came out with the startling revealation presented below, it shocked many a people.

These figures are corroborated by the figures from the Office of the Registrar General and Census Commissioner of India, found in *Polygynous Marriages in India - A survey and Peoples of India Project.*

Incidence of Polygyny in India

1. Tribal Communities	15.2%
2. Buddhists	7.8%
3. Jains	6.7%
4. Hindus	5.8%
5. Muslims	5.7%

As per the findings of this report the cultural motivation for plural marriage beside barrenness of wife, absence of son, the custom of marrying a brother's wife etc., the economic gain is also an important motivation for polygamy among communities where women contribute substantially to the family economy. Some artisan groups, both Muslim and Hindu, find it cheaper to have a number of wives as extra hands than hiring labour. Thus, the incidence of polygyny is directly related with the status and role of women in their respective societies.

As for as population growth is concerned it is true that the birth rate is marginally higher among the Muslims. The acceptance of family planning methods and birth rates is dependent upon a large number of factors. The major ones are occupation, income, access to technology, child survival, education and skills the economic value of children and security in old age (*Report of the Working Group on Population Policy, Planning Commission*). The significance of these and other factors lend credence to the possibility of Muslims having a marginally higher birth rate because they are relatively more disadvantaged in all these areas. If the facts are examined without prejudice, the inescapable conclusion is that religion is not the primary determining factor in population. In this background one must also note birth rates in the Malabar region of Kerala, an area with a Muslim population of 40 percent, are significantly lower than those in Uttar Pradesh with only about 18% Muslim population. For that matter Goa, with its large population of Catholics, has one of the lowest birth rates in the country. Then, if religion does not matter much, what accounts for the persistently higher rate of population growth of Indian Muslims besides the factors enumerated above? However, the 2011 census shows that the decline in total fertility rate among the Muslims is highest among all religious communities showing that they, too, have taken to small family norm in a big way. Thus, hoped that in the next or next two decades their birth would be at par with others. Swaminathan S. Anklesaria Aiyer (2001) comes out with more factors as given below:

- Traditional Hindus do not allow the remarriage of widows, while Muslims encourage it.
- A disproportionate number of migrant labourers are Hindus, and their long absences from home tend to reduce births per women. Literacy is lower among Muslims, especially Muslims women. Low female literacy is associated globally with higher birth rates.
- Failure of the state. The world over, government efforts have been important in persuading people to adopt contraception. The state has been able to persuade Muslims to use contraception in Iran, Libya, Bangladesh and many other countries. But state has not been able to carry conviction with Muslim in India. Do not blame this on the culture and religion of Muslims.

The debate on **Uniform Civil Code versus Muslim Personal Law** has also been a contentious issue steeped in misconceptions, sociological distortions and preconceived notions. Historically speaking, Islam in India functioned as a political entity rather than as a legal system. The *Shariat* was never really enforced during centuries of Muslim rule. Social, political and economic rather than religious factors were more important. As rightly pointed out by Rafiq Zakaria (1994), the Muslim Personal Law is merely a compilaton of some *moulvis* (religious priests/scholars) at the instance of Lord Macaulay; it is based in many respects on the *Futuhaat-i-Alamgiri*, the judicial pronouncements in the reign of the Moghal emperor Aurangzeb. It bristles with innovations and is known as 'Muhammadan Law' which itself is a misnomer. It has been considerably modified by the decisions of the Privy Council during the British rule and by some of the legislative measures introduced by the Muslim members of the pre-partition Central Assembly. Moreover, some sections continued to be governed by customary laws. Similarly, usury, which is prohibited by the *Shariat* was widely practiced by such orthodox, practicing Muslims as the Pathans, and the Arab immigrants. The theologians connived at these lapses because of worldly compulsions.

If we take a look at the demand often made by the secular sections of the Indian society for reforms in Muslim Personal Law there is hardly any evidence of an attempt to change the whole of it unlike the demand made by the *Hindutva* forces inimical to any Muslim identity. The demand for some required changes in Muslim Personal Law from the progressive and secular forces does not seem to be contrary to the spirit of Islam. Essentially, whatever controversy there has been, arose around the issues of polygamy and divorce. Islam can be shown to allow polygamy within certain restrictions, but it certainly does not enjoin it on everyone. This right has been severely restricted in most of the Muslim countries, and there is no reason why polygamy cannot be completely banned, for Muslims and non-Muslims alike, if the Indian Parliament so desires. It will be entirely in the spirit of Islam. As to the matter of divorce, in actual practice Muslim males are at some advantage compared with the females, though the concept of allowing women to get a divorce is in the books from the beginning. There is no reason why uniformity should not be established in this respect by simply requiring a uniform marriage contract, and by providing relevant safeguards to protect both the parties from economic hardships.

It is tragic and dangerous, as rightly pointed out by Mohammad Naim (1999), on the part of the present (largely self acclaimed) leaders of the Muslim community to assert that the national parliament is not competent to make these changes. They fear that if changes are allowed in one area, then more changes will follow in other areas too, and the Muslim Personal Law will be replaced by the present Hindu code. This fear is baseless. Even for highly religious Muslims any and every change should not be opposed as long as it does not violate the spirit of their religion. Do not let the male dominated society take away what Islam gave to women and weaker sections of the society. *"Can the minority rights be different from human rights*?"

Political Status

Indian Muslims enjoy all the civil and political rights enshrined in the constitution for all the citizens of India. They are an integral part of the socio-political fabric of Indian society. Their electoral behaviour has been a matter of great interest for the political scientists. It is heartening to see that, by the large, Muslims have preferred non-communal, political parties and except Kerala (where Muslim League has a different structure and character) they have never supported, after independence, any communal Muslim political party even in Muslim dominated constituencies. The Muslims, alongwith other religious communities, have been participating actively in the democratic political process. However, serious communal riots, specially after 1960s, have instilled a sense of insecurity among the Muslims and tend to push them into their narrow communal shell. The state sponsored anti-Muslim violence in Gujarat during Februrary-May 2002 supposedly in retaliation to the Godhra incident has shaken not only the Indian Muslims but all the concerned Indian citizens. This must be a thing of the past and Indian polity should never allow any similar episode otherwise the authority of the state shall lose it's legitimacy.

In his outstanding work of formidable scholarship - *Ethnic Violence and Civic Life* : *Hindus and Muslims in India* (2002), Ashutosh Vashney writes that "In Hindu - Muslim relations in India the State tends to act in a politically strategic, not a legally correct manner. The state in Gujarat acted in primarily strategic, not a legally correct manner...............citizens action in India has to take two forms: (a) while continuing to pressure the state for it's dereliction of constitutional duty it should (b) focus on building integrated civic structures. The first has been the primary strategy for citizen action in India thus far. Such action is necessary but not sufficient. Citizen initiative should follow a two tract strategy, combining (a) and (b). The state, otherwise, will continue to get away with utter misconduct and gross disrespect for human lives during communal riots."

Political integration does not mean political subordination. It means closer unity for political purposes in a heterogeneous country and multicultural society like India. Healthy regionalism, autonomy of cultures, free development of languages, liberties of social organization are the very life-blood of a federal democratic polity. This the majority - communal and political - more than the minorities ought to remember. Rasheeduddin Khan (1987) in his significant observation says that taking advantage of the constitutional possibilities and the establishment of the process of democracy and change, the Muslim leadership at all levels should encourage their co-religionists to discard their separatist tendencies and enter the area of competitive polity and its composite problems so as to accelerate the pace of modernization. Hitting at where it hurts most, an eminent human geographer Moonis Raza (1994) comments that the 'Indianness' and 'Muslimness' of the Indian Muslims are both defining characteristics and neither can be ignored nor underplayed in any nationally sound and scientific assessment of the situation. Thus, Indian Muslims are Muslim Indians as well.

In the past the Muslims had been either rulers or the ruled. Today, in India, they are co-rulers as joint sharers of national sovereignty. As Rashidduddin Khan (ibid) rightly points out, the majority community is bound to be the first beneficiary of nationalism in a democratic society, therefore the minorities in order to retain their identity, depend not merely on the promotion of nationalism but also on the simultaneous development of the sub-nationalism. And Kancha Iliah (2003) in his characteristically blunt and ruthlessly honest narration comments that "Indian nationalism is not the property of Hindus only. It is the property of Muslims, Christians,

Buddhists and Sikhs as well." Thus, religious minorities are the natural guardians of a secular state.

SACHAR COMMITTEE REPORT

In the post-independence period the Government of India, showing concern for the continued educational and economic condition of Muslims has been gathering information from various sources to taking up remedial measures. Thus Planning Commission, National Sample Survey Organization (NSSO), Gopal Singh Committee, among others have been providing inputs.

Not satisfied with the progress in the desired direction the Prime Minister constituted a high powerd committee in 2004 under the chairmanship of Justice Rajendra Sachar, former Chief Justice of Punjab and Haryana high court. For the first time eminent economists, sociologists and civil servants were taken as its members. The committee is now popularly known as Sachar Committee.

Salient Findings of the Sachar Committee

(i) Education:

(a) The literacy rate among Muslims was 59.1%, which was below the national average of 64.8%.

(b) The mean years of schooling (MYS) is lower compared to the average MYS for all children.

(c) 25% of Muslim children in the age of 6 - 14 year age group have either never attended school or have dropped out.

(d) The majority of Muslim girls and boys fail in their matriculation examination or drop out before that.

(e) Less than 4% of Muslims are graduates or diploma holders compared to about 7% of the population aged 20 years and above.

(f) There is a strong desire and enthusiasm for educating among Muslim women and girls across the board.

(g) Schools beyond primary level are few in Muslim localities. Exclusive schools for girls are fewer.

(h) Lack of hostel facilities is a limiting factor, especially for girls.

(i) Muslim parents are not averse to modern or mainstream education and to sending their children to affordable Government schools. They do not necessarily prefer to send children to madarsas. However, the access to government schools for Muslim children is limited.

(ii) Skill Development

(a) Skill development initiatives for those who have not completed school education may be particularly relevant for some sections of Muslims given their occupational structure.

(b) The skill demands in the manufacturing and service sectors are changing continuously and youth with middle school education would meet these needs.

(c) A rehabilitation package for innovative re-skilling and for upgrading the occupational structure in the wake of liberalization is seen as an urgent need.

(iii) Employment and Economic Opportunities

(a) Self-employment is the main source of income of Muslims. They are engaged more in self-employed manufacturing and trade activities compared to others.

(b) The share of Muslim workers engaged in street vending is the highest. More than 12 percent of Muslim male workers are engaged in street vending as compared to the national average of less than 8 percent.

(c) The percentage of women Muslim workers undertaking work within their own homes is much larger at 70 percent compared to all workers at 51 percent.

(d) The share of Muslims in the total workers engaged in the tobacco and textiles/garment related industries are quite significant.

(e) The share of Muslim workers in production related activities and transport equipment operation is much higher at 34%, as against 21% of all workers.

(f) More than 16 percent of Muslims were engaged as sales workers, while the national average was only about 10 percent.

(g) While the participation of Muslim workers is relatively higher in production and sales related occupations, their participation was relatively lower in professional, technical, clearical and to some extent managerial work.

(h) Muslims, by and large, are engaged in the unorganized sector of the economy and have to bear the brunt of liberalization.

(i) The participation of Muslims in regular salaried jobs is much less than workers of other socio-religious categories.

(j) Muslims are relatively more vulnerable in terms of conditions of work as their concentration in informal sector employment is higher and their job conditions, even among regular workers, are less for Muslims than those of other socio-religious communities.

(k) Percentage of households availing banking facilities is much lower in villages where the share of Muslim population is high.

(iv) Poverty and Development

(a) About 38% of Muslims in urban areas and 27% in rural areas live below the poverty level.

(b) Muslims are concentrated in locations with poor infrastructure facilities. This affects their access to basic services like education, health facilities, transport etc.

(c) About a third of small villages with high concentration of Muslims do not have any educational institutions.

(d) There is a scarcity of medical facilities in larger villages with a substantial Muslim concentration. About 40% of large villages with a substantial Muslim concentration do not have any medical facilities.

(e) Muslim concentration villages are not well served with pucca roads.

(f) Policies to deal with the relative deprivation of the Muslims in the country should sharply focus on inclusive development and mainstreaming of the community while respecting diversity.

(v) Social conditions

(a) A community-specific factor for low educational achievement is that Muslims do not see education as necessarily translating into formal employment.

(b) The Muslim population shows an increasingly better sex ratio compared with other socio-religious communities.

(c) Infant and childhood mortality among Muslims is slightly lower than the average.

(d) There has been a large decline in fertility in all the religious groups including Muslims.

Christians

The Christians constitute the second largest religious minority in India and they are around 3% of the total population of the country. The emergence of Christianity and Christians in India, as per popular belief, has been linked up with the advent of the British colonial rule. However, well established traditons and historical evidence tell us that Christians have been existing in the state of Kerala right from the first A.D. Therefore, the Christians can be considered not only the oldest religious minority, but Christianity also as one of the oldest religions in India. Thus, the 2 Crore plus Christian population has been an integral part of India.

Like the Muslims, they are widely distributed in the country forming a sizeable proportion of population in several states and union territories. Following are some of the important facts and figures about the Christian population in the country.

- The Christian poulation reveals a strong tendency of concentration in the southern states of Kerala, Tamil Nadu, Andhra Pradesh and Karnataka.

- About 56 percent of the total Christian population of the country lives in the four southern states mentioned above.
- Kerala alone has almost one third of the country's Christian population, while Tamilnadu takes care of about one sixth of the national total.
- A second major concentration of the Christians is seen in the north eastern states which together share 22 percent of the total Christian population of the country.
- Though at national level, they form around 2.5 percent, at state level they are in majority in three states viz. Nagaland (88%), Mizoram (86%), and Meghalya (65%). There are a few other states with a significant percentage of Christians. These are Manipur (34%), Goa (30%), Kerala (19%), Arunachal Pradesh (10%) and Tamil Nadu (6%). In Assam and Sikkim they form 3 percent of the state population. While in the remaining, states their population varies between 0.4 percent to 2 percent. Among the Union Territories, Andaman and Nicobar Islands has the highest Christian population (24%) and Pondicherry has a substantial Christian population (7%). In the rest of the Union Territories, it ranges between 1 percent and 3 percent.
- Among all the religious communities of India the ratio of female population among the Christians is the highest which is 994 females per 1000 males. Perhaps, that is why they are not only more 'visible' but also constitute significant segment of the workforce.
- Contrary to the popular belief Indian Christians too are largely rural. Seventy one percent of all Christians in India are of rural background. Interestingly while in the south and the north east the Christians are predominantly rural, in north India, they are predominantly urban.
- Among all the major religious minorities the Christians have the highest rate of literacy

mainly because of the untiring effort of the missionaries.

The Indian Christians like Indian Muslims do not constitute a 'cultural community'. They speak different languages, they maintain different lifestyles and do not occupy a common geographical space. Even in the matter of religion, like the Muslims, they are divided into several denominations. Of the multiple Christian denominations in India today, only five could be distinguished as the main groups from which the various sub-branches have emerged. There are the Syrian Christians or the St. Thomas Christians, the Latin or the Roman Catholics the Protestants, the Tribal and the Dalits. The last two are often fused together since many of their concerns are similar. However, for better reasons the two should be seen as separate groups. The fact that the Roman Catholics constitute a major chunk of the Indian Christian population is also evident from the number of catholic institutions such as churches, schools and colleges, and hospitals. The distribution of Catholic Church in India, related as it is with the concentration of catholic population, appears to be an outcome of the long history of diffusion of Christianity. The spread of Christianity owes much to the dedicated social work of missionaries in the area of education and healthcare.

Two very indigenous offsprings of the Christian movement are the tribal and Dalit Christians. As Bonita Aleaz (2002) points out, "the tribal Christians are geographically dispersed througout the territory of India. However, it is possible to be locationally specific about two of the largest segments, which constitute more than 80 percent of the tribal Christians in the country. These are the tribals of north-eastern India and the Santhals who in turn are scattered over Bihar, West Bengal, Orissa and Assam." In the remaining tribal areas the Christianity has touched the tribes only marginally. The Christianity has been as important agency of welfare and modernization among the tribal societies. It has brought some positive changes in a number of their customs and practices. Among all the Christians in India, the Dalit Christians are the most vocal today. Most of them come from the Hindu untouchable who found Christianity as a welcome relief from the tyranny of the caste system. C.B. Webster (1994) has meticulously traced the origin and gradual proliferation of the Dalit Christian movement. He mentions that, on the basis of 1881 census report, four main groups of dalits could be identified, viz, the Chuhra of Punjab, the Chamar of North India, the Mahar of central and western India and the paraiyar of south India. Even though these groups were not homogenous, certain common characteristics could still be distinguished among them. These were their main occupation as agricultural labourers, poverty, similar rituals concerning birth, marriage and death, and finally lack of sympathy or support to their cause from other social and caste groups. Of course, all of them were also untouchables and suffered from a number of socio-economic disabilities like lack of landownership, lack of services from other castes such as barbers, washermen, priests, etc, bondage, lack of access to education and so on. In the 1920s and 30s there was a tremendous spontaneous movement of Dalits towards Christianity. The detail escaped into the Christian fold to take advantage of up ward mobility through economic independence and education. But discrimination continued to persist, though on much lower scale, as the descendants of higher caste Christians continued to look at them from the higher pedestal of caste hierarchy. Sometimes even the church resorted to discrimination. As Bonita Aliaz (ibid) points out that even today the church is not free from caste prejudices. In the north, however, caste has been largely replaced by class within the church community. But the relationship of dalit Christians, with other communities is still defined by caste. In the south, the associational view of caste predominates within the Christian community.

Large number of Christian in rural areas, mainly converts from lower Hindu castes, follow their preconversion occupational patterns. Rowena Robinson (2001) making incisive comment on this aspect says that "the negotiation of caste differences within Christian groups constitutes an area of considerable historical and sociological interest. Wherever group conversions took place, the converts carried their caste identities with them even as they shed their religious affiliations. In contradiction to the popular understanding which is unable to come to terms with how an egalitarian religion condones inequality, it may be pointed out that Christian missionaries have not always and everywhere unequivocally opposed caste, or all its implicated distinctions. Converts themselves often resisted any misionary efforts to establish egalitarian relations. In Kerala, the converts from untouchable groups such as pulayas and parayas are largely landless labourers and work for Syrian Christians and other landed upper castes. There is no question of interdining or intermarriage between the Syrian Christians and the untouchable converts. In many cases, the latter worship in their own churches. In rural Tamil Nadu, untouchable converts often remain residentially segregated from the higher castes. Ideas of purity and impurity persist."

There is a small section of urban middle class Christians which has experienced upward mobility through the educational facilities made available by the missionaries. T.K. Oomen (2000) talking about their political status says that "Christians in India are not organized into a political party and this is due to two factors : First, their socio-cultural fragmentation based on denominations and language to which we have already referred; and, second, their conscious rejection of separate electorates initially and the subsequent non-communal approach they seem to have adopted in political affairs. Following the recent tradition of the modern west, Christians in India accept the separation between church and state. This, too, stands in the way of their being organized on a politico-religious platform on an all India basis. Further, their small size and physical dispersion does not equip them to acquire any political clout except in certain regional contexts - such as in Kerala or the north east." There is one area in which Christians dominate in India, notwithstanding their small size and economic disabilities, and that is in the area of service institutions, particularly in education and health. The last decade witnessed large scale attack on the churches and Christians in Gujarat, Orissa and several other states. The alleged 'large scale' conversions through 'coercion and fraudulent' means are said to be root cause of these atrocities. There are more than a million Christians in Bihar, Karnataka and Maharashtra but, significantly, the states targeted for the fundamentalist attack were Gujarat and Orissa having 0.44 percent and 2.1 percent Christian population respectively. Though there have always been some cases of conversion of dalits and tribals the issue has been blown out of proportion and the hate campaign against minorities especially Christian and Muslims is being used as political tool by a major political party and its various affiliates. B.K. Roy Burman (1999) analyzing the facts of conversion tell us "that the followers of Christianity among the tribal peoples of Gujarat were 0.09 percent of the total tribal population of the state in 1961, 0.24 percent in 1971 and 0.40 percent in 1981." The percentage of Christians in fact has decreased according to the census of 1991. If Christian missionaries were all the time busy with conversions, why is this decrease in numbers? If a person changes his religion on his own, that is his own choice and such a personal choice is respected all over the world. Yet in a multi-religious society like India surrounded by fundamentalist regimes even microscopic number of conversion to any non-Hindu faiths generates fears, apprehensions, insecurities and ill will. Under such circumstanced it is in the interest of the minorities to keep away from any such activities, however small scale it might be.

Sikhs:

The Sikhs are the third major religious minority in India. Originated in Punjab, they are found in all parts of the country carrying with them the vital elements of the Punjabi Culture.

The Sikhs constitute about 2 percent of the total population of India that comes to 16.26 million people. Significantly, the overwhelming majority of the Sikhs are still concentrated in Punjab of their total population 78.5 percent reside in Punjab, 6 percent in Haryana and the remaining in Himachal Pradesh, Rajasthan, Delhi, Chandigarh and Jammu & Kashmir. Significantly most of the areas in these adjoining states were once parts of the greater Punjab. The partition of the country in 1947 was a major event in the history of the Sikhs. There was almost a complete exodus of the Sikhs from the west Punjab and their resettlement on this side of the border. Analyzing the social geography of the country Aijazuddin Ahmed (1999) says that the "redistribution of Sikh population in the wake of partition introduced Sikh elements in the neighbouring Haryana and Rajasthan where the irrigated colonies, such as in Ganga Nagar and Kurukshetra districts, emerged as the new foci of Sikh resettlement. Sikhs also settled down in the *Terai* regions of Uttar Pradesh transforming this once malaria -infested wetland into a granary of northern India. This transformation came due to the sturdy Sikh farmer, an alien to the region and yet tied to the soil." The Sikh Jats became a symbol of irrigation agriculture and perhaps the most active agent of agrarian revolution that followed the construction of canals in Punjab.

The Sikhs are not a monolith community. They consist of several sects such as *Namdharis, Nihangs, Udasis, Nirankaris, Niranjanis, Nanak Panthis* etc. A Sikh Gurudwara is not merely a sacred religious place of worship. It is the religio-cultural hub of the community where so many rituals and ceremonies related with birth, nomenclature, marriage and death are performed. It is the most important place of congregation which has been used even for such secular activities as electoral politics. Though the devout Sikhs visit a village gurudwar or a city gurudwara as a matter of routine but the most important congregations may be seen on *Baisakhi* which marks the birth of the *Khalsa panth* and the two *Guru Parva* (birthdays of Guru Nanak and Guru Govind Singh).

The economic status of Sikhs has always been a matter of envy to others. In the rural areas, wherever they live, they are excellent cultivators and a substantial section of them are rich farmers. As stated earlier, these Sikh Jats have played a very important role in the 'Green Revolution' of the country. In urban areas most of them earn their livelihood in the trade and commerce sector. They have substantial presence in transport, autcmobile, spare parts and transport service sector such as garage etc. They have always maintained a larger share in defence forces, larger in ratio than their population.

Like Muslims and Christians the Sikhs are also internally segmented. They are divided into caste, class and urban-rural divides. The urban Sikh traditing community, popularly known as *Bhapas* (Khatris, Aroras, etc.) on the one hand, the daily wage earning Sikhs, generally of lower castes. Moreover, there are caste-class divisions among artisans, such as carpenters (*Ramgarhias*), blacksmiths (*lohars*), etc right from the cities to the towns and the villages. Then there are *Mazhabi* Sikhs, the scheduled castes.

After the partition turmoil, the post-Indira Gandhi assasination anti-Sikh violence was the second event that shook the entire Sikh community. Thousands of Sikhs were massacred in Delhi, Kanpur, Bokaro and elsewhere. But being a robust and vibrant community they have recovered from this trauma too. The Sikhs, in spite of their cultural pride, still closely identify themselves with India and except a microscopic minority, they are not tempted by secessionism.

26 Linguistic Minorities

Language is one of the greatest glories and achievements of humankind. It is indeed one of the greatest treasures of human civilization. It is the most important part of human culture and cultural expression. Language also gives any human group it's cultural identity and the preservation of all the components of culture is ensured through language.

India is the home of a very number of languages. Grierson in his monumental work, Linguistic Survey of India enumerated 179 languages and as many as 544 dialects in the country. Even if we take out several languages from his category of languages and put them in the category of dialects, the fact remains that India will be described as a land of great language diversity and linguistic pluralism. Describing the social geography of India, Aijazuddin Ahmed (1999) writes that "the prevailing situation in the country is not pluralistic but that of a continuum. One dialect merges into the other almost imperceptibly; one language replaces the other gradually.

Moreover, along the line of contact between two languages, there is a zone of transition in which people are bilingual. Thus, languages do not exist in watertight compartments. Linguistic pluralism is a state of mutual existence of several languages in a contiguous space and continues to be a distinctive feature of the modern India state."

When India became independent and different types of groups and communities in pluralistic India were craving for the fulfillment of their aspirations, India's national leaders had to confront several language problems in the first two decades of independence. These problems included the official language issue, demands for the linguistic reorganization of the provinces of India whose boundaries during British rule did not confirm to linguistic division, and the status of 'minority languages' within reorganized states. Thus, the issues and problems of 'linguistic minorities' are largely the by product of the re-organization of states.

What a Linguistic Minority means is clear from Articles 29 and 30 of the constitution. Thus, 'Linguistic Minorities' are minorities residing in the territory of India or any part thereof having a distinct language or script of their own. "The language of the minority groups need not be one of the languages mentioned in the Eighth Schedule of the constitution. In other words, a Linguistic Minority at the State level means any group of people whose mother tongue is different from the principal language of the state, and at the district and taluk levels, different from the principal language of the district or the taluk. It would thus be observed that the speakers of all the languages become eligible for being included among the linguistic minorities, in one or more states, districts or taluks, except for those where the principal language is the same as their own language." (Report of the Commissioner for Linguistic Minorities in India, 1988). Apart from the constitutional provisions as enshrined in Articles 29, 30, 347 and 350 of the constitution, the bulk of the safeguards for linguistic minorities were formulated during the period 1956 to 1961, i.e., immediately following the reorganization of states on the linguistic basis.

Talking about the prejudices and discriminatory tendencies among the dominant ruling class, Paul R. Brass (1955) rightly points out that "in constrast to the pluralist policies pursued by the government of India, many of the states have pursued discriminatory policies towards their linguistic (and other) minorities within their boundaries. Moreover, the Center has been unable to protect such minorities effectively against the opposition of the state governments concerned." The examples of Bengali speaking people in Assam, Kannada, Malyalam and Tamil speaking people of Andhra Pradesh and vice versa may be cited. Among the worst casualties have been Urdu in the north Indian states and the various so called "mother tongues" or "dialects" of Hindi and other larger languages which have not been granted official recognition by either the central or state governments. Moreover, even when official recognition has been granted grudgingly in some states, for instance to Urdu in Uttar Pradesh, Bihar and Andhra Pradesh, the discriminatory policies and practices continued unabated. The case of some of these dialects - example, the Maithli language of north Bihar may also be cited. These are separate languages in all but official recognition. To avoid the controversial issue of distinguishing between "languages" and "dialects", however, it is best to follow the practice of the Indian Census authorities and use the term 'mother tongue' to encompass both terms. Paul Brass (ibid) stretching the argument further says that the languages and mother tongues are, in effect, arranged in a hierarchy of official status. At the top are the two languages, Hindi and English, recognized as official languages of the Union. At the next level are the regional languages recognized as official languages in the linguistically reorganized states (such as Kannada, Marathi, Oriya, Tamil, Bengali etc.) all of which are also listed in the Eighth Schedule. At a third level are those languages listed in the Eighth Schedule which have no official status in any province, namely Sanskrit and Sindhi, the language of the province of Sindh now in Pakistan.

Since language is the most important marker of identity, the linguistic minorities in different states have to face discriminatory and sometimes hostile attitude of the dominant class in different states especially in the sphere of job competition and other economic grievances. The speakers of minority languages are always conscious of their cultural identity and when face a hostile state tend to come together and become a political force for the redressal of their grievances.

While the linguistic minorities are entitled to reasonable safeguards to protect their educational, cultural and other interests, it has to be borne in mind that such safeguards should not so operate as to perpetuate separatism. The best interest of both linguistic minorities as also the dominant linguistic majority can be secured only by promoting mutual understanding, goodwill and cooperation between them, rather than by mere insistence on rights and safeguards. After all, in the ultimate analysis, the welfare of the individual or groups of individuals, whatever be their mother tongue, depends on the progress made by the country as a whole and by defending the national independence.

The case of tribal languages and linguistic groups is also an important issue in any discussion on linguistic minorities. Paul Brass (ibid) taking a holistic view of the situation rightly says that recognition of a mother tongue by a state government is no guarantee that facilities will actually be provided for students in government schools to receive instruction through the medium of their mother tongue. State government rules and regulations generally require that the parents of the children who wish such instruction formally request it and that a certain number of children in each school and classroom must do so in order to receive such instruction. Even then competent teachers and textbooks in the language may not be available. Spokesmen for several other tribal languages, both in the predominantly Hindi speaking states and in other states with large tribal minorities, have demanded instruction for their children in their mother tongue.

Tribal Languages:

The most vulnerable among linguistic groups/minorities are the tribal communities. Hence the case of tribal languages and linguistic groups is also an important issue in any discussion on linguistic minorities. Taking a holistic view of the situation it may be said that recognition of a mother tongue by a state government is no guarantee that facilities will actually be provided for students in government schools to receive instruction through the medium of their mother tongue. State governments' rules and regulations generally require that the parents of the children who wish such instruction formally request it and that a certain number of children in each school and classroom must do so in order to receive such instruction. Even then competent teachers and textbooks in the language may not be available. Spokesmen for several other tribal languages, both in the predominantly Hindi speaking states and in other states with large tribal minorities, have demanded instruction for their children in their mother tongue, but most of the states have taken this matter very casually. Moreover, the state governments in general have tended to ignore the request of the Commissioner for Linguistic Minorities.

A lot remains to be done for our tribal linguistic groups. The problem of lack of script and the constraints of inadequacy of text books need to be tackled at the national level. Early action needs to be taken for evolving a common script for tribal languages/dialects with a view to promoting education among the tribal people, particularly at the primary stage of education. Devanagri(Hindi) may appear to be an appropriate script for adoption for the tribal languages and dialects in the country, as has been adopted by Bodos of Assam, and Bhils, Munda and Gonds of Madhya Pradesh-Chattisgarh

It is to be noted that many erstwhile developed and popular tribal languages are dying and with them their indigenous knowledge system preserved for centuries and millennia in and through these languages. It is high time that government take necessary steps to integrate the tribal languages, at least the major ones, into the education system.

National integration is not possible without emotional integration. Small minorities may be bulldozed into submission for the time being but in the long run it will lead to separatist tendencies among them. When any minority group feels that its language, religion, customs and traditions are safe in the country and the state is doing all for its conservation, it strengthens the sense of belonging and acceptance of the language and culture of larger society. Cultural pluralism has been the essence of Indian civilization. India's destiny lies in pluralism and 'Unity in diversity'. Moreover, among the determining criteria of any 'civil society' are the way minorities and women are treated in it.

India is an exemplary laboratory for the coexistence of languages and ethnic communities. Moreover, the essence of secularism in India is the recognition and preservation of different types of people, with diverse languages, cultures and beliefs, and placing them together so as to form a whole and united India. ❑

Select Bibliography

Abbi, B.L. & Satish Saberwal (Eds.): *Urgent Research in Social Anthropology*, 1969, Indian Institute of Advanced Study, Simla.

Agrawal, B.C. (ED.): *Anthropological Approaches to the Study of Complex Societies*, 1982, Ethnographic & Folk Culture Society, Lucknow.

—— : *Anthropological Methods for Communication Research*, 1985, Concept Publishing Company. New Delhi.

Agrawal, D.P.: *The Copper-Bronze Age in India*, 1971. New Delhi.

—— : *The Archaeology of India*, 1984, Select Book Service Syndicate, New Delhi.

Agrawal, D.P. & P.K. Chakrabarti. (Eds.): *Essays in Indian Prehistory*, 1979, New Delhi.

Ahuja, Amit : *Mobilizing the Marginalized: Ethnic Parties without Ethnic Movements*, 2019, Oxford University Press, New Delhi.

Aiyer, S.P. (Ed.): *Modernization of Traditional Society and Other Essays,* 1973, The Macmillan, Madras.

Allchin, B. & F.R. Allchin: *The Birth of Indian Civilization:* Indian and Pakistan Before 500 B.C., 1968, Penguin Books, Harmondsworth.

Ames, Michael: *Museums, The Public and Anthropology,* 1986, Concept Publishing Company, New Delhi.

Anderson, J.D.: *The Peoples of India,* 1913, Cambridge.

Anderson, Nels: *The Urban Community: A World Perspective,* 1959, New York.

Andreski, *Stanislav: Social Sciences as Sorcery,* 1972, Penguin Books, Harmondsworth.

Ansari, Ghous: *Muslim Caste in Uttar Pradesh,* 1959, Ethnographic & Folk Culture Society, Lucknow.

Asad, T. (Ed.): *Anthropology and the Colonial Encounter,* 1913, London.

Atal, Yogesh: *The Changing Frontiers of Caste,* 1968, National Publishing House, Delhi.

Aurora, G.S.: *Tribe-Caste Encounter,* 1972, Administrative Staff College of India, Hyderabad.

Bailey, F.G.: *Tribe, Caste and Nation,* 1960, Oxford University Press, Bombay.

—— : "Tribe" and "Caste" in India, *Contributions of Indian Sociology,* Vol.5, 1961.

Balsara, J.J.: *Problems of Rapid Urbanization in India,* 1964, Popular Prakashan, Bomaby.

Banton, Michael (Ed.): The social Anthropology of Complex Societies, 1966, F.A. Praeger, New York & Washington.

Bardhan, A.B.: Unsuljhi Janjatiya Samasya (Hindi), 1977. Communist Party of India, New Delhi.

Basham, A.L.: The Wonder that was India, 1957. London.

Beals, R.: 'Urbanism, Urbanisation and Acculturation'. *American Anthropologist,* Vol. 53:1, 1951.

Beattie, John: Other Cultures, 1974, Cohen & West, London.

Berreman, Gerald, D.: Behind Many Masks, 1962, Cornell University Press Ithaca.

—— : Hindus of the Himalayas, 1963, Cornell University Press, Berkeley.

Beteille, Andre: 'Our Villages and Cities: A Contrast between Tradition and Modernity', Yojana, Jan. 2, 1965.

—— : Six Essays & T.N. Madan (Eds.): Encounter and Experience: Personal Accounts of Fieldwork, 1975, Vikas, New Delhi.

Bhattacharya, D.K.: Archaeology and social Formation, 1984, *Spectra of Anthropological Progress*, Delhi.

Bodley, J.H.: Victims of Progress, 1982. Cummings Publishing Company, California.

Bose, A.: Urbanization in India, 1971. Academic Books Ltd., Bombay.

Bose, N.K.: Cultural Anthropology, 1929, Indian Associates Publishing Company, Calcutta.

—— :'Fifty years of Science in India: Progress of Anthropology and Archaeology', 1963, Indian Science Congress Association, Calcutta.

—— : Culture and Society in India, 1967. Asia Publishing House, Bombay.

—— : Problems of Natonal Integration, 1967. Indian Institute of Advanced Study, Shimla.

—— : Calcutta: A Social Survey. 1968, Lalwani Publishing House, Bombay.

—— : Tribal Life in India, 1971, New Delhi.

—— : 'The Hindu Method of Tribal Absorption'. *Science and Culture, Vol. 7*

Brew, J.O.(Ed.): One Hundred Years of Anthropology, 1972. Cambridge-Massachusetts, Harvard University Press, Harvard.

Briggs, G.N.: The Chamar, 1920, Calcutta Associated Press, Calcutta.

Burkitt, M.C.: *The Old Stone Age*, 1963, Bowes & Bowes, London.

Chakravarty, M.R.: 'Dermatogiyphics in Anthropology', *Journal of Social Research*, Vol. V, No. 1-2, 1963.

Cohn, B.S.: India: The Social Anthropology of a Civilization. 1971. Englewood Clifts, New Jersey.

Cohn, B.S. & Mckim Marriott.: 'Networks and Centres in the Integration of Indian Civilization', *Journal of Social Research*, 1958.

Cornwall, I.W.: The World of Ancient Man, 1964, London.

Dani, A.H.: Prehistory and Protohistory in Eastern India, 1960, Firma K.L. Mukhopadhyay, Calcutta.

Dey, A.K.: Geology of India, 1968, New Delhi.

Dey, S.K.: Community Development: A Bird's Eye view, 1964, Asia Publishing House, Bombay.

Dhillon, H.S.: Leadership and Groups in a South Indian Village, 1955, Planning Commission, New Delhi.

Dube, S.C.: India's Changing Village, 1958, Routledge & Kegan Paul, London.

——(Ed): Emerging Patterns of Rural Leadership in Southern Asia, 1965, National Institute of Community Development, Hyderabad.

—— :Explanation and Management of Change, 1971, Tata McGraw Hill, New Delhi.

—— : Social Science in Changing Society, 1973, Ethnographic & Folk Culture Society, Lucknow.

—— : Contemporary India and its Modernization, 1974, Vikas, New Delhi.

Dumont, Louis: Homo-Hierarchicus: The Caste System and Its Implications, 1970, Chicago University Press, Chicago.

Dymond, D.P.: Archaeology and History, 1974, London.

Elwin, Verrier: The Baiga, 1939, John Murrary, London.

—— : A Philosophy ofr NEFA, 1958, Shillong.

——— : The Tribal World of Varrier Elwin, 1964, Oxford University Press, Bombay.

Epstein, A.L.(Ed.): The Craft of Social Anthropology, 1967, Tavistock Publication, London.

Evans-Pritchard, E.E.: Social Anthropology, 1951, Cohen & West, London.

Fairsevis, W.A.: The roots of Ancient India, 1971, New York.

Ferriera, J.V.: 'Urban Anthropology; A radican Perspective', *The Eastern Anthropologists*, Vol. 31, No. 4, 1971.

Foote, R.B.: Collection of Indian Prehistoric and Protohistoric Antiquities, 1916, Madras.

Ganguly, Indrani: Urban Anthropology: A Critical Review, 1986, Unique Publications, Delhi.

Ghosh, A.K.(Ed.): *The Scheduled Tribes,* 1960, Popular Book Depot, Bomaby.

Ghosh, Biswajit(Ed.): *Social Movements: Concepts Experiences and Concerns,* 2020, Sage India, New Delhi.

Gordon, D.H.: The Prehistoric Background of Indian Culture, 1958, Bombay.

Gould, Harold: 'Lucknow Rickshawallas: The Social Organisation of an Occupational Category' in M.S.A. Rao (Ed.) *Urban Sociology in India,* 1974, Orient Longman, New Delhi.

Gore, M.S.: Urbanisation and Family Change, 1968, Popular Prakashan, Bombay.

Gutkund, Peter: Urban Anthropology, 1974, Van Gorcum, Assen.

Harris, Mervin: The Rise of Anthropological Theory, 1968, Thames & Crowell Co. New York.

Hasan, Amir: The Kols of Patha, 1972, Kitab Mahal, Allahabad.

——— : Meet the U.P. Tribes, 1987, Gurgaon.

Hasan, K.A.: Applied Anthropology in History of Medicine: *Journal of Social Research,* Vol. VI, No.1-2, 1963.

Hasan, Zoya Politics of Inclusion: Castes, Minorities and Affirmative Action, 2015 Oxford University Press, New Delhi.

Hasnain, Nadeem Sociology of Marginalised Communities and Weaker Sections of India, 2021 SAGE India, New Delhi.

Shia Muslims of India, 2021 New Royal Book Company, Lucknow.

Handbook of Sociology, 2020 Surjit Publications, Delhi.

Indian Society: Themes and Social Issues, 2019 McGraw Hill Education, New Delhi.

'The Kolta: A Study in the Ethnography of the Poor." 1975 , *The Eastern Anthropologist*, Vol. 28, No.4.

Bonded for Ever, 1982, Harnam Publications, Delhi.

Tribal India, 1991, Palaka Prakashan, Delhi.

General Anthropology, 1997, Jawahar Publisher and Distributor, Delhi.

Indian Anthropology, 1998, Palaka Prakashan, Delhi.

Introducing Social-Cultural Anthropology, 2003, Jawahar Publisher and Distributor, Delhi.

Indian Society and Culture: Continuity and Change, 2004, Bharat Book Centre, Lucknow.

OBCs in the Process of Change, 2005, Serial Publication, Delhi.

Anthropology in India, Ethnographic and Folk Culture Society, Lucknow. 2010

Contested Identities in the Globalised World, INCAA, 2013.

Indian Society and Social Issues, 2016, Palaka Prakashan, Delhi.

Hausar, P.M. (Ed.): Urbanization in Asia and Far East, 1951, UNESCO, Calcutta.

—— : Handbook for Social Research in Urban Areas, 1965, UNESCO, Paris.

Hutton, J.H.: Census of India, Vol.1, 1931, Government of India Press, Simla.

—— : Caste in India, 1951, Oxford University Press, Bombay.

Indian Council of Social Sciences Research (ICSSR): A Survey of Research in Sociology & Social Anthropology (3 Vols.), 1972-74, Popular Prakashan, Bombay.

Jain, K.C.: Prehistory and Protohistory of India, 1979, Agam Kala Prakashan, New Delhi.

—— : An Introduction to Anthropological Thought, 1983, Vikas, New Delhi.

Karwe, Irawati: Hindu Society: An Interpretation, 1953, Sangam, Poona.

—— : Kinship Organisation of India, 1953, Deccan College, Poona.

Kosambi, D.M.: Myth and Reality, 1962, Bombay.

—— : The Culture and Civilization of Ancient Indian in Historical Outline, 1970, Delhi.

Kothari, Rajni (Ed.): Caste in Indian Politics, 1970, Orient Longman, New Delhi.

Leach, E.R.: Rethinking Anthropology, 1961, Athlone Press, London.

Leakey, L.S.B.: Adam's Ancestors, 1960, Methuen & Co. Ltd., London.

Lewis, Oscar: Group Dynamics in a North Indian Village, 1954, Planning Commission, New Delhi.

—— : Anthropological Essays, 1970, Random House, New York.

Lynch, Owen M.: 'Some Aspects of Rural-Urban Continuumin India' in Bala Ratnam (Ed.) *Anthropology on the March*, 1963, The Book Centre, Madras.

—— : The Politics of Untouchability, 1969, Columbia University Press, New York.

Madan, T.N. (Ed.): Muslim Communities of South Asia: Culture and Society, 1976, Vikas, New Delhi.

Madan, T.N. & Gopal Saran (Eds.): Indian Anthropology: Essays in Memory of D.N. Majumdar, 1962, Asia Publishing House, Bombay.

Mahapatra, L.K.: Transformation of Tribal Society in India, 1970, Delhi University National Lecture, Delhi.

Majumdar, D.N.: A Tribe in Transition, 1937, Longmans, Green & Co. Ltd., London.

—— : The Affairs of a Tribe: A Study in Tribal Dynamics, 1950, Universal Publishers, Lucknow.

—— : Rural Profiles (2 Vols.), 1955, Ethnographic & Folk Culture Society, Lucknow.

—— : Caste and Communication in a North Indian Village, 1958, Asia Publishing House, Bombay.

—— : Social Contours of an Industrial City. 1961, Asia Publishing House, Bombay.

—— : Races and Culture of India, 1965, Asia Publishing House, Bombay.

Majumadar, D.N. & T.N. Madan: An Introduction to Social Anthropology, 1957, Asia Publishing House, Bombay.

Malinowski, B.: Argonauts of the Western Pacific, 1922, Dutton, New York.

—— : Sex and Repression in Savage Society, 1927, Kegan Paul, London.

Mandelbaum, David G.: 'The Study of Complex Civilization' in W.L. Thomas (E.D.), Current Anthropology, 1956, Chicago University Press, Chicago.

—— : Society in India, 1970, University of California Press, Berkeley.

Mandelbaum, David G.: Gabriel W. Laskar & Ethel M. Albert: The Teaching of Anthropology, 1967, University of California Press,. Berkeley.

Mariott, Mc Kim (Ed.): Village India, 1955, Chicago University Press, Chicago.

Marshall, J.: Mohanjodaro and Indus Civilization, 1931, London.

Mathur, H.M. (Ed.): Development Administration in Tribal Areas, 1976, The H.C.M. State Institute of Public Administration, Jaipur.

——(Ed.): Anthropology in the Development Process, 1977, Vikas, Bombay.

Mathur, K.S.: Caste and Ritual in Malwa Village, 1964, Asia Publishing House, Bombay.

Mathur, K.S. & S.C. Verma (Eds.) : Man and Society, 1972, Ethnographic and Folk Culture Society, Lucknow.

Mathur, K.S. & B.C. Agarwal (Eds.): Tribe, Caste and Peasantry, 1974, Ethnographic and Folk Culture Society, Lucknow.

Memoria, C.B.: Tribal Demography in India 1957, Kitab Mahal, Allahabad.

Misra, V.N. & M.S. Mate: Indian Prehistory, 1964, Poona.

Misra, V.N. & Malti Nagar: 'Twenty Five Years of Indian Prehistory', K.S. Mathur & S.C. Verma (EDs.) *Man and Society*, 1972, Ethnographic & Folk Culture Society, Lucknow.

Memoria, C.B.: Tribal Demography in India 1957. Kitab Mahal, Allahabad.

Misra, V.N. & M.S. Mate: India Prehistory, 1964, Poona.

Misra, V.N. & Malti Nagar: 'Twenty five Years of Indian Prehistory', K.S. Mathur & S.C. Verma (Eds.) *Man and Society*, 1972, Ethnographic & Folk Culture Society, Lucknow.

Misra, V.N.: Y. Mathpal & Malti Nagar, Bhimbetka, 1977, Poona.

Mitra, P.: Prehistoric India, 1930, Calcutta University, Calcutta.

Morley, Grace: 'Museums of Anthropology: Their Role in East, South and South-East Asia, *The Eastern Anthropologist*, Vol. 29, No.1, 1976.'

—— : Museums Today, 1967. Baroda.

Mukherjee, Radhakamal: Social Profiles of a Metropolis City Lucknow, 1961, Asia Publishing House, Bombay.

Murdock, G.P. *et al.* Outlines of Cultural Material 1950, Human Relations Area Files Inc., New Haven.

Nadel, S.F.: Anthropology and Modern Life, 1953, Australian National University, Canberra, Nair Kusum: Blossoms in the Dust: The Human Elements in Indian Development, Gerald Duckworth, London.

Narain, Iqubal & Yogesh Atal (Eds.): Social Sciences and the Government: the Asian Scene, 1987, Lancer International New Delhi.

Narain, Jai Prakash: 'Gandhism and Social Sciences'. AVARD, *News Letter*, Vol. 6, No. 5, 1964.

Orans, M.: The Santhals: A Tribe In Search of a Great Tradition, 1965, Wayne State University Press, Detroit.

Penniman, T.K.: A Hundred Years of Anthropology, 1965, Gerald Duckworth, London.

Piggot, S.: Prehistoric India, 1950, Pelican Books, Harmondsworth.

Redcliff-Brown, A.R.: The Andaman Islanders: A Study in Social Anthropology, 1922, Cambridge University Press, Illinois.

—— : Structure and Function in Primitive Society, 1952, Cohen & West Ltd., London.

Redfield, Robert & Milton Singer: 'The Cultural Role of cities', *Man in India*, Vol. 36, No.3.

—— : Royal Anthropological Institute: Notes and Querries on Anthropology, 1967, Routledge & Kegan Paul, London.

Roy Burman, B.K.: 'Third World Anthropology and Related Sciences: The Issues', *The Eastern Anthropologist*, Vol. 40, No.4, 1987.

—— : 'Dynamics of Persistence of Tribal Community in India' in B.C. Agarwal (Ed.); *Anthropological Approaches to the Study of a Complex Society*, Ethnographic & Folk Culture Society, Lucknow.

Roy, Sachin: Museum of Man in India: Problems and Prospects, 1972, New Delhi.

Saberwal, Satish: Mobile Man: Limits to Social Change in Urban Punjab, 1976, Vikas, New Delhi.

Sachchidanand: Cultural Change in Tribal Bihar, 1964, Bookland Pvt. Ltd., Calcutta.

—— : 'Planning, Development and Applied Anthropology in India', Indian Anthropologist, Vol. 3.

Sahay, K.N.: Under the Shadow of the Cross, 1976, Institute of Social Research & Applied Anthropology, Calcutta.

Sankalia, H.D.: Indian Archaeology Today, 1962, Asia Publishing House, Bombay.

—— : Prehistory and Protohistory of India and Pakistan, 1963, University of Bombay.

—— : New Archaeology: Its Scope and Application to India, 1977, Ethnographic & Folk Culture Society, Lucknow.

Saran, A.B.: Murder and Suicide among two Tribes of Bihar, 1975, National Publishing House, Delhi.

Saran, Gopal: 'Anthropology of Indian Civilization', *Journal of Indian Anthropological Society*, Vol. 5, 1978.

—— : 'Anthropological Method and Indian Anthropology', 1973, (The L.K. Ananthakrishna Aiyer Birth Centenary Lectures, 1972-73, University of Madras Press, Madras).

—— : 'Can We Be of Any Service at Our Village Folk'? *Journal of Karnataka University*: Social Sciences, 1978, Vol. XIV.

—— : 'Anthropology and Nation Building', *Journal of the Institute of Social Research and Applied Anthropology*, 1979, Vol. 5, No. 1-2.

——— : Sociology & Anthropology and Other Essay, 1983, Calcutta.

Saran Gopal & D.P. Sinha: 'Status of Social-Cultural Anthropology in India', *Annual Review of Anthropology*, Edited by Bernard J. Siegel 1976, Vol.5, Annual Reviews, Inc. Palo Alto, California.

Saraswati, B.N.: Contributions to the Understanding of Indian Civilization, 1970, Karnataka University, Dharwar.

Sharma, R.N. & Santosh Bakshi (Eds): Tribes and Tribal Development: A Select Bibliography, 1984, Uppal Publishing House, New Delhi.

Sharma, R.S.: Light on Early Indian Society and Economy, 1966, Bombay.

——— : Ancient India, 1977, NCERT, New Delhi.

Sheth, N.R.: The Social Framework of an Indian Factory, 1968, Oxford University Press, Bombay.

Singer, Milton & B.S. Cohn (Eds.): Structure and Change in Indian Society 1968, Aldine Publishing Company, Chicago.

Singh, Hajinder (Ed.): Caste among Non-Hindus in India, 1977, National Publishing House, New Delhi.

Singh, K.S. (Ed.): Tribal Situation in India, 1972, Indian Institute of Advanced Studies, Shimla.

Singh, P.: Burial Practices in Ancient India, 1971, Prithvi Prakashan, Varnasi.

Singh, Yogendra: Modernization of Indian Tradition, 1973, Thomson Press, New Delhi.

Sinha, D.P.: Culture Change in Inter-Tribal Market, 1968, Asia Publishing House, London.

Sinha, Surajit: 'Tribe-Caste Continuum', *Man in India*, Vol.45, No.1.

Spicer, E.H.: Human Problems in Technological Change, 1952, Russel Sage Foundation, New York.

Srinivas, M.N.: Religion and Society among the Coorgs of South India, 1952, Oxford University Press, London.

—— : India's Villages, 1955, Asia Publishing House, Calcutta.

—— : 'The Dominant Caste in Rampura', *American Anthropologist*, Vol. 6, No. 1, 1959.

Srinivas, M.N. & M.N. Panni: 'The Development of Sociology and Social Anthropology in India', Sociological Bulletin, Vol. 22, 1973.

Tax, Sol *et al.* (Eds.): An appraisal of Anthropology Today, 1973, Chicago University Press, Chicago.

Teltumbde, Anil : Dalits: Past Present and Future, 2020, Routledge India, New Delhi.

—— : Republic of Caste: Thinking of Equality in the Time of Neoliberal Hindutva, 2020, Navayana Publishing Pvt. Ltd., New Delhi

Turner, Roy: India's Urban Future, 1962, University of California Press, Berkeley.

UNESCO: Sociology and Social Anthropology in Asia and Pacific, 1985, Wiley Eastern Ltd., New Delhi.

Vidyarthi, L.P.: Indian Anthropology in Action, 1960, Council of Social and Cultural Research, Ranchi.

—— : Sacred Complex of Hindu Gaya, 1961, Asia Publishing House, Bombay.

—— : The Maler: A Study of Nature-Man-Spirit Complex in a Hill Tribe of Bihar, 1963, Bookland Pvt. Ltd., Calcutta.

—— : Cultural Contours of Tribal Bihar, 1964, Punthi Pustak, Calcutta.

—— (Eds.): Leadership in India 1968, Asia Publishing House Bombay.

—— : Applied Anthropology in India, 1968, Kitab Mahal, Allahabad.

—— : Cultural Configuration of Ranchi: Study of a pre-Industrial City of Bihar, 1969, Bookland Pvt. Ltd., Calcutta.

—— : Rise of Anthropology in India (2 Vols.), 1978, Concept Publishing Company, New Dehli.

Vidyarthi, L.P. & Makhan Jha (Eds.): Sacred Complex of Bodh Gaya, Institute of Social & Cultural Research, Ranchi.

Vidyarthi, L.P., B.N. Sahay & P.K. Dutta (Eds.): Aspects of Social Anthropology in India, 1980, Classical Publishers, New Delhi.

Vidyarthi, L.P. & B.N. Sahay (Eds.): Development of Researches in Anthropology in India, 1981, Concept Publishing Company, New Delhi.

Vatuk, S.: Kinship and Urbanization: White Colar Migration in North India, 1972, University of California Press, Berkeley.

Warner, W.Loyd: 'Social Anthropology and the Modern Community: *American Journal of Sociology*, Vol. 46:6, 1969.'

Watson, J.F.: Indian Museum and Library, 1874, London.

Wheeler, Mortimer: Early India and Pakistan, 1959, Thomas & Hudson, London.

—— : The Indus Civilization, 1968, London.

Winnick, Charles: Dictionary of Anthropology, 1957, London.

Worsley, Peter: Introducing Sociology, 1971, Penguin Books, Harmondsworth.

Whyte, William: Street Corner Society, 1955, Chicago University Press, Chicago.

Yengde, Suraj & Cornel : Caste Matters, 2019 Penguin Viking, New Delhi.

Zamora, Mario D.: 'Crisis and Concerns in Anthropology and the Validity of the Anthropological Enterprise', The Eastern Anthropologist, Vol. 40, No. 4, 1987.

Zenuer, F.E.: Dating the Past, 1958, London.

—— : Pleistocene Period, 1959, London.